D0856336

JUDGMENT
RESERVED

A Landmark
Environmental Case

JUDGMENT RESERVED

A Landmark Environmental Case

Frank D. Schaumburg

Oregon State University

With a Foreword by

Dr. Frederick Seitz

President of Rockefeller University
and Past President of the
National Academy of Sciences

RESTON PUBLISHING COMPANY, INC.
Reston, Virginia
A Prentice-Hall Company

Library of Congress Cataloging in Publication Data

Schaumburg, Frank D
  Judgment reserved.

  Includes bibliographical references and index.
  1. United States, plaintiff.   2. Minnesota,
plaintiff.   3. Reserve Mining Company.   4. Water—
Pollution—Law and legislation—United States.
5. Water—Pollution—Superior, Lake.   I. Title.
KF228.U5S35   344′.73′0463   75-42098
ISBN 0-87909-406-0

© 1976 by
Reston Publishing Company, Inc.
A Prentice-Hall Company
Reston, Virginia   22090

10   9   8   7   6   5   4   3   2   1

Printed in the United States of America.

IN MEMORY OF A GIVING PERSON

my sister Barb

Contents

Foreword

By the end of World War II, the city of Pittsburgh—beautifully situated at the confluence of two rivers—had been one of the grimiest cities in our country for nearly a century. Steel mills, coke ovens, railroad traffic, and soft coal furnaces in residences made its atmosphere black and acrid and covered its buildings with soot. In winter, it was not uncommon for the sun to be as hidden at noon as at midnight.

All of this changed in a few years through a remarkable program in which political, business, and academic leaders cooperated. Realizing that future improvement of the community depended upon radical improvement of the environment, they put into effect a plan for controlling atmospheric emissions at all levels. In a short time, Pittsburgh became one of the cleanest cities involved in heavy industry and a model by which others might be judged. The only opposition to this transformation came from an overanxious component of the blue collar community that associated clean air with economic depression and wondered if the two were irrevocably linked.

The Pittsburgh experience is not an isolated one. An extensive cooperative movement of a similar kind must have been undertaken to preserve the great forest lands of northwestern Europe—decisions now presumably lost in history, but clearly made with broad-based support from many levels of European society. In fact, this cooperative tradition, which contributed so much to the European landscape, helped to encourage movements in our own country, near the turn of the century, that led to creation of many state and federal preserves. This aspect of our national history is well documented, and we know that the advance was not made without controversy. Even among the conservationists, there were two schools of thought: those who wished to preserve the forest lands as wilderness, and those who wished to preserve them in a highly cultivated form for utilitarian purposes.

During the third of a century since the Pittsburgh community mobilized to clean its air, our country has become widely aware of the influence man can have on the environment in which he lives. With this realization has evolved a vast family of environmental movements—all designed for what is believed to be the common good. What distinguishes our present national situation from the conditions that made the Pittsburgh program an unmitigated success is the climate of uncompromising belligerence that surrounds so many of the participating groups. This makes it seem unlikely that the decisions made will serve the public interest optimally in the long run. We are made particularly aware of the need for cooperation as we move further into an era, long familiar to Europe, in which it becomes necessary to combine the aesthetic and the utilitarian in ways that do not ignore economic penalties and benefits.

The differences in policies governing the treatment of public and private forest lands are a case in point. When our national forests were created, the most influential group was the one concerned with the disappearance of wilderness areas—a group which clearly deserved a prominent place at the conference table. That they tended to dominate policy has guaranteed, however, that the federal forest lands are currently far less productive of useful timber than the private forest lands that are planted and harvested on a scientific basis. One cannot help feeling that a compromise solution at the turn of the century might have served our present economic, as well as aesthetic, needs more effectively—granting, of course, that there is good reason to preserve some wilderness areas as part of our heritage.

Judgment Reserved by Frank D. Schaumburg deals with an isolated, but by no means atypical, case in which environment groups concerned about possible changes in Lake Superior pressed their cause with such vigor that an important commercial enterprise had to change its mode of waste disposal completely. Yet when we look at the end result, we are by no means certain that the concessions achieved will do the most for the well-being of society. The changes that the mining company felt compelled to make, under the pressures exerted upon it, will not only add to the cost of its product but will also dampen its willingness, and that of other industries, to develop such resources.

It would seem to be in the interest of all concerned to find means for adjudicating cases like this one—means that depend not so much upon the routine procedures of law as upon an overall assessment of costs and benefits that involve the full range of factors related to economics, health hazards, aesthetics, and physical and biological changes. Perhaps the time has come to develop something in the nature of a superior court of judgment, that includes, but reaches well beyond, assessments based on legal statutes, and whose conclusions would be advisory rather than mandatory. Unless some such method of striking a balance is put into effect, we may well find that during times of national need the present wave of environmental concern will be followed by a strong counter movement in which many important gains are lost because they were achieved with too limited a perspective.

Dr. Frederick Seitz
*President of Rockefeller University
and Past President of the
National Academy of Sciences*

Preface

Rapid acceleration of the so-called environmental movement of the late 1960's and early 1970's resulted from a dramatic realignment in societal values relative to environmental quality. Many industries and other dischargers of pollutants were caught up in this movement and faced severe consequences. One affected firm was the Reserve Mining Company of Silver Bay, Minnesota—one of the nation's largest producers of iron ore.

This book is a documentary account of the Reserve controversy, the longest and most costly environmental controversy in U.S. history. It is a factual story of how a basic resource industry could be acclaimed in the 1950's as the savior of the Minnesota iron range country, then charged in the late 1960's as a heinous polluter, and finally condemned in the 1970's for allegedly creating a serious hazard to public health.

Since the beginning of the controversy in 1969, the myopic news media have characterized the Reserve Mining Company as a villain and have elected to publicize only negative aspects of the case. Perhaps to the news media, only bad news is news! But there is much more to the Reserve story. This book attempts to tell the Reserve story in balanced perspective, and then permit the reader to assess the degree of guilt or innocence of Reserve regarding the numerous charges and allegations.

The Reserve controversy followed a lengthy and arduous pathway of litigation, first in a Minnesota state court, then in a federal district court, and finally in a U.S. court of appeals. Even the Minnesota Supreme Court and the U.S. Supreme Court became tangentially involved in the case. Though some of the charges against Reserve were well-founded, others were unproved and based upon emotion rather than scientific fact. Regardless of the degree of guilt or innocence, the company was legally compelled to discontinue its discharge of process residue (tailings) into Lake Superior and convert to an onland disposal system at a cost of over $200 million—a cost ultimately to be borne by consumers of iron products, i.e., society. Will the environment benefits to be gained by society offset this enormous expenditure? Though a decision has been rendered in the case, final judgment must be reserved.

Grateful appreciation is extended to Ms. Jean Evashevski, attorney-at-law, who provided excellent assistance with the review of legal documents. The technical assistance offered by Richard Heggen is also appreciated.

Acknowledgment is made to the faculty of the Civil Engineering department at Oregon State University who were tolerant and supportive of my involvement with manuscript preparation.

Lastly, but most importantly, I am grateful for an understanding wife, Judy, and daughters, Susan and Cynthia, who surrendered many hours of family togetherness in support of this book.

FRANK D. SCHAUMBURG

Chapter 1

Introduction

The Reserve Mining Company of Silver Bay, Minnesota, began iron ore beneficiation operations on the shores of Lake Superior in the early 1950s. The company had received formal state and federal permits to discharge its huge quantity of process residue (tailings) directly into the lake. Though operations proceeded smoothly for several years, events in the late 1960s precipitated a controversy that was to have a profound impact upon the company, the taconite industry, the state of Minnesota, and the nation.

The following divergent and contrasting statements typify the controversy that surrounded the most lengthy, costly, and significant environmental case in history.

Stoddard Report (December 1968):

Pollution is occurring as a result of taconite tailings being deposited in Lake Superior by Reserve Mining Company. *(1)*

**Minnesota Pollution Control Agency Report
(November 1969):**

The overall water quality of Lake Superior . . . in the vicinity of Silver Bay was found to be excellent at all sampling stations. *(2)*

**Judge Luther Eckman, Minnesota District Court
(December 1970):**

. . . there has been no substantial or convincing evidence of deterioration (of Lake Superior) to date. . . . *(3)*

U.S. Justice Department, in filing suit (May 1973):

Reserve Mining's discharge is accelerating the process which has damaged the other Great Lakes. *(4)*

Headline, *St. Paul Dispatch* (June 15, 1973):

ASBESTOS–TYPE FIBERS FOUND IN DULUTH WATER *(5)*

Judge Miles Lord, U.S. District Court:

Reserve's discharge constitutes a very substantial public health hazard. . . . *(February 1974) (6)*

This Court cannot honor profit over human life and therefore has no choice but abate the discharge. *(May 1974) (7)*

U.S. Court of Appeals, 8th Circuit (June, 1974):

We believe that Judge Lord carried his analysis one step beyond the evidence. *(8)*

Scientists from the National Cancer Institute in testimony before the House Commerce Committee (June 9, 1975):

. . . we found no unusual cancer mortality patterns among
people residing where drinking water is contaminated by
asbestos. . . .

Who was right? Or was there a "right" or "wrong"? It has been
exceedingly difficult for an interested observer to draw an objective
opinion on the *Reserve* case because of biased reporting by the press,
radio and TV, and possibly conflicting statements by the industry, and
even respected members of the scientific community. Writers and com-
mentators have been engulfed in emotionalism and have often failed
to ferret out fact from unfounded supposition or charge. As a con-
sequence, the Reserve controversy has generated a trail of unwarranted
apprehension, fear, and enmity across the state of Minnesota and the
nation. There is much in the *Reserve* case that has not been told—but
must be told, and in a factual and balanced manner. Such is the objective of this book.

The Reserve story is not one of isolated events but rather an
entanglement of issues, actions, and inactions, many of which occurred
simultaneously. The story is complicated by both obvious and subtle
interrelationships among politics, law, economics, pollution abatement,
land use, public health, energy consumption, national and state policy,
and our affluent lifestyle. It is in a broader sense a landmark case testing
the exquisite balance between consumption and conservation, between
fact and assumption, and between conflicting elements in the trade-off
in minimizing the inevitable environmental degradation that accompanies
man's development and evolving civilization. Indeed, there are lessons
for government, for industry, and for the public that would be well to
learn and take to heart as we proceed into a second decade of environmental improvement.

Much of the animosity that emerged during the latter stages
of the federal trial in 1974 and 1975 was actually spawned in the late
1960s, incubated during confrontations in the "Federal Enforcement
Conference," developed during state and federal trials and nurtured during political campaigns. Half-truth reporting and the exploitation of fear
and emotion fueled the often irrational attitudes held and actions taken
by the industry, governmental agencies, conservation groups, politicians,
and the public. For example, Reserve threatened plant closure and loss
of jobs even though other alternatives were available. Environmental
groups, regulatory agencies, and even some prominent court figures

early over-dramatized ecological impacts and later public health concerns in spite of scientific evidence to the contrary.

The 27-year period (1947–1974) marking the growth and development of the Reserve company can be viewed as highly transient —an era of constant and rapid change. During this period, public attitudes toward environmental quality changed dramatically and provided the impetus for the development of new and more rigorous pollution control legislation. The period also featured industrial growth with increased demand for natural resources, including iron ore.

Public demands for products of resource utilization were soon to conflict with public demands for resource conservation. This competition for resource development and allocation was engendered without any national strategy for effective and equitable resource management. A similar exploitation of energy resources is presently occurring in this nation and the world in the absence of a comprehensive and workable national or global energy policy.

Issues in the *Reserve* case are viewed differently by different groups and individuals, depending upon inherent concerns and motivations or designated responsibilities. The court, state and federal regulatory agencies, environmental groups, politicians, Reserve, and the public consider this case from different perspectives. An attempt will be made in this book to evaluate key issues from all perspectives.

The following descriptions represent the author's perception of the responsibilities, motivations, and/or concerns of each of the pertinent groups in the *Reserve* case.

Regulatory agencies, both state and federal, respond to mandates from politicians, via the public, to abate existing pollution and to prevent future pollution. These demands generally call for prompt, decisive actions, often in the absence of adequate information for a rational and technically-defensible response. Technological, economic, time, and other "real-world" constraints are often minimized or simply ignored by those demanding rapid agency action. This frequently leads to superficial and ultimately ineffective solutions, undue hardships on dischargers, and even, at times, negative side effects of the actions—all of which tend to degrade public confidence and trust in the agency. Furthermore, some hasty and premature decisions that have far-reaching impacts are subsequently found to be in error and must be reversed. Examples of this dilemma include catalytic converters, NTA substitutes for phosphate detergents, and perhaps even the SST.

Though not clairvoyant, regulating agencies must gaze into the

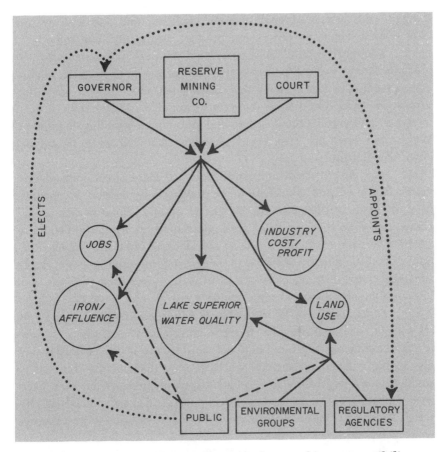

FIGURE 1   Interaction of motivations and/or responsibilities.

future to protect our environment for unborn generations. Yet abatement programs and regulations must be realistic within the framework of a modern technological society and scientific possibility. To be predictive, agencies often base policies on educated "gut-feelings" rather than on sound scientific facts. Definitive actions are often needed well in advance of adequate technical information. But realism must not give way to idealism. Predictive policies frequently seem, and sometimes are, arbitrary and tend to frustrate industries and other dischargers who generally base decisions on hard facts. The primary responsibility of regulatory agencies is environmental quality control. They are seldom charged with weighing environmental policies and decisions against such related factors as economics, product availability, and jobs.

Though the public and its elected political representatives may proclaim strong dedication and conviction for preserving a high quality environment, the fact remains that these same advocates are unwilling to pay the price for quality regulatory programs. They prefer instead to speak loudly from the soapbox and pass tough-sounding legislation. Words and laws are cheap and expedient but fall short of solving environmental problems.

The effectiveness of most federal and state environmental programs has been and continues to be thwarted by a lack of financial support. Even in the midst of this era of environmental consciousness, many state regulatory agencies are understaffed and underfunded. This situation is continually worsened as new federal laws and implementation directives burden states with needless forms and paperwork. In summary, regulatory agencies are continually confronted with an endless number of impossible tasks which were all due yesterday.

Politicians seem to be involved either directly or indirectly in all societal controversies—the Reserve controversy certainly is no exception. Politicians must respond not only to the needs of society but also to the demands of society, whether those demands are rational or simply emotional. Failure to respond to public pressures in some overt way generally spells doom to political futures. Elected officials at different levels of government can view controversies, such as the Reserve controversy, in different ways.

State governors are elected officials and consequently must remain sensitive to the sentiment of their constituency, yet they must weigh other factors in a decision-making process including jobs, economy, environment, and the health and well-being of all citizens of the state. An effective and responsible governor must be able to evaluate trade-offs of these interrelated issues, then be willing to bargain or compromise to obtain what is in the best interest of the entire state.

Legislators at both the federal and state levels, must respond to the needs of society by promulgating effective and equitable laws. Legislators must guard against succumbing to unfounded emotional arguments and should consider all factors impinging on a given problem. Legislators face constant pressures from all segments of society and rarely are able to assume a posture that is supported by all sides.

Conservation and/or environmental groups have played an effective role in changing public attitudes toward environmental legislation.

The words *conservationist* and *environmentalist* can take on a wide array of meanings. The broadest definition of environmentalist would be any person with a genuine concern for the environment. This could or at least should include nearly all Americans. A more appropriate and restrictive definition, the one used in this book, is any person who supports the preservation of a high quality environment regardless of cost or implication. A conservationist has concern for environmental quality but is more dedicated to the preservation of natural resources in the natural state.

Environmentalists and environmental groups press for tough legislation and stern enforcement and are generally uncompromising. They give little, if any, consideration to such factors as employment; economics; technological, physical, and time limitations; or the importance of products for the well-being of society. Such a narrow and biased perspective sometimes leads to chaos and confusion but must be considered an important ingredient in our checks-and-balances form of democratic government. Without the dedicated efforts of these groups, pollution abatement in this country would likely be lagging well behind its present state.

One serious weakness in the philosophy of many environmental groups is their myopic approach to environmental management. Well-meaning environmentalists frequently seek actions that, if implemented, would actually result in a net negative impact on the *total* environment. They fail to recognize that advocacy of any environmental plan should be preceded first by a careful evaluation of potential negative impacts and resource consumption.

Our democratic form of government provides a mechanism whereby differences in interpretation of laws and regulations can be settled—*the judicial system*. The courts have perhaps the most onerous, complex, and important function in any environmental confrontation. The court must weigh technical evidence, economic considerations, laws and regulations, and the general well-being of society in reaching a decision. Yet the court rarely possesses sufficient scientific expertise to pass independent judgment. Instead, the court must rely upon expert testimony introduced by plaintiffs and defendants or provided by the court itself. In some instances, since the court must rely upon expert testimony, a sound decision is only possible if experts are willing and able to present the whole truth—and if the court is willing to accept it. *Whole-truth* testimony is generally denied, however, by the adversary procedures followed in a court of law. The only information brought forward is that in response to direct examination or cross-examination. Judgments must be made on the basis of facts presented rather than upon emotional pleas and suppositions, and facts withheld by either side in a controversy, so as not to undermine a position, can be as important as facts provided.

Industry involved in environmental confrontation faces several competing constraints. The consumer (public) places a demand for industrial products in unlimited supply and at low cost. On the other hand, investors and the company's board of directors demand an acceptable profit from the operation. Because of investment risks involved, the rate of return must be greater than that obtainable from government bonds or other low-risk investments. Since an industry would be forced to close down if profits dipped below a minimum level, most costs incurred by the industry must be passed on to the consumer. Thus costs for pollution abatement, safety, labor benefits, etc., must be reflected in the price of the product.

Though many industries purport to espouse high environmental goals and ideals (and some genuinely do), they nonetheless tend to hold to a more liberal interpretation of pollution control legislation and regulation. Industry is generally willing to abate *provable* pollution but is less than eager to commit itself to programs based upon supposition and gut-feelings as opposed to sound scientific fact.

The *public* generally assumes an incongrous posture in environmental controversies. For instance, the public often demands an unlimited supply of an infinite variety of consumer goods of high quality and low cost. Increasingly, the public expects this to be accomplished with zero pollution of air, land, and water resources. It also expects the standard of living to improve, taxes to be reduced, and more and better jobs at higher salaries for everyone—with of course increased benefits and more leisure time. The Christmas list of *wants* continues well beyond the list of *needs* and *possibles*.

Against these considerations, the Reserve controversy is highly complex and far-reaching. It did not begin in Judge Lord's federal court nor end in the U.S. Supreme Court. The controversy had a much earlier beginning, and the precedents established during the case will cling to society for years in the future. This book endeavors to begin at the beginning with a story of the birth and growth of an industry and a company during an era of rapid industrialization, the dramatic change in public sentiment toward industry and the environment, and the continual changes in legal ground rules.

The book is divided into four distinct sections to minimize confusion of dates and issues and to facilitate readability. The first section focuses on important background material and attempts to establish a framework or perspective for evaluation of subsequent legal actions against Reserve. Part II is a documentary account of Reserve's legal encounters with the state of Minnesota and the federal government, beginning with its applications for permits in 1947 and ending with the judgment of the U.S. Court of Appeals. The third section briefly reviews the land tailings disposal alternative open to Reserve. The final section is devoted to an overview of important implications of this controversy to society. This case has established many landmarks, not all of which are in the best interest of industry, environment, or society.

PART I

IN
PERSPECTIVE

Background information on the changing moods of society, the natural resources involved, and the development of the taconite industry is important to an understanding of actions taken by the company, the government, and the public.

Chapter 2

Toward
Environmental
Consciousness

Well-meaning environmentalists of today seriously question the logic and foresight of a company that chose to locate a large iron ore beneficiating facility on the shores of beautiful Lake Superior. Certainly, they contend, such a decision showed callous disregard for environmental quality and public health. But the decision to locate the Reserve Mining Company facility at Silver Bay was made in the 1940s—an era philosophically removed from that of the '60s and '70s.

One must appreciate the historic reality that the years of growth and development of the Reserve Mining Company spanned a period of rapid change in public sentiment and action toward resource development and resource conservation. Based on prevailing attitudes of today and the prognosis for tomorrow, Reserve would undoubtedly not now choose to locate a new beneficiating facility at its present site.

NATURE AS A NATIONAL ASSET

From the founding of the United States to the beginning of the twentieth century, appreciation for and conservation of natural resources was more a philosophy than a practice. Early Americans like James Fenimore Cooper, George Catlin, and Oliver Wendell Holmes generated public awareness of nature as a national asset. Unfortunately, preoccupation with frontier expansion and economic accomplishment relegated the cause of conservationism to obscurity. Classical economics, well suited for a nation of expanding boundaries, assigned little or no real value to the perpetual preservation of natural resources. Resources appeared limitless in quantity and resilient in quality. Dollars and standard of living were held as the essential factors in decision-making processes. Railroad companies, land developers, and oil, timber, and minerals industries consumed resources at their pleasure with little regulation or control.

But by the mid-1800s, wanton abuse of resources had begun to leave visible scars—and the environmental consciousness of the nation began to stir. The first major battle over resource exploitation was waged in California and involved efforts to save the giant sequoia trees from extinction. This controversy, fueled by an emerging press and a determined public, led to the establishment of the national park concept. In 1864, the Yosemite Valley was granted to the people of California as a public trust to provide a refuge for the ageless sequoias. Less than 30 years later, in 1890, the Yosemite National Park was created. Conservationists had brought about a pioneer achievement in resource protection.

In the 1880s, the federal government expanded its role in environmental surveillance and protection by creating the Division of Ornithology in the U.S. Department of Agriculture. (This was later to become the U.S. Biological Survey and then the Fish and Wildlife Service.) In 1899, Congress passed the first pollution control law known as the Rivers and Harbors Act. This law decreed tremendous regulatory powers to the U.S. Army Corps of Engineers; however, the vagueness of several provisions of the law rendered it largely ineffective.

The changing attitudes of government and society toward resource conservation in the late 1800s was complemented by an increased awareness by resource-consuming industries that resource protection was in their best interest as well. Resource managers, economists, and natural scientists began to pool talents to develop programs aimed at preserving resources for future use.

By the turn of the century, conservationism was part of the Progressive reform platform. The movement became an active political issue with Theodore Roosevelt. Though T.R.'s accomplishments were limited, he did establish conservationism as a legitimate consideration in American development. Under his administration, public support for conservation took firm roots. A national conviction arose deeming it immoral to give away natural resources, which were the property of the nation's people. Roosevelt cautioned Congress that "the forest and water problems are perhaps the most vital internal problems of the United States." (9)

Theodore Roosevelt's interest in resource conservation carried on through subsequent presidents; however, none put philosophy to practice more definitively than his cousin, Franklin. President Franklin D. Roosevelt initiated the Tennessee Valley Authority (TVA), a revolutionary experiment in coordinated, multi-purpose resource development. Under his direction, the Civilian Conservation Corps took part in reforestation, soil conservation programs, and river control activities. Thus, the era of two Roosevelts (1901–1945) can be noted in history as a period during which environmentalism became a political reality. The development period of the Reserve Mining Company (1947–present) was to coincide with the next era of the environmental movement—the era of activism.

THE ERA OF ACTIVISM

The decade of the 1950s marked a deceleration in conservation gains. World War II recuperation and administrations geared to business interests impeded actions directed at water resource protection, although some weak congressional legislation was enacted. The '50s provided a lull period during which industries were allowed to become established with only minimal environmental responsibility. The environmental consciousness of the nation was not totally dormant, however. Dedicated environmentalists and numerous environmental and conservation groups began to solidify their goals and extend their lines of influence. The opposing forces met in the 1960s.

Politicians, pressured by special interest groups and a concerned constituency attempted to regain the momentum developed by the

Roosevelts. Tough federal and state laws were promulgated, implemented, and enforced. Some dischargers, themselves sensitive to environmental concerns and to public sentiment, independently modified
operations to minimize environmental degradation.

Early successes by environmentalists stimulated a rapid growth
of special interest groups and organizations. The number of non-govern-
mental conservation organizations founded in the United States increased from approximately 150 in 1947, to 300 in 1960, and over 550 in
1972. This trend in public support for environmental protection might
be measured by the phenomenal increase in Sierra Club membership,
from less than 10,000 in 1950, to nearly 140,000 in 1972. The Sierra
Club is one of the more politically active conservation groups in the
country.

These growth statistics could be interpreted as an indicator of

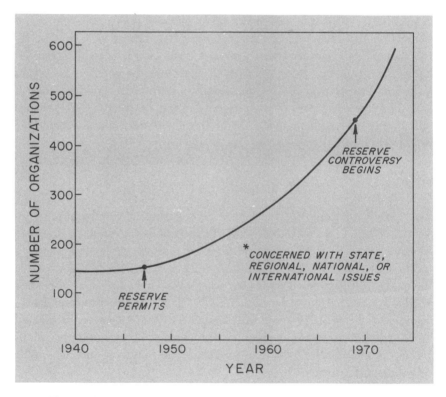

FIGURE 2   Nongovernmental conservation organizations *
in the United States.

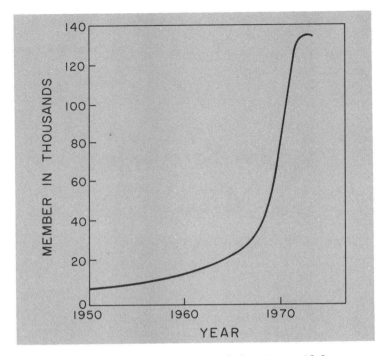

FIGURE 3   Membership of the Sierra Club.

the acceleration in national concern for conservation and environmental protection. This being the case, it is not difficult to perceive how an environmental decision made in good faith nearly 30 years ago could be contrary to societal demands of today.

Chapter 3

Lake Superior: A Multi-Use Resource

The multi-use development of Lake Superior is an historic example of changing societal values on natural resources. Since the days of the early French fur traders who coined the name "Lac Superieur," this great body of water has been used concurrently for transportation, water supply, residue disposal, commercial fishing, and recreation. Depending upon point of view or special interest, each of these activities might be considered to be a legitimate beneficial use of the resource. But when uses become incompatible, for real or imagined reasons, who is to determine priority? Currently, there is no formal mechanism for making this value judgment or for setting rational goals for the well-being of society. Consequently, special interest groups like industry, agriculture, business, environmentalists, and others lobby for their respective goals and aspirations.

Until the beginning of the Reserve controversy in 1968, the multiple uses of Lake Superior appeared compatible, compatible in terms of the then prevailing values of society. Changes in societal values and goals in the late 1960s and 1970s brought into question the informal and unofficial alignment of priorities for uses of the lake.

TRANSPORTATION

For many decades, the waters of Lake Superior have provided an important transportation route to America's heartland. Lake shipping has been used as an inexpensive and convenient mode of transport of metals, timber, grain, fish, and other products of the region. Over one-half of the nation's iron ore is transported on Lake Superior. For this reason, Duluth is now the nation's fifth largest shipping port.

The transportation use of Lake Superior, however, directly and indirectly affects other uses of the lake. Perhaps the most significant impacts relate to environmental quality. Transport vessels frequently discharge contaminated bilge waters and human wastes directly into the lake. In addition, unintentional (and perhaps some intentional) spills in harbors and in the open lake create environmental problems. Lake transport has several important positive environmental implications, however. One is that water transport is generally more efficient in terms of energy consumed per ton-mile than overland or air transport. Consequently, less environmental contamination results from energy production and consumption.

The water supply use of Lake Superior appears to pose minimal impact upon other beneficial uses, primarily due to the vastness of water volume. The some 200,000 inhabitants of the Lake Superior basin generate a water demand of 25 million gallons per day (mgd). By comparison, basin industries draw an estimated 560 mgd, of which nearly 90% is used by the Reserve Mining Company. Most of the water withdrawn from the lake is ultimately returned as an industrial or municipal effluent discharge.

FISHING

Commercial fishermen have chronically complained that the Lake Superior fishery has been negatively impacted by other uses of the lake. Records show, however, that overzealous fishermen, not industry, have been their own worst enemy, (*10*), overfishing being a major factor responsible for reduced fish catches in Lake Superior. Predation by the parasitic sea lamprey has also contributed significantly to the reduction of lake trout populations. One might argue that the transportation use of Lake Superior has negatively affected the lake fishery, since were it not for the development of the St. Lawrence Seaway for shipping purposes, the lamprey would not have gained access to the Great Lakes system from its native habitat in the Atlantic Ocean and tributary streams.

RESIDUES OF MAN AND NATURE

Lake Superior has also long served as a natural repository or sink for residues of man and nature. Fertilizers, pesticides, and other substances used extensively in agriculture and silviculture in the Lake Superior drainage basin have gained entry to the lake via surface runoff and subsurface flows. Furthermore, improper land and forest management practices have resulted in excessive soil erosion and large sediment loads in tributary streams. Cities, towns, and individual homes in the basin have discharged (and some continue to discharge) untreated or partially treated sewage into Lake Superior. And the U.S. Army Corps of Engineers has dumped millions of tons of contaminated dredge spoils in lake waters.

Numerous industries in the basin contribute unwanted residues to the lake. Undoubtedly the largest industrial contributor, at least in terms of quantity of residue, is the Reserve Mining Company at Silver Bay. But all residues from all sources, man-induced and natural, tend to degrade the quality and character of lake water because residue disposal is a use of lake water that inevitably affects other uses such as water supply, recreation, and possibly the lake fishery. Whether the impact of Reserve's discharge is minute, significant, or substantial is the subject of debate in the Reserve controversy.

RECREATION

The importance of Lake Superior as a recreational resource has never been disputed; however, in the 1940s, 1950s, and early 1960s, the recreation and aesthetic qualities of the lake were not given the high priority rating assigned today. Although by some standards the recreational potential of the lake is underutilized today, increased population pressure will likely make this area a prime location for future recreation development. In 1968, the annual recreation demand in the Lake Superior basin was an estimated 16 million person-days. This could double by the year 2000.

HOW TO PRESERVE LAKE SUPERIOR?

It is now the goal of many environmentalists that preservation of the lake in its *existing* natural state should supercede all other uses. The question is whether this idealistic goal is incompatible with parallel societal goals of economic growth, resource development, and consumerism—and which is to take precedence.

The multi-use importance of Lake Superior results from its many unique physical characteristics. Though the lake was formed in the Ice Age over 10,000 years ago, scientists refer to the lake as *oligotrophic*, meaning young in terms of chemical enrichment. As lakes become rich with nutrient chemicals such as nitrogen and phosphorus, algae and other more evolved plant forms develop causing a *eutrophic* condition. Even though all lakes age naturally, the residue-generating activities of man can rapidly accelerate the aging process.

Lake Superior is the largest, deepest, clearest, cleanest, coldest, highest, and least man-affected of the Great Lakes. It occupies a surface area of 31,789 square miles, or larger than the state of South Carolina. The volume of Lake Superior, 2927 cubic miles, is second only to Lake Baikal in the Soviet Union. The lake's bottom profile varies considerably from shore to shore, with a mean depth of 487 feet and a maximum depth of 1330 feet. Compared to its vast water surface, the Lake Superior watershed, or drainage basin, is surprisingly small, just over 9000 square miles. Though some 200 streams feed into the lake, none is particularly large. Outflows from the lake pass through the St. Mary's River to the lower Great Lakes, thus providing another reason for protecting the quality of Lake Superior water.

Since a relatively small amount of fresh water actually enters and passes through this vast lake volume, a long hydraulic residence time is inevitable. It has been estimated that a droplet of water entering Lake Superior may not be flushed from the lake for 500 years or more. This slow flushing rate is an extremely critical factor for consideration in any water quality management plan for the lake.

Prior to intensive field studies in the late 1960s and early 1970s, it was commonly assumed that current patterns in Lake Superior were either insignificant or non-existent. It is now known that significant currents are prevalent in the lake and play an important role in its ecological health and water quality. The horizontal and vertical mixing action generated by currents tends to disperse added contaminants and provide a vehicle for food, nutrient, and waste products exchange in aquatic ecosystems. The lake is well-mixed throughout its depth during the cold winter months; however, during the summer it becomes stratified into three distinct zones. The upper zone, or epilimnion, is well-mixed by surface currents and wave action and becomes several degrees warmer than

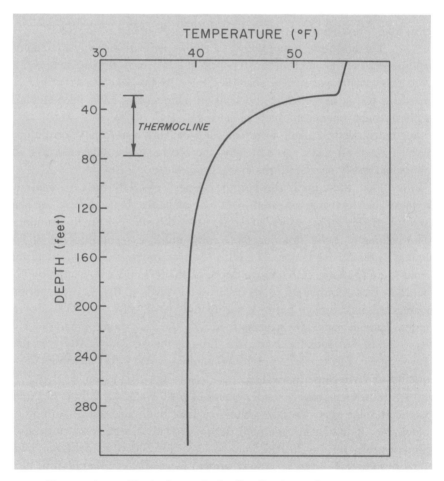

FIGURE 4   Typical vertical distribution of temperature, Lake Superior near North Shore, late September.

the poorly-mixed deeper waters, i.e., the hypolimnion. The transition zone, or thermocline, generally extends from 30 to 100 feet below the water surface.

Contrary to the expressed fears of environmentalists and the foreboding of uninformed politicians, Lake Superior is not on the verge of becoming another Lake Erie. The two lakes share common inclusion in the Great Lakes chain, but beyond that similarity ceases. Lake Erie has aged rapidly, i.e., become eutrophic, as a result of several factors, all of which are uncommon to its big sister lake. Lake Erie is very shallow (less than 100 feet deep) and small in volume. Because of these physical factors and its relatively low latitude, the waters of Lake Erie are considerably warmer than Lake Superior waters. Warm water temperatures accelerate the growth rate of algae, bacteria, and other aquatic organisms.

The fate of Lake Erie, however, has not been determined solely by its physical and geographic characteristics. Another significant factor has been the degree of shoreline and basin development. Nearly 60% of Lake Erie's shoreline (U.S. portion) has been developed for residential, industrial, and/or commercial uses. By contrast, only 20% of Lake Superior's shoreline has been developed. This becomes highly significant when one considers that 72% of the nutrient chemicals (nitrogen and phosphorus) added to Lake Erie gain access by way of municipal discharges, i.e., the public. Industry contributes approximately 4%, agricultural runoff, 17%; and urban runoff, 7%.

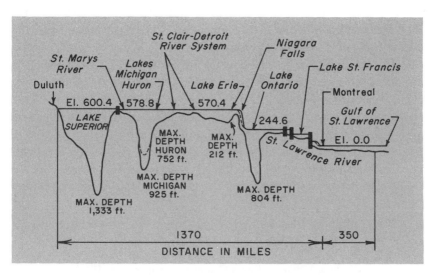

FIGURE 5   Great Lakes profile.

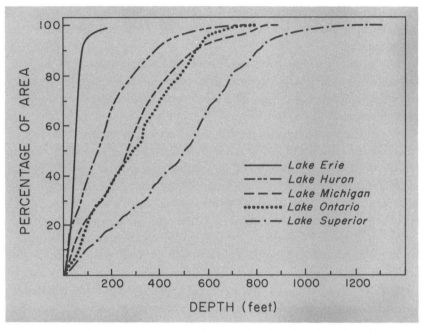

FIGURE 6   Depth–area relationships for the Great Lakes.

     But even though Lake Superior does not face incipient peril, con-
stant vigil, surveillance, and regulation must be exercised to minimize the
rate of degradation. The question is, How? Regulatory policies must reflect a recognition of societal demands for all of the compatible, beneficial
uses of this multi-use natural resource. Moreover, efforts to preserve this
valuable water resource may result in environmental pollution in other
forms and other places. In 1971, environmentalists and politicians strongly
urged that Reserve's tailings be deposited on land, anywhere on land,
rather than continue with any form of lake dumping. This environmental
management decision was made without a comprehensive evaluation of
potential impact on the land resource and of associated energy consumption. Technical representatives of the EPA, like Murray Stein[1] and Dr.
Donald Mount[2], together with experts from the U.S. Bureau of Mines,

---

[1] Murray Stein: Then assistant commissioner for enforcement, Federal
Water Pollution Control Administration, U.S.D.I., Washington, D.C.

[2] Dr. Donald I. Mount: Then director, National Water Quality Laboratory, Federal Water Pollution Control Administration, U.S.D.I., Duluth,
Minnesota.

attempted to caution these individuals and groups about the environmental hazards associated with land disposal. But, it wasn't until after the company agreed to convert to onland disposal that the environmentalists and politicians who had not heeded the warnings of experts began to recognize that the onland disposal they had so long espoused could also cause environmental degradation. At this point, they turned on their solution.

Chapter 4

Iron–The Fabric of National Development

The wealth and strength of a nation is generally derived from its natural resource base. The United States is a classic example. It has risen to a position of world economic and military dominance because of its vast wealth of natural resources including timber, arable lands, energy reserves, and metals. Iron ore deposits in the Lake Superior basin have long provided the sinew for industrialization. This bountiful resource also strengthened the U.S. position and effectiveness in both world wars.

STEEL BREAKTHROUGH INCREASES IRON ORE DEMAND

The importance of iron in American development can be traced to the days of Sir Walter Raleigh who established the first new world foundry in Falling Creek, Virginia, in 1610. By the 1700s, blast furnaces in eight colonies were forging iron from ore deposits in local swamps. Technical developments by Bessemer and others in the mid-1800s produced breakthroughs in the production of steel. The great utility of steel led to a greatly accelerated demand for iron ore and rapid expansion of markets. During the same period, prospectors in the Great Lakes region discovered enormous deposits of high-grade iron ore, seemingly enough to supply this nation's needs indefinitely. But who could have predicted the insatiable demand for resources that developed in the twentieth century?

In 1900, the U.S. ranked as the world's foremost producer of iron, with an annual production of 27 million long tons [1] ($\frac{1}{3}$ of world production). Though U.S. production continued to increase to a high of 118 million long tons in 1953, its dominance of the world market declined. Other iron-producing nations were rapidly developing facilities to exploit the world's growing demand for this valuable resource. By 1971, U.S. production of 82 million long tons represented only $\frac{1}{10}$ of the world's output.

The quality of iron ore reserves also has changed markedly since 1900. At the turn of the century, most of the iron ore was mined from high grade deposits (55% to 65% iron content) and shipped directly to blast furnaces. Later, increasing demand for iron required that poorer quality ores be mined as well. Though ore quality was less (35% to 50%), a variety of beneficiation or concentration processes such as crushing, screening, flotation, and gravity or magnetic separation were developed to produce blast furnace-grade iron concentrate (60% to 68%). Over 20% of Minnesota's Mesabi Range production in 1942 was in the form of concentrated low-grade ore. Reliance on this ore increased to 30% by 1950.

TACONITE

As the demand for iron continued to grow at an alarming rate, a small group of farsighted mining engineers and investors, anticipating a crisis in ore supply, began to explore radical alternatives in the 1940s. Led by the pioneering efforts of Professor E. W. Davis, then director of the

---

[1] The long ton is a common unit of measure in the mining industry. It is equivalent to 2240 pounds or 1.12 short tons.

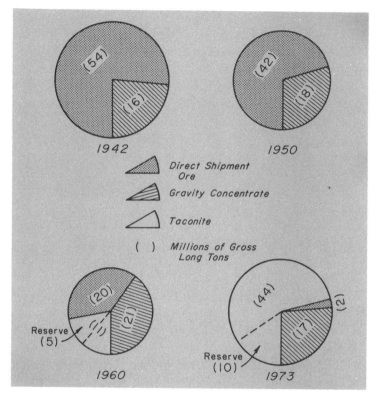

FIGURE 7   Iron shipments from the Mesabi Range.

Mines Experiment Station at the University of Minnesota, a new technology was developed to extract iron from taconite rock. Davis likened
the Mesabi iron deposits to raisin cake. The raisins were analogous to
high-grade iron, which could readily be plucked from the ore for direct
shipment; the remainder of the cake was taconite. By the late 1940s the
raisins were all but gone.

Taconite is found in commercial quantities only in Minnesota's
110-mile, Z-shaped Mesabi Range. The rock is embedded in a swath one
to two miles wide and to a thickness of 750 feet. Overburden is generally
less than 30 feet.

Taconite is a flint-like, sedimentary rock, hard enough to cut
glass. Minnesota law [2] defines taconite as

[2] Sections 1–4 inclusive of Minnesota Laws of 1941.

. . . ferruginous chert or ferruginous slate in the form of compact, silicious rock, in which the iron oxide is so finely disseminated that substantially all of the iron-bearing particles of merchantile grade are smaller than 20 mesh. Taconite may be further defined as ore-bearing rock which is not merchantable as iron ore in its natural state, and which cannot be made merchantable by simple methods of beneficiation involving only crushing, screening, washing, jigging, drying or any combination thereof.

The taconite industry emerged in the nick of time. The slack generated by declining production from high-grade ore deposits was picked up effectively by taconite iron. In 1950, before start-up of the taconite industry, 42 million tons of high-grade iron and 18 million tons of gravity concentrate were shipped. By 1960, however, high-grade iron production had dropped to just 20 million tons, gravity concentrate production remained about the same at 21 million tons, and the emerging taconite industry contributed just over 10 million tons. Five million of this was from Reserve. By 1973, high-grade iron production had dipped below 2 million tons, and the taconite industry contributed 44 million tons, or 70% of total Mesabi production. Mesabi taconite iron at this time

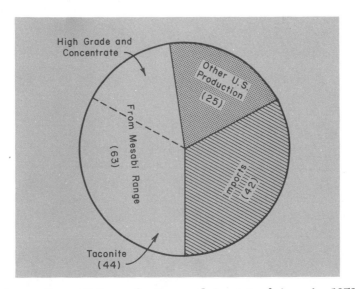

FIGURE 8   U.S. production and import of iron in 1973 (Total—130 million long tons).

accounted for ½ of total U.S. iron production of 88 million long tons. Reserve's production represented approximately 11% of total U.S. iron production.

In less than 100 years, Americans have used or sold over ⅔ of this nation's high-grade iron resources and the demand for iron-and-steel-containing consumer goods continues to accelerate. U.S. demand for iron is expected to exceed 150 million tons per year by 1980. Since the nation's high-grade ore deposits are nearly exhausted, this tremendous

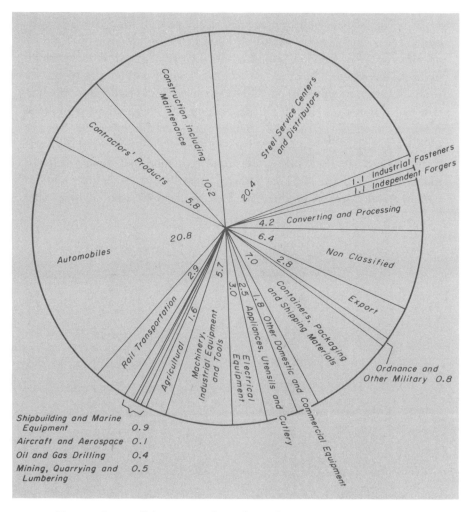

FIGURE 9   Shipments of steel products by market classification in 1973 (all grades percentages).

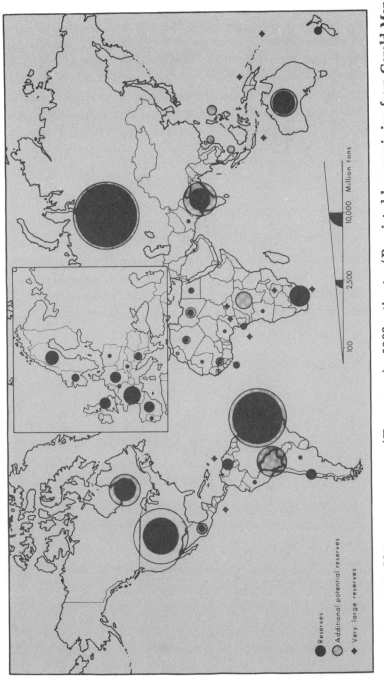

FIGURE 10   World iron ore reserves (Fe content)—1966 estimate. (Reprinted by permission from Gerald Manners' *The Changing World Market for Iron Ore, 1950-1980*, published in 1971 for Resources for the Future by The Johns Hopkins University Press, Baltimore, Maryland)

demand for iron will be met only by increasing taconite operations or by increasing imports. Both alternatives have serious implications to the nation. Though taconite and other low-grade iron reserves are in abundance in the Mesabi Range (an estimated 9 billion tons of crude ore), procurement of iron from taconite is highly costly, both in terms of dollars and perhaps more importantly, energy. Furthermore, production of any metal from low-grade sources must also result in large quantities of residue that must be disposed of *somewhere*. For every ton of iron pellets produced from taconite, two tons of residue (tailings) result. By contrast only one ton of residue is produced per ton of gravity concentrate, and essentially *no* tailings are left in mining high-grade, direct-shipment iron.

IMPORTS

The alternative source, imports, could pose even more serious problems. Though other countries of the world are well-endowed with iron reserves, reliance on imports would accentuate foreign trade deficits, impair U.S. self-sufficiency in a critical resource and thus encourage international

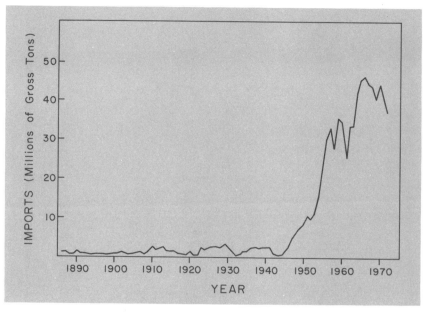

FIGURE 11   U.S. imports of iron ore, 1866-1972.

"resource blackmail." This nation's iron ore dilemma is directly comparable to its current tenuous international position with regard to oil reserves. In both instances, natural resources have been consumed by the *American public* at a rate that could deny these resources to later generations.

Chapter 5

Birth and Growth of an Industry, a Company, and a Community

Among the investors who foresaw the need for an assured iron source were Armco Steel and Republic Steel, the parent owners of the Reserve Mining Company. The corporate history of Reserve is a noteworthy saga of successful parent-company management. It is not one of instant success, but rather a story of years of bold commitment to financial risks.

DEVELOPMENT OF THE TACONITE INDUSTRY

In 1871 taconite rock was discovered at Babbitt, Minnesota, in the Great Mesabi Range. Although beneficiation of this ore was technologically impractical at that time, speculators staked their claims.

In 1875, the original Mesabi Iron Company organized and acquired rights to properties in the Babbitt region. It wasn't until 40 years later, however, that a concerted effort was made to develop the taconite resource. In 1915, the newly-organized Mesabi Syndicate, spearheaded by D. C. Jackling, acquired leases to the Babbitt site and built a 100-ton per day experimental plant in Duluth. Four years later, the Mesabi Iron Company incorporated and took over assets, processes, etc., developed by Jackling's group and started construction of a full scale beneficiating plant and town at Babbitt. The plant was completed in 1922 but operated just two years. Failure of the Mesabi Iron venture was attributed to the corporation's inability to compete economically with high-grade ores. This initial failure dampened the enthusiasm of other taconite investors to such an extent that it wasn't until 1937 that any new attempt was made to negotiate for leases on the Mesabi Range.

In a labyrinth of corporate dealings in 1939, the newly formed Reserve Mining Company emerged with the Babbitt property leases. This new company was organized by Oglebay-Norton Company as agents for Armco, Wheeling Steel Corporation, Montreal Mining Company, and Cleveland-Cliffs Iron Company. Reserve put the Babbitt site in order.

MINNESOTA TAX LAWS IMPEDE MINING DEVELOPMENT

However, until 1941 the Minnesota law relating to mine holdings discouraged the development of new mining operations. It taxed unmined ore. Thus, owners were motivated to extract high-grade deposits as rapidly as possible to reduce tax obligation. This short-sighted industrial tax policy had a catastrophic impact on the economy of northern Minnesota in the 1940s when high-grade ore deposits were exhausted and mining operations closed en masse. It also discouraged investment in vast reserves of taconite that would remain unmined for many years.

Investors refused to encourage the development of an active taconite industry in this undesirable tax climate. Clearly, a change was needed. Professor Davis became an outspoken advocate of the future of the taconite industry and was successful in rallying some public support for tax adjustment. Another key spokesman for a tax change was a school administrator from Chisholm, Minnesota, John A. Blatnik. Blatnik was later to become the U.S. Representative from the 8th Minnesota District and was to become known as a pioneer in developing federal water pollution control legislation.

In 1941, the Minnesota legislature passed a revised tax law which removed levies on unmined low-grade ore and established a tax of 6 cents per ton on taconite actually processed. The new law also permitted tax-free capital investment in taconite production. These changes removed initial tax obstacles standing the way of a new taconite industry.

TECHNOLOGICAL PROBLEMS

But early development was also impeded by technological problems that required solution before full-scale operations could be undertaken. The state and the industry turned to the University of Minnesota Mines Experiment Station for technical assistance. During the period 1941 through 1949, Dr. Davis, then director of the station, and his staff collaborated with Reserve personnel to develop an economic method of processing taconite from the Babbitt area. Davis also worked on a method to agglomerate the fine, pulverized taconite iron concentrates into pellets.

Finally it was through Davis' ingenuity and dedication that a feasible process was developed to recover marketable iron from taconite rock. The process he developed, with only a few minor changes, continues to be used today by Reserve and other companies. A flow diagram and description of the basic steps in this beneficiation process are shown in Appendix A.

In 1950–51, Armco and Republic each acquired 50% of the stock in the Reserve Mining Company and have been co-owners ever since. Construction of the taconite processing plant at Silver Bay was essentially completed in the summer of 1955. On October 20 of that year, after a few tune-up operations, the first pellets were produced. By April 10, 1956, production at Silver Bay had exceeded 1 million tons.

BIRTH OF A COMMUNITY

The birth and growth of Silver Bay closely paralleled the development of the Reserve Mining Company. Prior to the start of plant construction in the early 1950s the area was essentially a wilderness with less than one inhabitant per square mile. Soon, however, the giant taconite plant attracted over 1000 employees and another 2000 persons who earned their livelihood through support of the plant or its employees. Including dependents, the population of Silver Bay rapidly grew to over 3500.

Silver Bay is quite unlike most "company towns." From the beginning, it was professionally designed and developed. It rests on a gentle hillside above the plant and overlooks Lake Superior.

Though Reserve bore the cost of constructing the community's wide streets, its modern school, and its recreational facilities, over 95 percent of the homes are individually owned. The company also provided, at the outset, secondary sewage treatment and water filtration facilities, unique to northshore communities at that time and for many years to come.

STATE SUPPORT OF TACONITE AMENDMENT

The taconite industry immediately began to pick up the slack in U.S. iron production and at the same time infused new life into the dying economy of northern Minnesota. Even with these accomplishments, the future of the taconite industry in Minnesota was unassured. The industry complained that it was viewed as a treasure chest from which state and local governments could freely draw to balance their budgets. Taxes on mining operations had provided up to 95% of the funds to operate public schools. Taxes were assessed considerably more heavily on mining than on other manufacturing operations. For the industry to irrevocably commit itself to further growth, Minnesota would have to substantially reduce its traditional heavy tax assessment on mining activities. Pressure was again brought to bear on the Minnesota public and politicians.

After a futile attempt in 1961, the 1963 state legislature overwhelmingly approved a constitutional amendment to limit future tax increases on taconite to the same level applied to other state manufacturing operations. The proposed amendment required a ⅔ affirmative vote in the general election. Would the public show such strong support for this growing state industry?

To achieve voter support, divergent groups came together as never before. The Steelworkers swung the AFL-CIO behind the measure. Vice President Hubert Humphrey and Governor Karl Rolvaag brought along the DFL [1] Party. State chairmen of both political parties, together with the renowned Dr. Charles Mayo (then chairman of the University Regents), leaders of the Federation of Women's Clubs, Chambers of

---

[1] DFL: Democrat Farm Labor.

Commerce, Rotary Clubs, and other citizens groups campaigned vigorously for the measure. Even the Minnesota Vikings played a football game in support of the referendum. Either the public relations firm hired to promote voter support wasn't needed or it did its job well!

In November 1964, Minnesota voters approved the taconite amendment by a landslide seven to one margin.[2] Just four years later the Reserve Mining Company was to see its public and political support undercut by alleged negative impacts of its process residue on the waters of Lake Superior.

[2] The day after the election, as an indicator of growth to come in the taconite industry, the U.S. Steel Corporation announced that it would build a $120 million taconite plant at Iron Mountain, Iron, Minnesota.

PART II

DOCUMENTARY HISTORY OF THE RESERVE CONTROVERSY

This section traces the involvement of the Reserve Mining Company in securing permits, in a federal enforcement conference, and in state and federal trials.

CAST OF CHARACTERS

RESERVE

EDWARD FURNESS
President

KENNETH HALEY
Vice President

ED FRIDE
Chief Outside Counsel

DR. G. F. LEE
Technical Consultant

COURT

HON. C. LUTHER ECKMAN
Judge
Lake County District Court

HON. MILES W. LORD
Judge, U.S. District Court
5th District

DR. ARNOLD BROWN
Chief Medical Witness
Appointed by District Court

JUDGE WEBSTER, JUDGE BRIGHT, JUDGE ROSS
(left to right)
U.S. Court of Appeals, 8th Circuit

42

U. S. GOVERNMENT

CHARLES STODDARD
formerly with
Dept. of Interior

DR. GARY GLASS
EPA—Duluth NWQL

DR. DONALD MOUNT
EPA—Duluth NWQL

DR. I. SELIKOFF
Chief Medical Witness
Government

DR. PHILIP COOK
EPA Enforcement
Duluth

STATE OF MINNESOTA

GOV. WENDELL ANDERSON

GRANT MERRITT
Director, MPCA

Chapter 6

Permits

The regulatory foundation for the birth and growth of the vast Reserve Mining complex at Silver Bay was not laid carelessly or, in fact, without consideration for its possible impact on the waters of Lake Superior. Following the formation of the company, Reserve spent nearly eight years in engineering investigation and planning before it applied for permits from the State of Minnesota. On January 28, 1947 the company formally sought to begin large-scale iron ore beneficiation on the northern shore of Lake Superior. The company and parent owners were taking a substantial risk at this stage, but only, it was assumed, because the taconite beneficiating process was not yet perfected for large-scale application.

Development and operation of a manufacturing facility of this

45

type required, under state and federal statutes, several types of permits. First, the company had to obtain a permit from the Minnesota Department of Conservation to appropriate water from the lake for ore processing and power plant operation. A permit was also required from the Minnesota Pollution Control Agency, to discharge process wastewaters (tailings) and cooling water back into the lake. Lastly, the company needed to construct dock and harbor facilities adjacent to the shoreline at its plant site to facilitate the transport of the finished taconite iron pellets. Because these facilities could pose a potential impingement or hazard to lake navigation, a permit was also required from the U.S. Army Corps of Engineers.

Minnesota state statute required that public hearings be held to provide an opportunity for organized groups and individual citizens to air their views and concerns regarding the potential impact of the proposed project. In response to this mandate, the commissioner of conservation, then Chester A. Wilson, issued an order on May 9, 1947, for public hearings. The first hearing was held on June 5 in the courthouse at Two Harbors, a community approximately midway between Duluth and the area soon to be known as Silver Bay.

Although the state statute required only two hearings, a total of nine were held because of the significance of the issues to the citizens and to the preservation of natural resources. The first and fourth hearings were held in Duluth and the other seven were held in St. Paul, the state capital.

Reserve proposed initially to construct and operate an ore beneficiating plant capable of producing 5 million long tons of concentrated pellets per year. The operation would yield approximately 10 million tons of solid residue each year for disposal or "storage" in Lake Superior. The process was to require 130,000 gallons per minute of lake water to operate both the beneficiating plant and the power plant. This quantity of water, 187 million gallons per day, is roughly equivalent to that required by a city with a population of one million inhabitants.

Early in the public hearings Reserve stated its intentions ultimately to expand its production to 10 million long tons per year, as the demand for iron ore increased. Such expansion could only be undertaken, however, upon issuance of new or revised permits from the state agencies and the U.S. Army Corps of Engineers.

According to Reserve, location of the beneficiating operation on the shores of Lake Superior rather than at the Babbitt mine site, was necessary because of the peculiar lack of a reliable supply of water [1] and the unsuitability of land near the Babbitt mine for onland tailings disposal. But there were also economic reasons that led Reserve to seek the Lake Superior site. H. S. Taylor, mines manager affiliated with Reserve in 1947, stated frankly that "We have shown one of the primary reasons why we are going to Lake Superior is to try to reduce our costs so that we can compete with direct shipping [high-grade] ores. . . ." (11)

Though the mere mention of utilizing Lake Superior as a sink for mining residue based on economic considerations may be repugnant to conservationists of today, the prevailing attitude of most Minnesotans and the general public in the 1940s, '50s, and early '60s was motivated by growth and economic considerations.

Success of the entire Silver Bay beneficiating operation was predicated upon two factors: the presumed effectiveness of a *heavy density current* phenomenon [2] and the existence offshore of the 600- to 900-foot deep Great Trough. Though the principle of the heavy density current was not new in 1947, the application of this principle for waste-water disposal was new and untried.

Reserve attempted to relieve the concern of citizens and, to some extent its own reservations, by retaining as consultants two leading experts on this subject, Dr. Lorenz Straub, director of the University of Minnesota St. Anthony Falls Hydraulics Laboratory, and Dr. Adolph Meyer, a prominent hydraulics engineer. They considered the properties of the expected tailings suspension and the properties of Lake Superior receiving water and made predictions based upon theoretical considerations, field observations of existing density currents, and laboratory experiments. In subsequent years, critics and opponents of Reserve charged

---

[1] The ore body at Babbitt is situated on the Laurentian Divide. Land area to the south of the mine lies in the Lake Superior drainage and the land to the north lies in the Hudson Bay drainage. Consequently, all precipitation drains away from the mine site and precludes the development of a *reliable* water supply. During the federal court trial, water recycle was suggested by government witnesses as a method of minimizing the water requirement.

[2] A heavy density current refers to a flow of liquid which is denser (or heavier) than the surrounding fluid. In this instance, tailings solids in Reserve's discharge results in a fluid slightly more dense than lake water. It does not readily mix with lake water and tends to flow undisturbed to the lake bottom.

that this testimony had limited credibility. Of course, a similar charge could be made by the company regarding expert testimony obtained by regulatory agencies, special interest groups, and other antagonists in later confrontations.

During the hearings, Straub described how the heavy density current would carry tailings to the bottom of the Great Trough. He stated,

> That stream [heavy density current] would then continue along the bottom of the lake and would seek the lowest point of the lake, carrying with it whatever is in the stream. In other words, we have there a stream of greater density than the surrounding fluid, and that stream with the entrained material would carry substantially as a stream to the lower depths until it reached the lowest point, and at the same time the particles, first the coarser ones and then the finer ones, would gradually deposit from the stream. (12)

He demonstrated the phenomenon at the hearing with a small hydraulic model.

Very little rebuttal was offered to the strong scientific testimony offered by Straub and Meyer. The public and representatives of state and federal regulatory agencies participating in the hearings apparently were convinced that the heavy current would function as described, and accepted Reserve's proposal. For several years, up to 1968, there appeared little contrary evidence to suggest that the heavy density current was not functioning as efficiently as Straub predicted. Today, simple observation of the wastewater flow across the tailings delta and into the lake leads one to conclude that the entire residue load is, in fact, descending to the huge natural storage vault in the lake bottom. However, recent sophisticated monitoring techniques and equipment have shown that a portion of the fine suspended particles escape from the density current and is transported under certain conditions outside of the specified discharge zone.

Chairman Wilson discussed the density current issue in his findings of fact. He was convinced, he said, that all tailings particles, including fine particles, would settle out in the deeper portions of the lake and would not cause surface water discoloration or clouding for more than one mile in any direction from the point of discharge. He also expressed confidence that the tailings would not materially affect fish life, public water supplies, or navigation. He further concluded that the project would "provide for the most practical and practicable use of the waters of the lake . . . and will not be materially detrimental to any public interests." (13)

One cannot legitimately question the fact that a heavy density current can and does work at Silver Bay. The point of contention between Reserve and opponents in later years was the degree of efficiency with which the current carries tailings to the lake's bottom.

Surprisingly little testimony was offered during the original hearings regarding lake currents and the potential for sediment transport via these currents. This is especially significant in light of the relatively large quantity of very fine particulate matter in the tailings discharge. Testimony introduced was more speculative than factual, since very few current measurements were made in Lake Superior prior to 1947. Dr. John Moyle, an aquatic biologist with the Minnesota Department of Conservation, testified at the early hearings, "I think that it is highly probable that there is no strong current flowing south close to the shore." (14)

Dr. Mario Fischer, director of public health for the city of Duluth, noted in a letter to the Duluth City Council on October 27, 1947, that there was a lack of information regarding deep currents in Lake Superior and that a study of these currents would be desirable. Fischer concluded in his letter,

> Because of the magnitude of a proper study of deep lake currents in Lake Superior, it appears logical that an appropriate federal agency should be requested to undertake such a study. The results of such a study would have considerable value for other reasons not associated with the tailings problem, one of which would have to do with the location of water supply intakes.

Though obviously desirable, the study of lake currents by a federal agency was delayed for several years—until *after* evidence of tailings was found in water supplies of lake shore communities, including Duluth.

Moyle also offered testimony on the potential impact of tailings in fish spawning grounds. "I should judge," he said, "that as far as permanent effects of the real fine silt in this operation on Lake Superior as a whole [it] would have no more effect than the St. Louis River has had, and that is not very much." [3] There is some question whether Moyle based his calculations on the original 10 million tons per year of tailings residue or the 20 million tons per year released when the plant was to begin operation at its maximum design capacity. Moyle compared the impact of sediments on Lake Superior fish life with the impact of high turbidity waters in smaller inland lakes in Minnesota. He noted that fish production in the latter, especially Red Lake, had not declined as a result of high turbidities. And he said that if the density current did, in fact, function as well as it was originally described, the zone of turbid water would be restricted to the nine square mile discharge zone.

Summing up the turbidity issues, Moyle said:

So, as far as the turbidity created from this plant goes and its effect on fish, it is my opinion that it would have no effect on fish except close to the shore; there might be an area along the shore where the fish wouldn't come in because the turbidity was too high, and I should just judge that wouldn't be extended out more than about a half a mile. (*14*)

Dr. Samuel Eddy, now professor emeritus of zoology at the University of Minnesota, in a preliminary study on the impact of tailings as a consultant for Reserve, had found that tailings deposition would significantly reduce spawning areas in the *immediate* vicinity of the plant. He also noted that tailings would upset the delicate balance of the fish population in a 10–15 square mile area near the plant. But while these conclusions appear noteworthy at first glance, they are not greatly significant because of the inherent problems associated with any effluent mixing zone. Most regulatory agencies recognize that all liquid discharges require a mixing zone wherein kinetic energy of the flowing water can be dissipated, and concentrations of contaminants can be diluted. Consequently, water quality in the mixing or discharge zone is generally not expected to meet the rigorous water quality standards of the remainder of the receiving water body. Furthermore, the impacts on the aquatic ecosystems in the limited discharge zone would be expected to be more pronounced.

[3] Reference 11, p. 78.

The impact on the chemistry of the lake was the subject of some testimony, though basic factual information was again lacking. Reserve's opponents in 1947 expressed their concern that 67,000 tons of anything added to a watercourse must somehow affect water quality. But these individuals and groups were unable to generate solid technical arguments to support their position because of a lack of organization, money, and technical expertise. Several technical experts offered opinions but few facts. Dr. Davis stated, "chemically, of course, they [tailings] will have no effect whatever on the lake." (15) Commenting on his small-scale laboratory studies, Moyle stated,

> [T]he conclusions I draw from my analysis of the water is that, from the chemical point of view, the wash water will have no effect on fish and will have no appreciable effect on the chemistry of Lake Superior. It is just too low in salts of all kinds. (14)

In later years, Reserve built a pond entirely from taconite tailings and stocked it with lake trout. Certainly one of the objectives of this pond project has been to convince visitors that a very active and healthy stock of trout can flourish in the plant effluent.

It is interesting to note that concern for public health was not overlooked as an issue in 1947. Only the nature of the concern was different. Opponents in 1947 argued that the addition of large quantities of silica into the lake could show up in public water supplies and possibly could produce silicosis, or be otherwise harmful when ingested. Dr. Fischer attempted to set this concern to rest in his October 27, 1947, letter to the Duluth City Council. He stated:

> It is a well-known fact that *inhalation* [4] of silica dust is capable of producing a distinct disease known as silicosis, but there is no evidence to support the belief that the *swallowing* [4] of silica is particularly harmful to the human system. This statement is not to be construed as an argument in support of the Mining Company's request for permission to run the tailings into Lake Superior, but is offered merely as one of the reasons why we find ourselves unable to offer a conclusive or irrefutable reason for its denial.

[4] Emphasis provided by author.

No mention was made in the 1947 hearings about the potential dangers from asbestos fibers, which were not then identified in the tailings. This is understandable, since most of the scientific studies done to identify asbestos and medical studies on asbestosis and the carcinogenicity of asbestos were undertaken after 1947 and followed development of electron microscopy which made detection of the submicroscopic particles possible.

On December 16, 1947, nearly one year after Reserve applied for permits and after extensive consideration, the Minnesota Water Pollution Control Commission (MWPCC) issued its permit. Two days later, the Department of Conservation published its findings and conclusions and authorized the appropriation of 130,000 gpm of lake water. Four months later, on April 22, 1948, Reserve received the U.S. Army Corps of Engineers' permit to construct dock and harbor facilities. Now the taconite industry was on its way as a major factor in U.S. resource development.

The permits issued by the Department of Conservation and the MWPCC were similar in terms of effluent discharge requirements and specified several important conditions for the discharge.

1 / The tailings, including power plant return water, were not to include any *material*[5] quantities of water-soluble matter, organic matter, oil, sewage, or other waste except taconite residue.

2 / The tailings were to be discharged into a designated nine-square-mile *zone of discharge*.

3 / The tailings were not to result in *material*[5] clouding or discoloration of the water at the surface outside of the discharge zone except as caused by natural phenomena, including storms.

4 / The tailings were not to exert any *material*[5] effects on fish life or public water supplies.

5 / The tailings were not to result in any *material*[5] interference with navigation or in any public nuisance outside of the discharge zone.

In practice, however, these permit conditions, while appearing at first glance to be rigorous and enforceable, proved weak and nearly

---

[5] Emphasis provided by author.

unenforceable. The conditions were much more qualitative than quantitative in nature. The word *material*[6] can have as many meanings as the number of persons asked to define the term. On one end of the scale, *material* can refer to any measurable, detectable, or quantifiable amount. This ultraconservative interpretation would be difficult to enforce because of limits on analytical techniques and methodologies. Furthermore, natural background conditions might mask any water quality change brought about by a wastewater discharge. On the opposite end of the scale, *material* might be interpreted as any significant, obvious, or substantial change in quality condition. Regulation efforts based upon this interpretation would be stymied until such time as pollution problems would become severe and possibly irreversible. Therefore, the absence of a quantitative definition of the word *material* rendered this permit nearly unenforceable.

The definition of *discharge zone* is equally ambiguous. The definition presented in the permits specifies a nine square-mile surface area zone, i.e., a two-dimensional definition. In fact, the permit specifically prohibits "any material clouding or discoloration of water at the *surface* outside said zone. . . ." This definition could be interpreted to exclude any restriction on *subsurface* movement of tailings in the lake.

In its findings and conclusions, the Department of Conservation appeared to have acknowledged the fact that tailings would migrate to the Great Trough that extends outside of the three-dimensional zone bounded by the vertical projection of the nine square-mile surface area. Again, lack of specificity in writing definitions seriously weakened the significance and enforceability of the state permits, a problem that became more evident in later legal actions.

Another significant provision of the permits extended their effective life "without limitation" until the permittee surrendered them or until they were revoked for violation of permit conditions.

The last provision of the permit clearly specifies that "the permit shall be subject to revocation only for violation of the conditions hereinbefore set forth." This provision gave the Department of Conservation and the MWPCC a mechanism to revoke the permit and stop plant operation if a *material* violation was observed.

The State Department of Conservation also issued a permit to Reserve on August 12, 1947, for the construction of breakwaters in Lake

---

[6] *Webster's New Collegiate Dictionary* defines *material* as having real importance or great consequences.

Superior. Even with this permit in hand, however, Reserve was unable to begin construction until the Army Corps of Engineers' permit was received, and actual construction of the breakwater did not commence until 1952.

Review of the old records shows that the Reserve project was either supported or viewed as unobjectionable by several prestigious conservation groups, state and federal agencies, and private citizens. Included were the U.S. Fish and Wildlife Service, the State Executive Committee of the Izaak Walton League, and the governor's Conservation Committee. The city of Duluth, which originally raised objections regarding the proposed project, withdrew these objections after a public hearing was held in Duluth at the request of the city council. The Wisconsin Conservation Department and the Wisconsin Water Pollution Control Commission (WWPCC) had no major objections. Support of the project also came from the North Shore Commercial Fisheries Association, the North Shore Resort Owners Association, and a number of individual citizens.

The U.S. Army Corps of Engineers' only involvement in 1947 was due to potential interference to navigation posed by the project. Its permit, granted to Reserve in 1948, dealt only with the proposed construction of dock and harbor facilities at Silver Bay and did not address the issue of water pollution. Yet it had the authority also to consider environmental matters associated with the project. The reluctance of the Army Corps to intervene on environmental issues in this case can be traced to the passive attitude of the Army Corps and Justice Department regarding enforcement of Section 13 of the 1899 Rivers and Harbors Act. Section 13, commonly referred to as the Refuse Act, provided the Corps with ample legal muscle to deal with environmental issues. The *Reserve* case was certainly not the first instance in which the Army Corps elected to forego implementation of Section 13 however. In fact, up to 1968, the Army Corps rarely, if ever, exercised this provision against *any* dischargers including industry or municipalities. Section 13 states,

> It shall not be lawful to throw, discharge or deposit . . . from the shore . . . manufacturing establishment of any kind, any refuse matter of any nature or description whatever other than that flowing from streets and sewers and passing therefrom in a liquid state, into tributary of any navigable water. . . .

Up until 1968, the Corps of Engineers acknowledged that "action under Section 13 has . . . been directed by the Department principally against the discharge of those materials that are obstructive or injurious to navigation." This applied to all dischargers, not just Reserve. The Army Corps simply complied with its longstanding tradition of issuing permits under Section 10 of the 1899 act, which pertains only to the construction of any potential obstruction in navigable waters. Thus, the permit issued to Reserve Mining in 1948 was based solely on Section 10 as it applied to the construction of dock and harbor facilities in Lake Superior.

During the period 1948–1955, Reserve was busy constructing the beneficiating plant, the railroad link between Babbitt and Silver Bay, docking and harbor facilities, and the town of Silver Bay itself. Some relatively minor changes in the Army Corps permits were required during the construction period to accommodate alterations in building plans and locations. Changes of this type are not uncommon during the construction of a large industrial complex such as that developed at Silver Bay.

In the fall of 1955, the first load of taconite ore reached the Silver Bay plant, known as the E. W. Davis Works, for processing. At that time, only one of the 2.5 million ton-per-year production units was completed and operational. Within a very few months, Reserve found that the taconite beneficiating process pioneered by Dr. Davis could be effectively operated on a large-scale basis. It immediately launched into the next phase of its project, the construction and operation of a second 2.5 million ton per year concentrator. The operation of this second unit also required approximately 130,000 gpm of water for process and power plant cooling. In order to secure rights to appropriate this additional lake water and discharge a comparable amount of wastewater into the lake, Reserve had to apply to the appropriate state agencies for an amendment to the original 1947 permits.

On July 6, 1956, the commissioner of conservation granted Reserve an amended permit that authorized the increase in water appropriation from 130,000 gpm to 260,000 gpm. Apparently, this action was taken without a formal hearing. The MWPCC, however, did hold a public hearing on September 25, 1956, in Duluth. Little objection was raised to the request by Reserve to increase discharge into the lake. On November 12, 1956, the MWPCC issued an amended permit to Reserve that simply increased the allowable effluent discharge from

130,000 gpm to 260,000 gpm. The amended MWPCC permit further ordered Reserve to "submit semi-annual reports to the Commission [on] the effect of tailings deposits in Lake Superior."

By 1960, the nation's increased demand for iron coincided with a further decrease in high-grade iron ore. Fortunately, the taconite beneficiating process had stimulated a whole new industry and several new plants emerged in the Lake Superior region to tap this substitute iron source. And the time had come for Reserve to initiate the third and final stage of its plant expansion program, the doubling of production from 5 to 10 million tons of pellets per year. Of course, plant expansion meant a need for more water and a corresponding increase in effluent discharge. Consequently, Reserve went to the Department of Conservation and the MWPCC a third time to seek amendments to the company's permits. Following a public hearing on the applications, the MWPCC issued an amended permit to Reserve on September 8, 1960. The amendment changed the allowable effluent discharge to 502,000 gpm. The permit also required that Reserve establish a more intensive lake monitoring program. A week earlier, the Department of Conservation issued an amended permit to the company to provide for appropriation of 502,000 gpm of water from Lake Superior.

In June of 1960, Reserve applied to the U.S. Army Corps of Engineers for a permit amendment that would allow for an increase in tailings disposal into the lake. Reserve requested that the amended permit be extended for an indefinite period, i.e., the life of the mining operation at Silver Bay. On July 22 of that year, Reserve received both good news and bad news from the Army Corps of Engineers. The good news was that their request for increased tailings discharge had been approved. The bad news, however, was that the permit was restricted to a 10-year period, i.e., through December 31, 1970.

Reserve was not satisfied with this ruling. The company argued that the large capital investment needed for plant expansion could not be justified to independent lending groups without a firmer long-term permit. Reserve renewed its request for an indefinite permit. After consultation with the Minnesota state regulatory agencies, the Army Corps changed its earlier position and on October 11, 1960, granted the indefinite extension. The state agencies had previously granted indefinite permits pointing out that these permits could be revoked at any time for cause. Apparently, the Army Corps felt that such revocation provisions provided ample safeguard against resource exploitation by the company.

With indefinite discharge permits now in hand, Reserve undertook the third and final phase of plant expansion at the E. W. Davis Works. The completed plant began full operation in 1963, producing approximately 30,000 tons of pelletized iron each day, using over 500,000 gallons per minute of water, and producing nearly 67,000 tons of tailings residue daily for disposal in Lake Superior.

Shortly after receiving discharge permits in 1960, Reserve began experimenting with flyash in the beneficiating process to improve product recovery. Because this material got into the tailings that entered the lake, Reserve sought and received permission for the additional discharge from the Minnesota State Department of Health. At that time, however, the Army Corps was not informed of the change in discharge character, since, according to Reserve officials, the flyash experiments were only experimental and temporary in nature. It was not until 1965 that Reserve formally notified the Army Corps of the flyash additive in the tailings discharge. In the spring of 1970, the Minnesota Pollution Control Agency required that Reserve discontinue its discharge of flyash with tailings and deposit it instead on land.

Thus during the period of 1947 through 1960, the Reserve Mining Company followed a comprehensive development plan, which the company outlined during the initial permit hearings in 1947. It appears that the company acted responsibly and in good faith throughout to secure bonafide permits from appropriate state and federal agencies to implement its plan. The company also invested extensively in a lake monitoring program.

On the other hand, the obvious lack of any sound scientific studies by the state or federal agencies during this period is readily apparent. No significant attempt was made by these agencies to establish pre-operation baseline conditions in the lake or determine the fate or impact of tailings subsequently discharged into the lake. Many valid explanations could be developed in defense of these agencies, however; the principal one is that the prevailing attitude of the populace in the 1940s, 1950s, and early 1960s was pro-business and pro-growth, with only passing concern for environmental quality. Consequently, agencies were not urged to action by citizen groups or politicians. Also, during this period of environmental moderation, agencies' budgets were tight and few funds were available to invest in costly monitoring programs such as that required for Lake Superior. Moreover, there was no question at that time that Reserve was acting in good faith and was making a significant contribution to the well-being of all Minnesotans.

CHRONOLOGY OF PERMIT HEARINGS
AND AWARDS

May 9, 1947	Commissioner of Conservation Wilson called for public hearings
June 5, 1947	First hearing held in the courthouse in Duluth
June 17, 1947	Second hearing held in St. Paul
July 3, 1947	Third hearing held in St. Paul
July 11, 1947	Fourth hearing held in Duluth
July 22, 1947	Fifth hearing held in St. Paul
August 12, 1947	Department of Conservation issued a permit to Reserve for the construction of breakwaters in Lake Superior
September 4, 1947	Sixth hearing held in St. Paul
September 30, 1947	Seventh hearing held in St. Paul
October 21, 1947	Eighth hearing held in St. Paul
November 4, 1947	Ninth and last hearing held in St. Paul
December 16, 1947	Permit issued to Reserve by the MWPCC
December 18, 1947	Permit issued to Reserve by the Dept. of Conservation
April 22, 1948	Permit issued to Reserve by the U.S. Army Corps of Engineers
Fall 1955	First taconite ore reaches Reserve's E. W. Davis Works at Silver Bay
July 6, 1956	Reserve received an amended permit from the Department of Conservation that authorized an increased water appropriation from 130,000 gpm to 260,000 gpm
September 25, 1956	MWPCC hearing in Duluth regarding Reserve's request for permit modifications
November 12, 1956	MWPCC issued amended permit to Reserve with authorized increase in wastewater discharge into the lake from 130,000 gpm to 260,000 gpm
September 1, 1960	Department of Conservation issued amended permit to Reserve allowing for an increase in water appropriation from 260,000 gpm to 502,000 gpm
September 8, 1960	MWPCC issued an amended permit to Reserve authorizing an increase in wastewater discharge to 502,000 gpm

Chapter 7

Federal Enforcement Conference: Statutory Prelude

Though apparent quiet prevailed on the northern banks of Lake Superior through 1968, several key pieces of federal legislation were being promulgated and orders issued in the Minnesota state capital and in Washington, D.C., which were to have a profound impact upon Reserve in later years. Simultaneously, a "Save the Lake" movement, aimed at Reserve, was born and started to gain momentum.

Under a directive from President Lyndon Johnson, the Department of the Interior initiated a series of water quality investigations on important rivers and lakes. A study of Lake Superior, launched in 1968, produced charges that Reserve's effluent was polluting the lake. This marked the beginning of the end of Reserve's exhalted image in the eyes of the public. Shortly after the release of this study, the Secretary of the

Interior called for a federal enforcement conference to further investigate charges of pollution by Reserve and other dischargers in the Lake Superior basin.

Statutory authority for this conference can be traced back to the initial Federal Water Pollution Control Act (FWPCA) promulgated in 1948, ironically just one year after Reserve received its initial permit to operate at Silver Bay. The 1948 FWPCA was very general in its provisions and placed primary responsibility for pollution abatement on the states. The act also stressed the importance of considering economics and technical practicability and feasibility in securing pollution abatement. This basic concern was retained through all subsequent amendments of the act, up to the amendments of 1972.

The 1948 FWPCA was renewed in 1952 and made a permanent law in 1956. The 1956 amendments gave the Surgeon General of the United States authority to call a conference if he found that serious pollution problems warranted enforcement action. Congressman Blatnik of Minnesota was one of the principal architects of the 1956 law. It specified that following a conference, dischargers found to be polluting navigable waters were to be given six months to take corrective action. Though the earlier act was strengthened by the 1956 amendments, enforcement provisions were still weak and not well defined. The 1956 act also failed to adequately extend jurisdiction to all navigable waters including coastal waters and most of the Great Lakes.

Congress moved again in 1961 to modify the act, overcoming some of the shortcomings of the 1956 act and extending federal jurisdiction to all navigable waters in the United States, including the U.S. portion of the Great Lakes. Administration of the act was transferred from the Surgeon General to the Department of Health, Education, and Welfare (HEW).

A much more comprehensive change in environmental rules emerged in 1965 when the FWPCA was amended for a third time. These changes, enacted as the Water Quality Act of 1965, incorporated the concept of water quality standards for all navigable waters. Section 10 (C) of the act gave the states the responsibility of developing these standards subject to federal approval. Failure by a state to develop satisfactory standards gave the Secretary of Health, Education, and Welfare authority to override and develop appropriate standards for that state. Shortly after passage of the new act, the newly created Federal Water Pollution Control Administration (FWPCA) was transferred from HEW to the Department of the Interior.

Originally the bill, as introduced in the Senate by Senator Edmund Muskie, of Maine, had charged the Secretary of the Interior with the responsibility and authority of setting water quality standards for all navigable waters. This usurpation of environmental quality control powers from the states was not acceptable in the House of Representatives. Congressman Blatnik succeeded in returning water quality standards-setting and regulatory functions to the states.

Almost immediately, though, the Secretary of Interior initiated a move to implement the water quality standards-setting provisions of the act. The FWPCA was also renamed the Federal Water Quality Administration (FWQA).

The mandate of the Water Quality Act for standards-setting placed an enormous burden on the states. Many, because of insufficient staff, budget, and/or inadequate organization, were ill-prepared to respond to the secretary's call for state water quality standards by June 30, 1967. Minnesota was no exception. Since the task could not have been effectively undertaken by the existing Minnesota Water Pollution Control Commission (MWPCC), the state legislature established the Minnesota Pollution Control Agency (MPCA). The MPCA immediately began developing water quality standards for all lakes and streams in Minnesota, including Lake Superior.

The weak enforcement provisions that plagued the Federal Water Pollution Control Act from its enactment in 1948 were addressed in the water quality standards concept introduced in 1965. This appeared at the time to enhance the enforcement provisions of the act. Section 10 (C) (5) of the 1965 act stated that "the discharge of matter into such interstate waters or portions thereof which reduces the quality of such waters below the water quality standards established under that subsection—is subject to abatement." This section provided a direct mechanism for obtaining compliance by dischargers. If the water quality standards developed and approved for a navigable watercourse were violated, and if the pollution endangered the health or welfare of persons in a state other than the one in which the discharge originated, the Secretary of Interior could request the Attorney General to bring suit on behalf of the United States against the discharger. A suit could also be initiated for intrastate violations if the governor of the state sought such action from the secretary.

Legal action under this section required, however, that the court give "due consideration to the practicability and to physical and economic feasibility of complying with such standards," then pass judgment "as the public interest and the equities of that case may require." This reservation provided a mechanism whereby a pollution problem could be placed in broader perspective and weighed against other important societal needs.

The second type of enforcement procedure specified by the act appeared in Section 10 (D) and involved enforcement conferences. This approach was complicated and lengthy but did insure a more rational technical basis for decision-making. Enforcement conferences could be called by the secretary of interior in response to:

1 /   A request from the governor of a state that was being affected by pollution generated by another state;

2 /   A request from the governor of a state experiencing intrastate pollution that endangers or could have endangered persons in that state; or

3 /   Without a request from a governor, when interstate pollution endangers public health and welfare.

The secretary could not intervene in a case involving *intrastate* pollution unless he received a formal request from the governor (or a pollution control agency) of that state.

Enforcement conferences once requested, were to be convened three weeks after public notice. Upon completion of a conference, the secretary was required to prepare a summary of findings and make recommendations for remedial action.

The discharger was then to be given six months to develop and implement corrective actions. Should the discharger not satisfy the specified abatement requirements, the secretary was required to call a public hearing before a hearing board of five or more persons appointed by the secretary. Following this hearing, the board was to recommend measures to be taken by the secretary, who in turn, specified actions to be taken by the state and the discharger. A second six-month implementation period was then given. If no action or inadequate action was taken by the discharger, the secretary could then request the Attorney General to bring suit against the discharger. Interestingly, if the pollution problem did not constitute an interstate health hazard, the governor of the state in which the discharge originated could *prevent* legal action.

The enforcement conference approach for pollution abatement had been invoked less than 50 times up to 1969, with varying degrees of success. Many now believe that this slow and often ineffective enforcement procedure weakened the otherwise sound Water Quality Act of 1965 and spelled its doom.

The FWPC Act of 1972 dramatically changed not only the basic concept of environmental quality control from water quality standards to effluent quality standards but also included more direct and decisive enforcement provisions. Whether this rigorous and tough 1972 act will be effective and enforceable remains to be seen. Because of its weak scientific base and unrealistic economic and timing provisions, it appears that major problems lie just ahead for this act as well.

Chapter 8

The Stoddard
Report

The image of Reserve as an industry operating in harmony with the environment suffered its first serious blow in January 1969 when the so-called Stoddard Report was leaked to the press in Washington, D.C. This report was prepared under the direction of Charles Stoddard, then a regional coordinator of the U.S. Department of the Interior.

The report described tailings from the Reserve operation at Silver Bay as seriously polluting the waters of Lake Superior. Though only a preliminary document, and not accepted by the Department as an official document, the calculated leak of the paper triggered an avalanche of criticism of Reserve by state and federal regulatory agencies, conservation groups, and the public. It did what it was apparently intended by its author to do. It precipitated the subsequent federal enforcement conferences and court cases.

The "Stoddard Affair" had its roots in the issuance of "Executive Order No. 11288" by President Johnson on July 7, 1966. That order implemented the Federal Water Pollution Control Act. The order directed that the "Secretary of the Interior shall, in administering the Federal Water Pollution Control Act, as amended, provide technical advice and assistance to the heads of other departments, agencies, and establishments in connection with their duties and responsibilities under this order." One federal agency in obvious need of technical assistance in the environmental protection area was the U.S. Army Corps of Engineers. The Army Corps had significant undischarged environmental responsibilities under Section 10 of the 1899 Rivers and Harbors Act. There are many possible explanations for the Army Corps' reluctance to enforce the act. First, this section of the act, referred to as "The Refuse Act," was too general and lacked clarification of purpose, scope, and enforcement procedures. Second, the Army Corps lacked trained personnel and the administrative machinery to effectively and equitably enforce the water pollution abatement provisions. This second limitation was partially overcome by President Johnson's order for inter-agency cooperation.

In response to the executive order, a "Memorandum of Understanding" was entered into between the Department of the Interior and the Department of the Army. This document, signed on July 13, 1967, by Secretary of the Interior Stewart Udall and Army Secretary Stanley Resor, acknowledged the responsibilities of the U.S. Army Corps of Engineers under Sections 10 and 13 of the 1899 Rivers and Harbors Act. It also recognized the interrelationships of those Army Corps responsibilities with responsibilities of the Secretary of the Interior under the Federal Water Pollution Control Act and other federal acts relating to the control and prevention of water pollution and the conservation of natural resources.

The memorandum outlined procedures for implementing cooperative efforts between the two federal agencies. They included:

1 / The district engineer was authorized to send notices to officials of the Department of the Interior and other interested persons or agencies when a permit application was received.

2 / The regional directors of the Department of the Interior were authorized to make "such studies and investigations as they determined necessary or desirable . . . and advise the District

Engineer [about] the work proposed by the permit applicant, including the deposit of any material in or near navigable waters in violation of applicable water quality standards or unreasonably impair natural resources or the related environment."

3 / In certain difficult cases, the Secretary of the Army could seek advice and counsel from the Secretary of the Interior on matters relating to environmental or wildlife damage and then could "either deny the permit or include such conditions in the permit as he determined to be in the public interest."

4 / There should be "full coordination and cooperation . . . at all organizational levels" including the resolution of differing views "at the earliest practicable time, and at the field organizational unit most directly concerned."

5 / The district engineers were ordered to "avail themselves of the technical advice and assistance which the Directors may provide."

The Army-Interior memorandum was quite explicit regarding procedures for dealing with new permit applications—but not so explicit about *existing* permits. After some deliberation, the Army Corps elected to extend the strict review procedure to existing permits, including those granted for indefinite periods. As a result the Army Corps on November 1, 1967, sent a notice of revalidation for the *Reserve* permit to the regional directors of the Department of the Interior. Shortly thereafter, the department issued a manual specifically designed to assist its regional directors in implementing the provisions of the memorandum.

On the authority of this directive, the regional coordinator for the Lake Superior region, Stoddard, initiated a study to determine the influence of taconite tailings on the water quality of Lake Superior. Stoddard began by soliciting the assistance of several federal and state agencies. He first convened these groups in February of 1968, then reassembled them a month later to map out a study plan. The agencies, which came to be known as the Taconite Study Group, included representatives of the Bureau of Sport Fisheries and Wildlife, Federal Water Quality Administration, Bureau of Commercial Fisheries, Bureau of Mines, and the Geological Survey. All were administratively controlled by the Department of the Interior. The Taconite Study Group was chaired by Stoddard. State regulatory agencies from Minnesota and Wisconsin were invited to participate as members. Even though they declined to become members, they did offer their assistance. The Minnesota

Department of Conservation elected to design and conduct a lake study of its own. The conclusions of its study interestingly were in substantial conflict with those outlined in the Taconite Study Group's Stoddard report. The U.S. Army Corps of Engineers also joined in the meetings, but as a nonparticipating observer.

Because of an apparent press for time, representative agencies of the Taconite Study Group were required to conduct all of their field studies on Lake Superior during the summer months of 1968, an incredibly short time to gather meaningful information considering the paucity of existing field data and the vastness of Lake Superior.

Nonetheless, preliminary findings from all participating agencies were received and analyzed in September and a preliminary report was drafted. This draft report was circulated for review and comment among the Taconite Study Group. On December 31, 1968, the group's report, the Stoddard Report, was completed. Part I of the report, which included a summary of data, conclusions, and recommendations, was forwarded to the district engineer, in accordance with the provisions of the Army-Interior memorandum. Part II of the report contained supporting documents that included reports from the participating federal agencies, the two state agencies, and the Reserve Mining Company.

It would appear so far that Stoddard simply responded in a straightforward manner to ground rules established by the Departments of the Interior and Army. Much criticism was yet to come, however.

First, the study, while in progress, was attacked by conservationists as being inadequate and superficial. After the study and report were completed, Reserve reacted negatively to the findings and conclusions, claiming that the report contained "serious errors." The intensity of Reserve's reaction was no doubt, at least in part, fueled by the contrary findings and conclusions contained in the Minnesota Pollution Control Agency report.

The Stoddard Report was never officially released by the Taconite Study Group, the U.S. Army Corps of Engineers, or the Department of the Interior. The details surrounding its leak remain a mystery, despite many disclaimers, accusations, claims, and counterclaims by high officials in the Department of the Interior, prominent politicians, Reserve officials, and Stoddard. Never accepted by the Department of the Interior as an official document, it remained an internal staff report. Interior officials held that it had not undergone proper departmental review. Stoddard and his supporters argued that the procedures for report preparation and dissemination followed the guidelines set forth in the Army-Interior memorandum and implementation manual. In addition to procedural criticisms, the Department of the Interior also questioned the validity of the study and certain conclusions in the report. One high department official, Max Edwards [1], stated, "I think there are some conclusions in that report which are obviously incorrect." (16) Congressman Blatnik (author of the 1956 Water Pollution Control Act) also questioned its validity and accuracy. This position cost Blatnik support from conservation groups and others in opposition to Reserve. Accusations and innuendos were published in the print media, which suggested that Blatnik compromised his position as a staunch environmentalist because of pressures from Reserve, the major industry in his congressional district.

Though several other politicians and high agency officials joined in the criticism of the Stoddard Report, there were others who supported Stoddard and his report, including the agencies in the Taconite Study Group. Some opponents of Reserve charged publicly that the Stoddard Report was "suppressed" in Washington through political pressures by Reserve. Several interesting accounts have been written that blend supposition and theory with a limited amount of documentation to develop a case for political suppression of the report. (17)

Regardless of the official or unofficial status of the Stoddard Report, or the validity of any or all of its findings, conclusions, and recommendations, or its procedural irregularities, the fact remains that this document was the primary catalyst that prompted the "Federal Enforcement Conference" and ultimately the state and federal court cases against Reserve.

This was the first major technical report that openly accused Reserve of polluting Lake Superior and of violating its state and federal permits. Interestingly, the conclusions reached in this report were in conflict with those presented a few months later by the Minnesota Pollution Control Agency. Which group was right—the Taconite Study Group comprised of federal agencies, or the state agency? Obviously, Reserve considered its position vindicated by the state report, which found no pollution of Lake Superior by tailings discharge, whereas Reserve's opponents considered the Stoddard Report to be valid and infallible. Each side rallied around the portion of the document that supported its position.

The Stoddard Report presented 15 separate conclusions on key

---

[1] Max Edwards: Then Assistant Secretary of the Interior for Water Quality and Research.

technical issues. These issues were subsequently debated in the "Federal Enforcement Conference," in the state court, and to a limited extent in federal court. A brief elaboration of these issues follows.

The Stoddard Report concluded (Conclusion No. 1) that the total discharge of solids from Reserve's E. W. Davis Works in just 12 days was equivalent to the sediment contributed to Lake Superior by all U.S. tributary streams during one year. (This is not surprising since large quantities of solid residue from a taconite operation are inevitable. It takes three tons of ore to produce one ton of high-grade iron pellets. The remainder must be discharged as an unwanted residue. Therefore, to produce 10 million tons of iron pellets per year (30,000 tons/day), approximately 65–70,000 tons of residue is produced daily for ultimate "disposal.")

Conclusion No. 2 of the Stoddard Report was that a portion of these solids escaped the density current and moved downshore in prevailing lake currents.

Stoddard alleged in Conclusion No. 5 that the vagrant tailings carried by lake currents were distributed "at least 10 miles off shore and 18 miles southwest of the plant." The issue of tailings identification in lake bottom deposits was hotly contested in subsequent confrontations between the government and the company.

Stoddard further charged (Conclusion No. 6) that lake currents were sufficient to carry sub-micron tailings particles long distances, even into interstate waters. (Sub-micron particles are produced by the abrasive grinding actions essential to the taconite beneficiating process. Such particles, referred to by scientists as colloids, do resist gravity settling especially in a turbulent environment. Lake currents provide a degree of turbulence.)

In Conclusion No. 8, Stoddard charged Reserve with violation of their state permits since some of the escaped tailings solids caused surface clouding or discoloration outside of the discharge zone specified in the permit. Suspended solids, whether from taconite tailings or river sediment, tend to restrict the passage of light through a water column. One of the intrinsic values of Lake Superior water is its extreme clarity, i.e., low turbidity. A slight increase in turbidity of these waters as a result of added suspended solids may not be visible to the naked eye, but does restrict light penetration and hence could alter the photosynthetic ecosystem in the lake.

Stoddard claimed (Conclusion No. 3) that turbidity was three to five times greater southwest of the plant (in the direction of the prevailing lake current) than in the waters northwest of the discharge. He also stated that subsurface turbidities were 10 to 60 times greater than that of surface waters.

(The purpose of specifying a discharge zone is to provide a transition zone in which the kinetic energy of a wastewater can be dissipated by a more quiescent receiving water body. Further, it provides a buffer zone for mixing and dilution. Water quality in the discharge zone should not be expected to be as high as that in the remainder of the receiving water.)

The *green water* phenomenon was observed in several parts of Lake Superior and for many years before the E. W. Davis Works became operational. Green water is a perceived color rather than a true color. This phenomenon results from the refraction of sunlight from particles suspended in surface waters of the lake. Taconite solids can produce this apparent color and thereby impair the aesthetic qualities of the lake. However, green water is more a visual nuisance factor than a water quality problem.

Stoddard concluded (No. 4) that "tailings suspended in water cause green water for distances at least 18 miles southwest from the point of discharge."

Soluble substances in the tailings discharge were an issue of considerable debate in the subsequent enforcement conference and state court case. Like many rocks, taconite contains a number of different elements (in addition to iron) including copper, lead, chromium, phosphorus, etc. These elements are chemically bound and are not readily released into solution as a result of crushing operations. Though these elements are toxic or otherwise biologically active in soluble form, they are essentially inert in the chemically bound state.

Stoddard charged in Conclusion No. 7 that federal-state water quality standards for iron, lead, and copper were violated as a result of tailings discharge.

Conclusion No. 9 claimed that the criteria recommended by the National Technical Advisory Committee for zinc and cadmium had also been exceeded. (Water quality standards and/or criteria generally refer to the soluble or biologically active form, not the total content as reported by Stoddard.)

Algal stimulation also drew immediate interest and concern, especially in light of the ecological disaster in Lake Erie and incipient problems in Lake Michigan. Algae are microscopic, photosynthetic plants that cannot grow without a number of basic elements. The nutrients, nitrogen (N) and phosphorus (P), are needed in relatively large quantities, whereas other elements such as copper, iron, cobalt, etc., are required, but only in trace amounts. Waters deficient in one or more of these essential elements will not support significant algal growth. These elements gain entry into surface waters from the natural dissolution of rocks and from man-induced sources such as domestic sewage, industrial wastes, and agricultural drainage. Given all of the essential elements, algal growth rates can be further enhanced by the presence of suspended matter, which provides a solid surface for attachment, nutrient release, and/or physical protection. Stoddard's Conclusion No. 10 stated that sufficient phosphorus is discharged in the tailings to stimulate algal growth. Further, Conclusion No. 12 charged that sub-micron particles of taconite tailings also stimulate the growth of algae in Lake Superior waters.

Some types of benthic fauna [2] are important in the fish food chain. These organisms thrive in the photic zone, i.e., where light penetrates the water column. Very few important benthic fauna exist offshore in the deep waters of Lake Superior. The issue in the Reserve case was the degree to which tailings physically covered or displaced important bottom fauna. Were all tailings deposited in the Great Trough as originally thought, then only those organisms on the bottom of the discharge zone would be affected. Stoddard claimed (Conclusion No. 11) that benthic fauna were reduced in numbers southwest of the plant for at least 15.5 miles.

Toxicity of tailings to aquatic life was a major Reserve issue as far back as the 1947 permit hearings. Acute toxicity is measured by standard bioassay procedures in which selected test organisms are exposed to different concentrations of a suspected toxicant or wastewater for a specified exposure period, generally 48 to 96 hours. The number of organisms remaining alive in each test tank are compared to those in a control tank that contains only dilution water (in this instance water from Lake Superior). Stoddard reported in Conclusion No. 13 that taconite tailings at a concentration of $\frac{1}{4}$ and $\frac{1}{10}$ of full strength were found to be lethal to rainbow sac fry in a few days. These are concentrations that are found only in the immediate vicinity of the heavy density current.

Stoddard's Conclusion No. 14 appeared to suggest that the tail-

---

[2] Benthic fauna: A term that refers to aquatic life that inhabits the bottom zone of a body of water.

ings discharge was responsible for some changes in commercial fish catch. He acknowledged, however, that much larger changes were brought about by lamprey predation and overfishing.

Stoddard's fifteenth and final conclusion stated that "Alternative disposal methods are available." Even though he was not explicit, support documents available to the Taconite Study Group referred to possible onland disposal. This issue surfaced in the latter stages of the conference proceedings and continued throughout the controversy.

In sharp contrast to the negative findings and conclusions of the Stoddard Report, the Minnesota Pollution Control Agency Report (published in November 1969) (2) were supportive of Reserve's claims. The MPCA study compared water quality measurements taken during the survey period of November 3–7, 1969, with results of similar surveys undertaken in 1948, 1953, 1955, and 1966. The four conclusions were:

1 / The overall water quality of Lake Superior at the time of the survey in the vicinity of Silver Bay was found to be excellent at all sampling stations.

2 / No significant difference was found in the quality of the water outside of the Reserve Mining Company permit area and that inside the area at the time of the survey, except for the 5-day biochemical oxygen demand which was significantly higher outside the area. These higher values are probably attributable to the rivers flowing into the lake south of the permit area.

3 / One sample taken approximately 15 miles southwest of the permit area had a lead concentration slightly in excess of the limit prescribed for Lake Superior by Regulation WPC 15. There was no apparent reason for this high value, and further investigative work is indicated to establish its significance.

4 / Every effort should be made to preserve the excellent quality of the lake.

Which report correctly appraised the effect of Reserve's discharge remained the overriding issue—that is, the overriding issue until the company's opponents abruptly introduced the asbestos issue in June 1973.

Chapter 9

Federal Enforcement Conference: First Session

At 9:30 A.M. on May 13, 1969, the Honorable Carl L. Klein, Assistant Secretary of the Interior for Water Quality, opened the "Conference in the Matter of Pollution of the Interstate Waters of Lake Superior and its Tributary Basin—Minnesota, Wisconsin, Michigan." The conference was held in the ornate old ballroom at the Hotel Duluth in Duluth, Minnesota, before a packed audience.

The call for the conference had been issued on January 16, 1969, by Secretary of the Interior Udall under Section 10(d)(1) of the Federal Water Pollution Control Act, as amended. The secretary was authorized to initiate a conference "whenever, on the basis of reports, surveys, or studies, he has reason to believe that any pollution referred to in subsection (a)[1] [endangers] the health and welfare of persons in a State other than that in which the discharge or discharges originate or are occurring."

It is important to recognize that this conference was initiated by the Secretary of the Interior, not by the governor of any one of the three states that border the U.S. portion of Lake Superior. In the absence of hard evidence of interstate pollution or harm to public health and welfare, the secretary stressed that this conference was to be of a fact-finding and exploratory nature. The call for a conference came less than one month after the unofficial release of the Stoddard Report which accused Reserve of causing interstate pollution.

Twelve official conferees were designated, three from each state pollution control agency and three federal representatives. Key members were:

Honorable David D. Dominick, commissioner of the FWPCA (Co-chairman)

John P. Badalich, executive director, Minnesota Pollution Control Agency

Thomas Frangos, administrator, Wisconsin Department of Natural Resources

Ralph Purdy, executive secretary, Michigan Water Resources Commission

During the three-day conference over 120 persons presented testimony as expert witnesses, representatives of special interest organizations, or concerned citizens. In addition, over 400 persons registered as interested observers.

In opening remarks, Klein reminded conferees and observers that the FWPCA delegated the primary rights and responsibilities of water pollution abatement to the states. He said that the purpose of the conference was to

. . . bring together the state water pollution control agencies,

[1] Subsection 10(a) states, "The pollution of interstate or navigable waters in or adjacent to any State or States (whether the matter causing or contributing to such pollution is discharged directly into such waters or reaches such waters after discharge into a tributary of such waters), which endangers the health or welfare of any persons, shall be subject to abatement as provided in this Act."

representatives of the U.S. Department of the Interior, and other interested parties to review the situation, the progress toward abatement, to lay a basis for future action by all parties concerned, and to give the states, localities, and industries an opportunity to take any indicated remedial action under state and local law.[2]

He further noted that the federal government lacked jurisdiction to even invite appropriate Canadian agencies to the conference.

Minnesota's Governor Harold Levander, the lead-off speaker, voiced his concern for keeping "a vigilant watch over the water quality of one of the largest, purest, youngest, and most delicate lakes in the world."[3] He also stressed the importance of seeking facts in order to "pursue the most proper and vigorous course in fighting pollution."[4]

Critics of Governor Levander and of Reserve point to the Governor's unwillingness to initiate a state call for a conference as a pro-Reserve delay tactic. However, at that point there was little solid evidence of "material" pollution of Lake Superior from the discharge of taconite tailings or any other source of contaminant. Further, the Stoddard Report had just been released and was unofficial and controversial. Also, the state's own pollution control agency was in the process of preparing a report on Lake Superior, and the results had not yet been compiled nor conclusions reached. Thus, a call from the governor for an enforcement conference would have been premature and technically indefensible.

The governor cited with pride: "All municipalities and industries on the lake were given orders of compliance. Each municipality and every industry is now required not only to provide secondary treatment of their wastes, but we have also gone a step further to require tertiary treatment."[5] Although Reserve has carried the brunt of the attack by environmentalists, regulatory agencies, and the public for non-compliance, as of 1974, *all* municipalities along the lake had failed to comply not only with the tertiary treatment requirement but some, the secondary treatment requirement as well; *all* municipalities—except

---

[2] Proceedings of "Federal Enforcement Conference in the Matter of Pollution of Lake Superior and Its Tributary Basin, Minnesota–Washington–Michigan," First Session, U.S.D.I.–FWPCA, May 13–15, 1969, p. 7.
[3] Ibid., p. 11.
[4] Ibid.
[5] Ibid., p. 12.

one, Silver Bay, which put in secondary treatment in 1953 and tertiary treatment in 1973.

Next to speak was Congressman Blatnik, author of legislation which provided the authority for the conference. Blatnik related his early personal experiences and acquaintance with Lake Superior. He recalled his long record of environmental activities and accomplishments in Congress, and stressed the importance of following the legal machinery provided in the Water Pollution Control Act. Although he defined the purpose of the Duluth enforcement conference as "to study the pollution problems of the entire Lake Superior Basin," he fully recognized that the focal point of the conference was the discharge of tailings from Reserve's E. W. Davis Works at Silver Bay. He said also that if the tailings discharge was polluting Lake Superior, then "the mining company . . . should and must take corrective actions." [6]

The Reserve question posed a real dilemma for the congressman. On one hand, Reserve's mining operation had rejuvenated the dying economy of his congressional district, and provided many jobs. On the other hand, he was committed as a public servant and long-recognized defender of natural resources to protect the high quality of Lake Superior for future generations. Though he attempted to keep these responsibilities in proper perspective, his actions and statements regarding the Reserve case drew constant criticism from Reserve's opponents.

The conference proceeded with more political dignitaries, the Honorable Warren Knowles, governor of Wisconsin, and Michigan's Governor William Milliken. Both governors spoke of Lake Superior's great beauty and intrinsic value and pledged support in preserving its high quality. Like many successful politicians, the governors' remarks were rich in superlatives and generalities but sidestepped the specific issues to be raised at the conference.

Colonel R. J. Hesse, district engineer for the U.S. Army Corps of Engineers, then outlined the Corps' pollution abatement responsibilities on Lake Superior—from the Army Corps' perspective. He spoke of the dredging activity in harbor areas and acknowledged that for 40 years the Army Corps had deposited dredge spoils in deep water areas of the lake. He acknowledged the pollution potential of this activity and indicated that the Army Corps had begun to study alternative disposal areas. Apparently, alternative methods have not been feasible since the Army Corps continues to dump polluted dredge spoils in Lake Superior.

[6] Ibid., p. 27.

Colonel Hesse next addressed the relationship of the Army Corps and Reserve Mining at Silver Bay. He reviewed the sequence and substance of permit granting by the Army Corps. He also verified that on November 1, 1967, a notice was sent to all interested parties regarding the Army Corps' intent to revalidate Reserve's permit for a 5-year period. He commented on several portions of the Taconite Study Group Report, although he did not mention it by name.

The conference proceedings got more specific with the presentation of Dale S. Bryson, director of the FWPCA's Lake Superior basin office. Bryson introduced into the record the *official* study prepared by the Department of the Interior entitled "An Appraisal of Water Pollution in the Lake Superior Basin." This report considered existing and potential pollution problems of all types in the Lake Superior basin. Even though portions of the report dealing with Reserve's tailings disposal were obviously strongly influenced by the findings of the Taconite Study Group, there were significant differences in the tone and substance of many of the conclusions. For example:

Stoddard Report:

Tailings suspended in the water cause "green water" for distances at least 18 miles southwest from the point of discharge.

FWPCA Report:

The occurrence of tailings was evident in "green water" masses. In *one instance* [7] the "green water" containing tailings was visibly present 18 miles southwest of the plant. "Green water" was observed along the Wisconsin shore line and did not contain tailings.

Furthermore, the FWPCA report did not support Conclusions 7, 9, and 10 of the Stoddard Report, which dealt with the release of toxic substances and phosphorus from tailings. FWPCA investigators apparently were not convinced that adequate scientific data was available to support these serious charges. Subsequent federal studies have shown that the FWPCA restraint was warranted and that those conclusions in the Stoddard Report were not technically supportable. The

[7] Emphasis provided by author.

FWPCA report also attenuated the concern over fish toxicity caused by tailings. Note the difference in the following conclusions:

Stoddard Report:

Taconite tailings discharged from the effluent launders [8] diluted to one-fourth and one-tenth of the original concentration were found to be lethal to rainbow trout sac fry in a few days.

FWPCA Report:

High concentrations (10 percent and 25 percent) of taconite wastes caused mortalities among sac fry trout in 4-day exposure. The wastes were not acutely toxic to fingerling sized coho salmon, rainbow trout, white suckers, black bullheads, bluegills, and yellow perch in 96-hour, static bioassays.

Interestingly, both conclusions were based upon the same report, a report prepared by the U.S. Bureau of Sport Fisheries and Wildlife, a member of the Taconite Study Group. Subsequent federal studies confirmed that taconite tailings do not pose a significant toxicity problem to aquatic life at concentrations normally found in Lake Superior.

Finally, the FWPCA refused, based upon scientific and engineering evidence available in 1968, to support the Stoddard Report conclusion that "alternative disposal methods are available." In this instance, later studies by agencies and the mining company have shown that viable alternatives for tailings disposal were available.

Recommendations presented in the two reports also provide an interesting comparison. The Stoddard Report directly accused Reserve of polluting Lake Superior and recommended that the Army Corps of Engineers permit be extended conditionally for a 3-year period, during which time an alternative disposal method could be studied and implemented. The FWPCA report, by comparison, showed less confidence in existing evidence of lake pollution, recommended continued surveillance of the tailings discharge, and urged the state of Minnesota to "take such regulatory actions as necessary to control the intrastate pollution resulting from these discharges, if any."

---

[8] Launder: Flume that conveys tailings from the plant to the tailings delta.

Again the tone and substance of these recommendations is significant. Anti-Reservists naturally preferred the strong, direct approach of the Stoddard Report, even though several of the conclusions (7, 9, and 10) were not technically defensible and others (4, 6, 12, and 15) were subject to differing expert opinions regarding their significance.

Also significant, the Taconite Study Group failed to obtain reliable evidence of interstate pollution and consequently could not recommend direct federal abatement intervention by the Secretary of Interior. The group's recommendation was, therefore, keyed to the Army Corps of Engineers' responsibilities for permit revalidation based upon the 1899 Rivers and Harbors Act and the Army-Interior "Memorandum of Understanding" of 1967. In the absence of evidence of interstate pollution, the FWPCA elected to hold the state of Minnesota responsible for pollution abatement . . . if such were necessary.

FWPCA testimony continued as Dr. Donald Baumgartner, a sanitary engineer and chief of the National Coastal Pollution Research Program for the FWPCA, took the stand. Baumgartner discussed the effectiveness of the heavy density current in carrying tailings to the bottom of the lake. Much of his statement was based upon laboratory model studies and theoretical considerations rather than field measurements. These were the same bases used in 1947 by hydraulics experts to describe and defend the heavy density current method of tailings disposal. At that time Reserve's opponents attempted to discredit the 1947 testimony as lacking field data.

Baumgartner concluded, however, that "Reserve's discharge most likely results in an unstable density flow which spreads out and becomes diluted as it flows down the face of the delta, shedding clouds of finely-divided particulate matter . . . [which] can then be transported with the currents of the lake." [9] He also concluded that "The main portion of the density current will probably descend to the lake bottom, except that when a strong thermocline [10] exists, a significantly large portion of the stream may be carried off into the lake near the thermocline." [11] He did not supply scientific definitions for the terms *main portion* or *significantly large*. He concluded, however, that "the

[9] Proceedings of "Federal Enforcement Conference," First Session, p. 183.
[10] A thermocline: Refer to Figure 4 on p. 22.
[11] Proceedings of "Federal Enforcement Conference," First Session, p. 186.

currents and topography of the lake are such that suspended solids concentrations would increase more rapidly in the Duluth embayment than in the lake generally. . . ." [12]

Later, an expert witness for Reserve, Dr. R. A. Ragotzkie, director of the Marine Studies Center at the University of Wisconsin, rebutted Baumgartner's analysis. First, he cautioned against the use of hydraulic models for quantitative evaluation. He then argued that Baumgartner's analysis of the buildup of suspended solids in the Duluth embayment was based upon "several assumptions which are unrealistic when applied to the real Lake Superior." One of Baumgartner's assumptions was that fines, once suspended, remain suspended indefinitely. Ragotzkie stated that this assumption "was not true . . . otherwise all surface waters of the lake would be highly turbid." [13] Ragotzkie also pointed out that "during the 13 years (1956–1969) that Reserve Mining Company has been disposing of tailings in Lake Superior, *no detectable* [14] increase in turbidity in the Duluth water intake has been observed." [15]

Subsequently Ragotzkie provided additional testimony regarding heavy density currents. He concluded that "most of the tailings are being carried directly into the trough where the material is deposited" and that "once deposited, the tailings material would not be expected to become resuspended because of the sluggishness of the currents near the bottom." [16] Again the question arises of the meaning of the term "most of the tailings."

A comparison of statements by Baumgartner and Ragotzkie, the former as an FWPCA witness and the latter testifying for Reserve, shows that both well-known and respected experts agreed that "most" of the tailings descend to the bottom of the lake via the density current. However, because of the constraint of insufficient field data, neither expert was able to place an accurate quantitative value (pounds or tons of tailings per day) on that material that escapes from the heavy density current. One had to conclude that the heavy density current does function; the question was how effectively or efficiently.

Dr. A. F. Bartsch, then director of the FWPCA's Pacific North-

---

[12] Ibid., p. 186.
[13] Ibid., p. 1352.
[14] Emphasis supplied by author.
[15] Proceedings of "Federal Enforcement Conference," First Session, p. 1352.
[16] Ibid., p. 1377.

west Water Laboratory and a widely acclaimed expert on eutrophication (lake aging), discussed the subject as it related to Lake Superior. He devoted the majority of his statement to the definition of the term eutrophication, causes of the problem, and the potential of this problem in Lake Superior. He elected to stay with generalities rather than focus on any specific eutrophication problem in the Lake Superior basin. He did, however, offer several statements worthy of note. He stated, "Fortunately for Lake Superior, only the slightest evidence of increasing fertility or other clues to eutrophication have so far made their appearance." He explained that: "A principal factor that affects the rate of eutrophication is the extent to which nutrients needed by algae enter the body of water. Elements of most concern are phosphorus and nitrogen." [17]

In response to questions from the conferees, Bartsch discussed the importance of controlling eutrophication in Lake Superior. He stated, "there is no reason to believe that Lake Superior is in some peculiar way immune to the forces of eutrophication." He continued, "Lake Superior and Lake Michigan are at the headwaters of the remaining Great Lakes. Whatever character this lake is permitted to acquire, it will have great impact on the success of protecting or restoring the lakes downstream." He then added, "Lake Superior is said to have a self-purging rate estimated to be well in excess of 500 years. This means that it acts like a trap, and any persistent nutrient such as phosphorus will tend to accumulate." He closed by stating, "if there is pride in the uniqueness and splendor of Lake Superior, keep it that way." [18]

Who could argue with the logic and importance of Bartsch's appraisal? But was he taking aim at Reserve Mining or any of the other nutrient contributors in the basin? During the executive session of the first conference, conferee Stein of the Department of the Interior addressed a specific question to Bartsch regarding Reserve's contribution of phosphorus to Lake Superior.

Stein: By the way, not to disillusion you all, I don't think that Reserve Mining is a significant contributor of phosphorus. Is that right?

Bartsch: As nearly as I can tell from data I have seen, I would say that is correct.

[17] Ibid., p. 192.
[18] Ibid., p. 198.

Stein: That is right. In other words, this [phosphorus] largely comes from organic wastes.

This observation was later corroborated by a leaching study conducted by Dr. Gary Glass, a chemist with the National Water Quality Laboratory (NWQL) in Duluth. Glass reported that several elements tended to leach or dissolve from the tailings after prolonged contact with water. Conspicuously absent from his listing was the nutrient, phosphorus. These statements and the laboratory studies confirm that Conclusion No. 10 [19] in the Stoddard Report was not technically defensible.

The FWPCA line-up of witnesses continued with Dr. Donald Mount, director of the National Water Quality Laboratory, at Duluth. Mount presented evidence to prove that cummingtonite can be used to "definitively identify and trace the tailings at any appreciable distance from the discharge." He explained that taconite tailings are composed of quartz, cummingtonite, some non-crystalline iron oxides, and small quantities of the clay minerals chlorite, vermiculite, and some montmorillonite. Cummingtonite comprises approximately one half of the fine fractions of taconite tailings and are not often found, he said, in the finer fractions of natural soils and sediments in the Lake Superior basin. Thus, he concluded that the presence of cummingtonite in the waters of Lake Superior was evidence of tailings. To further establish the validity of using cummingtonite as a taconite tracer, Mount cited a statement contained in a letter from Dr. William C. Phinney, a geology professor at the University of Minnesota: "All of the streams from Duluth northeastward and draining into Lake Superior have their entire courses in rocks which do not contain cummingtonite." He went on, "The only known occurrence of cummingtonite in the drainage area within Minnesota leading into Lake Superior is at the eastern end of the Mesabi Range [site of Reserve's Babbitt Mine and source of taconite ore]." [20]

Once the government had shown, at least to its satisfaction, that cummingtonite was a reliable tracer of taconite tailings, Dr. Charles Collier of the U.S. Biological Survey was called to discuss his findings regarding the distribution of tailings in Lake Superior. Collier stated that the tailings crossing the delta are carried downward by the density current. He added: "The extent and direction of this current is not

[19] Conclusion No. 10: "The widely accepted criteria of 0.10 mg/1 of phosphorus to limit algae growth is exceeded."
[20] Proceedings of "Federal Enforcement Conference," First Session, p. 252.

known. The material does not spread over the surface of the lake but sinks rapidly from sight within a few feet from the edge of the delta." He went on, "some of the material has been observed to break away from the density current by the action of local lake currents and form what appears to be clouds of fine tailings." He noted further that "the lake currents . . . are sufficient to carry the particles for long distances before they are deposited on the lake bed." [21] Collier attempted to measure the depth of tailings on the lake bottom, based upon the presence of cummingtonite. His results revealed a maximum thickness 6¾" at a point 5 miles southwest of the discharge and 2 miles off shore. A one-inch thick layer was found to extend from the discharge point 15 miles in a southwest direction and 5–6 miles offshore. However, he was unable to define the extremities of the deposit.

The issue of toxicity of tailings to aquatic life was raised by Clifford Resley, Jr., director of the Lake Michigan basin office for FWPCA. He reported on a Lake Superior water quality study in the vicinity of Silver Bay in June and July of 1968. The study reported values for total iron, lead, copper, cadmium, nickel, and chromium at levels exceeding "commonly accepted levels" for the protection of aquatic life. Unfortunately, this study failed to consider the chemical state or biological activity of the substances measured. In a water sample taken 100 feet offshore from the tailings delta and at a 100-foot depth (i.e., in or near the heavy density current), a copper value of 0.119 mg/l was found. When filtered through a 0.45 micron membrane filter, the sample gave a reading of 0.051 mg/l. Bioassays on this filtered water failed to show any toxicity, however. This observation led Resley to conclude, "Apparently, some of the particulate copper is not biologically active in a bioassay of short duration." [22]

Approximately one year later, at the second conference session, FWQA's Glass reported his findings on leachate from taconite tailings. His study showed little or no increase in concentration of soluble zinc or cadmium resulting from the presence of taconite tailings in water. His study for some unexplained reason failed to consider the dissolution of copper, nickel, chromium, lead, and other heavy metals that were associated with Reserve's discharge. Apparently, Glass found that these substances existed in a non-biologically active state in the tailings and/or did not leach or dissolve in measurable quantities.

[21] Proceedings of "Federal Enforcement Conference," First Session, p. 252.
[22] Ibid., p. 284.

Mount returned to the stand to comment on water quality criteria which the NWQL had been asked to develop for Lake Superior. He explained that terms like *trace* and *no material addition* were replaced with numbers in order to establish limits in clearly definable terms. In some instances, a range of acceptable or limiting values was given. The standards were established to achieve several different objectives, including: preservation of the present appearance of the lake, protection of aquatic life, and effective monitoring of the lake's aging process.

The second day of the conference was opened with a rousing and emotional speech, prepared for Minnesota's Senator Gaylord Nelson, and read by a stand-in. He urged strong action to upgrade water quality standards and to preserve the quality of Lake Superior for future generations. He stated, "These Great Lakes, once a magnificent example of the works of nature, are now a sad monument to the follies of man. And it can happen on Lake Superior." [23] He called for action to clean up municipal effluents, wastes from 61 industries, Army Corps of Engineers' dredge spoils deposits, dumping of shipboard wastes from commercial and pleasure craft, and sediment resulting from inadequate soil conservation measures. His most vigorous attack, however, was reserved for Reserve, stating, "I think there is ample evidence that action in this matter is justified and necessary for the protection of Lake Superior." [24] His "ample evidence" was the FWPCA report and the Stoddard Report.

"If there isn't adequate authority to properly control this massive tailings discharge," the Senator added, "I will ask that Congress amend the pollution control laws." [25] He added: "The same technological ingenuity which produced the marvel of the taconite process must be put to work to prevent pollution by the taconite wastes." [26] Senator Nelson's statement concluded that costs should not be a consideration and that "It is time this Nation established a policy that says pollution control must be part of doing business." [27]

[23] Ibid., p. 319.
[24] Ibid., p. 324.
[25] Ibid., p. 326. (In 1974, Senator Nelson together with Senator Hart of Michigan introduced an amendment in Congress that was aimed specially at the control of pollution from Reserve's operation. It would have permitted courts to close the operation down upon a finding of suspicion of health hazard.)
[26] Ibid., p. 327.
[27] Ibid., p. 328.

The applause had barely subsided when a telegram from Senator Walter Mondale of Minnesota was read into the record. The senator asked the conferees to act decisively to save Lake Superior, and said that the governors of Wisconsin, Minnesota, and Michigan endorse the conference (thus adding to its authority). He cited *two* official reports, one published in January (obviously the Stoddard Report) and the FWPCA report. Thus, in Senator Mondale's eyes, the Stoddard Report was an "official" Department of the Interior document, to be accorded full weight as incontrovertible.

The Minnesota Pollution Control Agency spoke through its executive secretary, John Badalich, a key member of the conference. Badalich acknowledged that the water quality standards promulgated by his office for Lake Superior were among the most stringent in the nation. He then remarked, "Inasmuch as these are Federal as well as State standards, this conference should address itself to the primary question of whether these established standards are being met, and, if not, where and to what degree are they being violated." He went on, "The manner of water quality management at both the State and Federal level is established by law and cannot be subject to arbitrary or whimsical action. The former provides for order and equity to all under the law, the latter for chaos and litigation. Therefore, we make the point that this must be a fact finding conference as it was stated to be." [28] This somewhat profound expression of logic was not well received in those quarters that were advocating rapid action before all of the facts could be assessed, and Badalich was immediately labeled pro-Reserve by some environmentalists and politicians.

The second speaker to represent the Minnesota position was Robert Rygg, assistant commissioner of the Minnesota Conservation Department (MCD). Rygg traced the history of the MCD's involvement in permits to Reserve. He spoke of extensive hearings held during 1947 to assist the department in arriving at its decision to grant a permit to Reserve. He noted that the technical advisory board of the MCD conducted a series of tests between 1948 and 1955 on Lake Superior waters in the vicinity of the plant site at Silver Bay. The tests included "bottom sampling, turbidity and temperature measurements, bacteriological studies, air photo studies; lake current studies . . . biological studies of fish and fish food, and inventories of fish catches in the area." [29] Based upon these studies and those conducted by other state agencies and the com-

[28] Ibid., p. 341.
[29] Ibid., p. 347.

pany from 1955 to 1966, Rygg concluded that, "To date, there has been no evidence of violation of the conditions of the original permit, P.A. 47-12, issued in December 1947." [30] Rygg also reported on a fish food chain study conducted by his department during the summer of 1968. The study findings revealed that, "fewer fish food organisms (scud or the small fresh water shrimp of the genus *Pontoporeia*) were found on the bottom covered with tailings below the plant than above the plant . . . [but] total production of bottom organisms was greater below than above the plant." His group concluded that the reduction of fish food organisms on the bottom "could possibly result in a reduction of the total annual fish catch . . . of 5 percent or less for the area having tailings on the bottom. This reduction would amount to 25 to 65 pounds of fish per square mile of water and probably be mostly smelt." [31] Rygg found the affected zone to be an area extending one-mile wide for a distance of at least 15.5 miles along the shore. He was quick to explain that these findings were sketchy and preliminary, stating, "It should be emphasized that the foregoing calculations on the possible effect of the fewer fish food organisms found are theoretical only. There is no evidence from data on the commercial or sports fishing catch along the north shore of Lake Superior to show that there has been an actual reduction in fish production." He continued, "Twenty years of commercial catch records show that great changes have taken place in the fish populations of Lake Superior. Most changes have been lakewide and began before the plant went into operation." [32] Later in his report, Rygg noted that the variations in lake trout catches had no relation to the plant operation. He stated, "Other commercial species, such as smelt and chubs, have increased during the period of plant operation. . . . Here again the timing of these changes cannot be related to the taconite plant, as the change in trends started in the early 1950's." [33] This MCD report was made available to the Taconite Study Group in 1968. The findings prompted two very interesting conclusions in the Stoddard Report:

Conclusion No. 11:

Bottom fauna, especially one species important as a fish food, show progressive reduction in numbers southwest of the plant.

[30] Ibid., p. 348.
[31] Ibid., p. 358.
[32] Ibid., p. 359.
[33] Ibid., p. 360.

Beyond the limits of bottom fauna collection (15.5 miles south-west of the plant) there are no data to establish how much further such effects continue before recovery begins.

Conclusion No. 14:

Even moderate changes in commercial fish catch due to tail-ings discharge would be masked by much larger changes due to lamprey and overfishing.

The link, or lack of a link, between these conclusions is obscure. Furthermore, it bears noting that none of the *positive* statements that tend to attenuate the impact of taconite tailings on Lake Superior were included as conclusions.

The first strong pro-Reserve voice to be heard at the conference was that of the company president, Edward M. Furness. Furness traced the history of Reserve and emphasized its beneficial impact on Minnesotans, especially those in the mining district. He pointed out that in 1968, "Reserve's state and local taxes paid totaled more than $3.7 million. Annual payroll for our 3,200 employees, including fringe benefits, was $29.4 million. Our purchases of goods and services were about $40 million." He added, "Today Babbitt and Silver Bay have a combined population of about 9,000 persons—people entirely dependent on Reserve's operation for their existence." He went on to explain that Reserve's use of Lake Superior results in "no waste of water, no injury to water, and it incorporates harmless, permanent deepwater deposition of inert tailings." He likened tailings to fine and coarse sand, "physically similar to the material which has been entering the lake from the rivers and streams along the Minnesota, Wisconsin, and Michigan shores for centuries." He stressed that, "No oils, no chemicals, no toxic materials are used in the processing to taconite by Reserve." [34] (Though perhaps a technicality, Reserve began adding calcium chloride to its raw ore during the winter months to prevent freezing during ore transport from Babbitt to Silver Bay. This addition was approved by the Minnesota Department of Health.) Furness renewed Reserve's claim that location of the beneficiating plant at Silver Bay was necessitated by the lack of a reliable supply of process water near the Babbit mine site.

The subject of tailings build-up on the lake bottom was addressed by Furness when he stated, "This deep area, a great depression extend-

[34] Ibid., p. 375–78.

ing for many miles parallel to the shore, is 600 to 900 feet deep. Its properties are immense: up to 8 miles wide, 59 miles long—big enough to hold our entire Babbitt ore body without raising the bottom more than a few feet. It is here that our tailings settle." [35] Perhaps a more technically correct statement would have been, "It is here that 'most' of our tailings settle."

Furness underscored his presentation with numerous quotes from state and federal reports that supported Reserve's position regarding the lack of significant impact of tailings on fish and fish food organisms. Furness' closing remarks were: "No agency, industry, or individual—public or private—is more interested in preserving the high quality of Lake Superior than is Reserve Mining Company. . . . In all our operations, we have followed good conservation practices. We pledge to continue." [36]

Edward Schmid, assistant to President Furness, followed and echoed sentiments similar to those of his boss. His testimony suffered somewhat from his attempt to explain in layman's terms that green water is not green but colorless. His testimony was reinforced with a series of color slides to show that the green water phenomenon occurred naturally in Lake Superior. The fact that green water can and does occur at several scattered locations in Lake Superior and can occur naturally was not refuted by any witnesses for the federal government. The basic argument was whether the tailings discharge increased the frequency of the appearance of the green water phenomenon.

Several individuals and groups read statements into the record in support of Reserve. Included were the mayors of Silver Bay and Babbitt, representatives of the Lake County Board of Commissioners, Duluth Chamber of Commerce, and the Northeastern Minnesota Development Association.

When Wisconsin's turn came, Frances Schraufnagel, of the State Department of Natural Resources, presented a summary of actions taken by the DNR during the period from 1964 to 1968 to curb pollution and improve water quality in the Wisconsin portion of the Lake Superior Basin. He pointed to the establishment of water quality standards and the development of a pollution abatement compliance program for all dischargers in the basin. His remarks did not reveal a significant concern over the potential impact of Reserve's tailings discharge on Wisconsin's waters.

[35] Ibid., p. 369.
[36] Ibid., p. 380.

Another spokesman for the Wisconsin regulatory agency was Frangos, an official conferee at the conference. Frangos first observed that under present state statute, a mining operation similar to Reserve's would not be permitted in Wisconsin. He then addressed his remaining remarks to the jurisdictional problems of the conference. He noted, "This conference is a legal proceeding. Therefore, we must make some specific technical findings for federal jurisdiction to apply. Up to very recently, we have not had information which would indicate to us that taconite tailings are causing interstate pollution." [37] He went on to say that new evidence being presented might significantly change this situation.

A long series of non-technical presentations by conservation groups and organizations followed. These included the Sierra Club, Wisconsin Conservation Council, Wisconsin Division of the Izaak Walton League, Wisconsin Wildlife Federation, Wisconsin Conservation Conference, League of Women Voters, and many others from Wisconsin, Minnesota, and Michigan. The thrusts of their messages were similar: Stop polluting Lake Superior now and in the future! Possibly because they did not have the financial resources, these groups were unable to present technical data to support their pleas and arguments.

To the surprise of some and the delight of many, Stoddard himself appeared at the conference and presented testimony. This time he was not speaking in an "official" federal capacity but rather as a private citizen and a resource consultant. He attempted in vain to introduce into the record the report he had authored a few months earlier. Dominick, now presiding, accepted it as an exhibit only, rather than as evidence. This action by Dominick had considerable significance and precipitated a critical attack by the anti-Reserve forces. A document entered into the record is reproduced in full and is made available to all who request a transcript of the conference. Exhibits are kept on file in the FWPCA Regional office in Chicago and at headquarters in Washington, D.C. Though still available to the public, an exhibit document was much less readily available for review. Dominick's action is difficult to understand, since he admitted all types of documents of marginal validity and relevance into the record. Yet the Stoddard Report, a key document that precipitated the conference, was not entered into the record.

Obviously resentful at what he felt was the ill-treatment accorded his report, Stoddard sharply criticized the Department of the Interior, the FWPCA, the Army Corps of Engineers, and the state regulatory agencies of Minnesota, Michigan, and Wisconsin. He asked this basic

[37] Ibid., p. 540.

and pungent question: "Can our complex legal and administrative machinery really enforce pollution control laws in the face of heavy economic and political pressures to study, to postpone, to discredit, and yes, even to use improper influence not to act?" [38] Stoddard acknowledged the differences between his report and the official FWPCA version. He even praised the FWPCA document.

Concluding, Stoddard offered these strong words: *"Make no mistake—a recommendation for continued surveillance in place of land disposal will represent a retreat and public demonstration that the law is bent to favor big polluters."* [39]

The conservation group known as the "Save Lake Superior Association" was represented by Dr. Louis Williams, a biology professor at the University of Alabama and formerly a research scientist with the National Water Quality Laboratory in Duluth. While with the NWQL, Williams had undertaken studies dealing with the enhancement of algae in the presence of mine tailings. But he had apparently committed two procedural errors with the study that jeopardized his position with the FWPCA. First, he had not been authorized to undertake a study of this type, and, second, he had spoken publicly of his preliminary findings before all loose ends had been nailed down. Williams' testimony at the conference was highly emotional and larded with statements that were technically unsupportable. In fact, many of his statements have been shown to be invalid by studies previously and subsequently conducted at the NWQL in Duluth. Some examples:

1 /   Williams: "The water quality [in the vicinity of taconite tailings] has been markedly deteriorating based on more and more green algae, and especially nuisance blue green algae. . . ." [40] Bartsch of the FWPCA, an expert on eutrophication, earlier testified that the cold water temperature in Lake Superior was limiting to blue green algae. He also stated that Reserve's tailings are not a significant contributor of the nutrient phosphorus that leads to algal blooms.

2 /   Williams: "While nitrogen and phosphorus are minor problems for Lake Superor, the major pollution threat to the purity of Lake Superior [is] from metabolic trace metals in circulating taconite from the Reserve Mining tailings. These trace metals, on

[38] Ibid., p. 667.
[39] Ibid., p. 675. (Emphasis is Stoddard's.)
[40] Ibid., p. 770.

reaching threshold concentrations, bring about enrichment and blooms of unwanted blue green algae. . . ." [41] Elementary textbooks that describe the eutrophication phenomenon explain that an algae bloom cannot be triggered by any trace element if either nitrogen or phosphorus is limiting. Williams admits that both of these basic nutrients are limiting. Furthermore, it appears that none of the prior or subsequent studies conducted by the state or the FWPCA have shown algal blooms to be even a potential problem in Lake Superior.

3 / Williams stated that molybdenum could well be the element that triggers algal growth in Lake Superior. He further stated, "Colloids of taconite were found to have a relatively high content of this trace metal, which might explain the enormous blooms of nuisance blue green algae." [42] Williams appears to be the only scientist to link molybdenum with taconite tailings and the only scientist to find "enormous blooms of blue green algae" in Lake Superior. Glass of the NWQL did not show any molybdenum in his analysis of leachate from taconite tailings. Little wonder that FWPCA officials became upset with Williams for transmitting information to the public that was preliminary and based upon weak, if any, scientific evidence.

On the final day of the conference, W. G. Turney, of the Michigan Department of Natural Resources commented on a document entitled, "Report on Water Pollution Control in the Michigan Portion of the Lake Superior Basin and its Tributaries." [43] The report explained generally how the state of Michigan intended to seek abatement of pollution problems in the Lake Superior basin. No mention was made of the Reserve discharge or its potential impact, if any, on Michigan's portion of the Lake Superior waters.

Later in the day, the conferees heard from representatives of the U.S. Forest Service, U.S. Bureau of Outdoor Recreation, Great Lakes Basin Commission, Soil Conservation Service, National Park Service, U.S. Bureau of Sport Fisheries and Wildlife, Bureau of Commercial Fisheries, Bureau of Water Hygiene, and numerous citizens and representatives of special interest groups.

[41] Ibid., p. 767.
[42] Ibid., p. 772.
[43] Ibid., p. 819.

Reserve's vice president for engineering, Dr. Kenneth Haley, took the stand and presented technical arguments to support Reserve's position on the heavy density current, distribution of tailings in the lake, bottom fauna, cummingtonite as a tracer, and the impact of tailings on fish life. His arguments were based on federal and state reports, buttressed with data collected by the company. One new observation was brought to light. Haley pointed out that the Minnesota Highway Department used large quantities of taconite tailings, mostly from Reserve's delta, to sand roads on the north shore during winter months. He claimed that this material washed from the highway into drainage ditches and streams that ultimately flowed into Lake Superior. He argued that this source of taconite tailings together with the cummingtonite found in natural streams on the north shore reduced the validity of cummingtonite as a reliable tracer of taconite tailings from Reserve's discharge.

Reserve's principal expert witness dealing with water quality matters was Dr. G. Fred Lee, then a professor of water chemistry at the University of Wisconsin. Lee is recognized nationally and internationally as a competent water chemist and pollution control consultant for industry and governmental agencies. But because he had been retained by Reserve and because many of his statements supported Reserve's position, Lee was immediately categorized by environmentalists as pro-Reserve and not a credible witness. Lee's critics failed to recognize that most of his early observations regarding water chemistry-related matters were later corroborated by federal studies. For example, Lee was critical of allegations that Reserve's tailings contained biologically-active phosphorus, copper, and other heavy metals. Statements by Bartsch and data presented by Mount and Glass supported Lee's contention that, though these elements were present in the particulate matter, they did not enter into solution at a significant rate.

Another key scientific witness for Reserve was Dr. Robert Bright, an associate professor of geology and ecology at the University of Minnesota. Bright examined existing state, federal, and company reports that dealt with the effect of tailings on lake water quality. He concluded from his analysis that "toxic metals are not increased in Lake Superior by disposal of tailings" and that "algae in the lake, which are a critical part of the fish food chain, are not affected by the tailings in the water area studies." [44]

On the final afternoon of the conference, a long line of witnesses

[44] Ibid., p. 1398.

representing individual opinions and reactions to the Reserve operation were heard. Some spoke in favor of Reserve; others were in opposition. Perhaps the most significant presentation was by Grant Merritt, significant not just because he was then the director of MECCA (Minnesota Environmental Control Citizen's Association) but because he was soon to be appointed as the top pollution abatement official in Minnesota. Merritt, a young lawyer and vigorous advocate, developed a lengthy argument that included the introduction of several letters and reports into the record. He was highly critical of Reserve's operation and urged *immediate* corrective measures.

The question of onland tailings disposal arose near the end of the first conference session. Reserve's attorney, Ed Fride, of the Duluth law firm of Hanft, Fride, O'Brien, and Harries, read into the record several direct quotes from a U.S. Bureau of Mines report developed for the Taconite Study Group. The report stated, "The second suggestion, to deposit the tailings in a pond on high ground above the plant, creates many problems. Objectionable effects of a tailings pond would have to be carefully weighed against the effects of depositing the tailings in Lake Superior. The area nearest Reserve is valued as a resort and recreation area; most of the area further removed is in Superior National Forest. A tailings pond would create a serious air pollution problem due to dust unless properly designed and operated." The Bureau of Mines report continued, "When considering alternatives to tailings disposition in Lake Superior, benefits gained should be compared to possible losses; i.e., would a tailings pond and possible air pollution problems in a particular area be less objectionable than depositing tailings in Lake Superior?" [45]

This sound and rational appraisal of the total environmental impact concept offered by the Bureau of Mines was important, especially considering the mission of its investigators for the Taconite Study Group. It was the same Bureau of Mines report that Stoddard relied upon to conclude, "Alternative disposal methods are available." He was obviously referring to onland disposal as the alternative method available.

The cost of onland tailings disposal was accorded a cursory investigation by the Bureau of Mines. Its report stated, "It is estimated on a *very preliminary basis* [46] that the capital investment in dike construction, pipelines, pumps and thickeners would be $7½ million for an initial capacity of 55 million tons of tailings (about 3 years production). Average

[45] Proceedings of "Federal Enforcement Conference," First Session, p. 1639.
[46] Emphasis added by author.

annual operating and dike costs would be $3.3 million. Assuming a 10-year depreciation on the initial $7½ million capital investment ($750,000/year plus an operating cost of $3.3 million per year), the added unit cost would be roughly $4 million, or 40 cents per ton, or 3% of the value ($112.80/ton) of taconite end products." [47]

Reserve hired an independent consultant to determine the feasibility and costs of disposing of tailings by overland pumping to an onland disposal site. Its consultant, Trygve Hoff and Associates, of Cleveland, Ohio, has a national and international reputation for conducting studies of this type. Stig Forssmark, president of the firm, made a brief presentation of findings on the final day of this first conference session. He stated, "The estimate of cost that we have come up with for this job is $253,256,000, with an operating cost per year of $13,236,000. This method of operation would be good for 22 years before it would be absolutely necessary to dump water into Beaver River, in which case it would get back into Lake Superior again." [48]

A comparison of the Bureau of Mines report with the Trygve Hoff report provides the reasons for this fantastic differential. The Trygve Hoff report is very detailed and comprehensive, whereas the governmental report, by admission of the Bureau of Mines, is superficial and incomplete.

At the close of the first conference session on May 15, 1969, Chairman Dominick announced that the conferees would reassemble in one month for an executive session to develop a conference summary as required by law.

The executive session did not convene until September 30, 1969. Official conferees included John Badalich and Robert Tuveson from the Minnesota PCA; Donald Mackie and Thomas Frangos from the Wisconsin Department of Natural Resources; Ralph Purdy from the Michigan regulatory agency; and three FWPCA representatives, H. W. Poston (the Great Lakes regional director for EPA), Dale Bryson, and the session chairman, Murray Stein.

Protocol for the executive session called for an open meeting and permitted audience observation but not participation. The first topic considered was the fate of tailings in Lake Superior. Dr. R. W. Andrew, a research scientist from the NWQL in Duluth, was asked by the conferees to present a summary of his studies on the identification of cum-

[47] Part II of "Stoddard Report," U.S.D.I., December 1968.
[48] Proceedings of "Federal Enforcement Conference," First Session, p. 1641.

mingtonite and its validity as a tracer of taconite tailings from Reserve's discharge. He reiterated the finding that cummingtonite was in sediment samples taken from the Wisconsin portion of Lake Superior. When this evidence was first presented in the May conference, the FWPCA had not established whether Wisconsin streams carried significant quantities of cummingtonite in their sediment load. Andrew, and later Mount, now stated that studies undertaken since the May conference revealed the absence of significant quantities of this substance in the major Wisconsin streams in the Lake Superior basin. This finding had a significant impact on the future of the federal case against Reserve, since a finding of interstate pollution (or at least alleged interstate pollution) transferred jurisdiction and responsibility for pollution abatement from the state of Minnesota to the federal government. (At the May conference, Reserve had adamantly refused to accept this cummingtonite evidence as proof of taconite tailings, especially in the Wisconsin waters. The company argued that certain Minnesota streams and highway drainage discharged sufficient cummingtonite into the lake to invalidate the use of cummingtonite as a positive tracer of tailings.)

The second question raised at the executive session was that of solubility of tailings. Glass, of the NWQL, was asked to comment on this subject. He challenged statements made at the May conference by Reserve witnesses, Lee and Bright, regarding the leaching of phosphorous and heavy metals from taconite tailings. Glass insisted that both scientists based their comments on theory and not on laboratory tests. But in the next few months, Glass was to undertake a leaching study at his Duluth lab and find that both Lee and Bright were correct.

The question of adverse impact of tailings on aquatic life was addressed by NWQL biologist, John Arthur. Arthur limited his remarks to the impact of tailings on lake shrimp. He found a twofold decrease in this fish food organism in the tailings discharge zone southwest of the Reserve plant.

Bartsch appeared before the conferees to reaffirm his attitude on eutrophication and its potential in Lake Superior. He reiterated his concern for limiting phosphorus levels in Lake Superior as a means of controlling eutrophication. In response to a question from Stein, Bartsch acknowledged, however, that Reserve was not a significant contributor of phosphorus, which comes mostly from organic wastes.

Following a series of questions directed at Bartsch, Mount returned to the conference table to offer some general statements relating to the phosphorus question.

"I think we have a tendency at times," he said, "to close our eyes to the multiple-use concept of water and I don't really think that we want a distilled water basin in Lake Superior, either. We have to have some phosphorus in the water in order to provide nutrients for the necessary amount of algal growth that must take place in the lake in order to sustain a commercial fish crop." Mount went on, "The point I am making is that our goal is not zero phosphorus but some appropriate value which will permit sufficient plant growth and still maintain the aesthetic appearance of the lake." [49]

After hearing all witnesses from whom clarification was solicited and after receiving new data (all from the FWPCA), the conferees began a discussion of their proposed summary, conclusions, and recommendations.

The 18 conclusions listed and agreed upon by all conferees covered a wide gamut of considerations, from the recognition of Lake Superior as a priceless natural heritage to evidence of pollution from municipal, industrial, and agricultural sources. Only those conclusions that impinged directly on the *Reserve* case are cited and commented upon here:

"Because of the low mineral content of Lake Superior waters, manmade changes in the range of parts per billion of heavy metals such as copper, chromium, zinc, and cadmium may have deleterious effects upon the lake." [50] Though a valid conclusion, the statement fails to consider the form of the heavy metal and whether it is biologically active. This is an extremely important distinction in the *Reserve* case.

"The extreme clarity and cold temperature of the waters of Lake Superior are a necessity to support its present ecology. A reduction in light penetration will significantly alter the types of life therein. The clarity of the lake is extremely susceptible to being reduced by pollutants." [51] This conclusion is significant as it relates to any discharge of particulate matter, including the Reserve discharge, which would increase turbidity.

"The portion of Lake Superior shallow enough to provide suitable fish spawning areas is limited to a small band around the shoreline. This area is most susceptible to the influence of natural and manmade sedi-

[49] Proceedings of "Federal Enforcement Conference in the Matter of Pollution of Lake Superior and Its Tributary Basin, Minnesota–Wisconsin–Michigan," First (Executive) Session, U.S.D.I.–FWPCA, September 30, 1969, pp. 118–19.
[50] Ibid., p. 129.
[51] Ibid.

ments. Deposition on the bottom of fine particles discharge to Lake Superior is a threat to the inshore food producing area and to the incubation of important fish species." [52] This statement bears direct relationship to the distribution of tailings along the north shore of Lake Superior.

"Water quality criteria can be established to protect the aesthetic value, recreational uses and unique aquatic life of the lake and yet such that reasonable allowance is made for future municipal and industrial expansion." [53] This statement is significant in that it recognizes and supports the multiple-use concept of Lake Superior.

"Lake Superior is an oligotrophic lake. Nutrient values in some areas of the lake have been reported at levels approaching those commonly associated with nuisance algae growth. However, other factors, such as temperature, are limiting." [54] Although the Reserve discharge does not add a significant amount of phosphorus to Lake Superior, some federal studies have shown that the tailings accelerate eutrophication by other mechanisms.

"Outflow from Lake Superior passes through Lakes Huron, Erie, and Ontario. Dissolved chemicals in this outflow contribute to the levels found in these downstream lakes." [55] Reserve discharges approximately 60,000 pounds per day (20 tons) of dissolved solids into the lake. By comparison, an estimated 1 million pounds enter the lake daily from tributary streams.[56]

"The discharge of taconite tailings to Lake Superior from the Reserve Mining Company . . . has a deleterious effect on the ecology of the portion of the lake by reducing organisms necessary to support fish life." [57] This conclusion was, for the most part, reached on the basis of one state and one federal study that showed a slight reduction of fish food organisms, most notably the lake shrimp, in areas where tailings were present in significant quantities.

"There is presumptive evidence in the record to indicate that the discharges from the Reserve Mining Company endanger the health or welfare of persons in states other than those in which such discharges originate and that this pollution is subject to abatement under the provisions of the Federal Water Pollution Control Act." [58] The word pre-

[52] Ibid., p. 130.
[53] Ibid.
[54] Ibid., p. 142.
[55] Ibid., p. 132.
[56] Ibid., p. 581.
[57] Ibid., p. 148.
[58] Ibid., p. 162.

sumptive is a key word, because it greatly reduces the impact and significance of the final conclusions. Obviously, the conferees felt that the evidence presented in the May conference and supplemental evidence presented at the executive session were not conclusive. But this conclusion, though diluted with the word *presumptive,* provided sufficient reason for the Secretary of the Interior to continue the enforcement conference.

On the second and final day of the executive session, the conferees delivered their recommendations for future action. Of the 21 recommendations, the following were aimed most specifically at Reserve:

"The FWPCA and the States keep the discharge of taconite tailings to Lake Superior from the Reserve Mining Company, E. W. Davis Works, under continual surveillance and report to the conferees at six-month intervals on any findings that interstate pollution is occurring or is likely to occur and the state of Minnesota is urged to take such regulatory actions as necessary to control the intrastate pollution resulting from these discharges, if any." [59]

"Reserve Mining Company be requested to undertake further engineering and economic studies relating to possible ways or means of reducing [to] the maximum practicable extent the discharge of tailings into Lake Superior and submit a report on progress to the Minnesota Pollution Control Agency and the conferees within six months of the date of issuance of the Summary of Conference by the Secretary of the Interior." [60]

Stein closed the executive session, stating, "I really think we have achieved a breakthrough. We really have developed something in the very difficult field of Federal-State relations. Also we are dealing with the kind of resource where our responsibility is so great that we can't permit ourselves a serious mistake." [61]

[59] Ibid., p. 172.
[60] Ibid., p. 179–80.
[61] Ibid., p. 248.

Chapter 10

Reserve in State Court

On Christmas Eve, 1969, Reserve filed suit in Minnesota State Court against the Minnesota Pollution Control Agency (MPCA). The suit challenged the validity of certain provisions of the federal-state water quality standards as applied to the company. The new standards, WPC 15, included effluent restrictions and an anti-degradation clause that, if immediately enforced against Reserve, would have prohibited the discharge of tailings into Lake Superior and consequently closed the processing facility.

The adoption of this water pollution control regulation by the state of Minnesota was the result of a lengthy and complicated set of procedures and guidelines prescribed by the federal government. Under the Water Pollution Control Act of 1965, states were delegated the primary responsibility and authority to control interstate pollution by

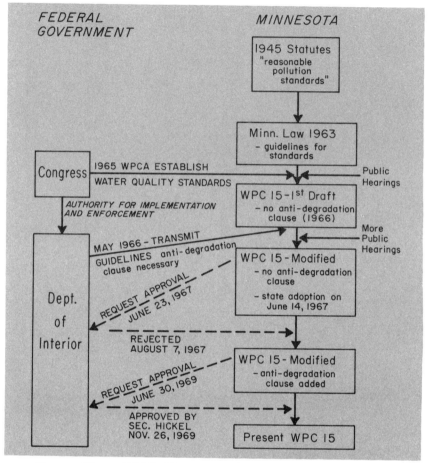

FIGURE 12   WPC 15 statutory history, federal/state inter-relationship.

adopting water quality standards. These standards were to be established by June 10, 1967, then submitted to the Department of the Interior for final approval. Once approved, they were to become federal as well as the state standards.

Minnesota was not lacking in legal authority to promulgate adequate water quality standards of its own. Since 1945, its statutes had contained a provision that authorized the adoption of "reasonable pollution standards" by the MPCA and its predecessor agency. Subsequent enactment of the Minnesota laws of 1963 established procedures and additional guidelines for the adoption of water quality standards. Those guidelines were further established and reiterated by the Minnesota statute in 1967 that required that "public hearings upon due notice" be held prior to adoption of water quality standards.

The Minnesota Water Pollution Control Commission (MWPCC) got to work early in 1966 to develop water quality guidelines for both interstate and intrastate waters. The commission held several hearings during the first few months of 1966, then began to draft regulations. Their effort was interrupted in May 1966, however, when the Department of the Interior issued its "Guidelines for Establishing Water Quality Standards for Interstate Waters." The Secretary of the Interior wanted to insure that a uniform system of standards would be established nationwide. These guidelines included the controversial anti-degradation requirement, which meant that "in no case will standards providing for less than existing water quality be acceptable. . . ." This document also laid down an effluent standard essentially prohibiting the discharge of "any wastes amenable to treatment or control . . . into any interstate water without treatment or control regardless of the water quality criteria. . . ."

The MWPCC's draft regulations had failed to include an anti-degradation clause or a rigorous effluent standard. Consequently, the commission was forced to hold more hearings across the state and develop a new set of standards and regulations. The second set of hearings was convened in April, 1967, and the revised regulations were adopted by the MWPCC shortly thereafter, on May 8. This modified version of WPC 15 still failed to include the strong anti-degradation language called for by the Department of the Interior. Reserve later challenged in state court the procedures followed by the MWPCC in adopting standards. This challenge was unsuccessful.

On June 14, 1967, WPC 15 was adopted by the state as a binding regulation, and nine days later, the regulation was submitted to the federal government for review and approval. On August 7 the state received a reply from Secretary of the Interior Udall that praised the standards but declined to approve the MWPCC's proposal because it was lacking in "a few . . . details."

At this point the MWPCC was succeeded by and its functions transferred to the newly created MPCA, (Minnesota Pollution Control Agency.)

For nearly two and a half years following the secretary's refusal to approve Minnesota's version of WPC 15, federal and state agencies argued back and forth. Most of the controversy centered around the rigor of the effluent standards and perhaps more importantly, over the efficacy of the anti-degradation clause. The MPCA was reluctant to adopt more stringent provisions, but finally on April 8, 1969, it agreed to include the controversial clauses with the potency required by the federal guidelines. On June 30 the amended regulation was again forwarded to the Department of the Interior for approval. But rapid approval was not forthcoming. It took five months of continued negotiations and language changes before newly appointed Secretary of the Interior Walter Hickel approved WPC 15 as amended.

Meanwhile, in July 1969, the MPCA formally requested Reserve to comply with the provisions of WPC 15, though it still lacked federal approval. Subsequent to federal approval of WPC 15, which in effect established it as both the federal and the state water quality standard, Reserve challenged the validity and the application of the standard. Reserve's notice of appeal was served upon the MPCA and filed with the clerk of the state court on December 24, 1969, Christmas Eve. This date was to become important later in determining whether or not Reserve's appeal was timely; the time to appeal a final order being only 30 days. Reserve acted in the belief that the date of federal approval of the regulation (November 26, 1969) started the 30-day period, so filing of the appeal on December 24 was just under the wire. The state, however, contended that Reserve's appeal was too late, because more than 30 days had lapsed since the regulation was adopted by the state on June 30, 1969. The question was ultimately determined by the Minnesota Supreme Court.

Reserve alleged in its appeal that

1 / the requisite statutory procedure for the adoption of WPC 15 had not been complied with and that, therefore, the regulation was not enforceable, and that

2 / the anti-degradation clause and the effluent standards were illegal, unreasonable, arbitrary, and invalid as applied to Reserve, but if the standards were applicable to Reserve, then

3 / the MPCA should be ordered to issue a Variance pursuant to subdivision (a)(5) of the regulations, because enforcement would cause undue hardship, and strict conformity would be unreasonable, impractical, or not feasible under the circumstances.

The state filed its answer on February 13, 1970, denying Reserve's allegations and counterclaiming that the company was polluting Lake Superior in violation of Minnesota Statutes Chapter 115 and Regulation WPC 15, thereby creating a public nuisance. The court was requested to set a time schedule for compliance with WPC 15 and other relevant pollution laws.

The MPCA's counterclaim against Reserve is noteworthy. Up to the adoption of WPC 15 by the state in June of 1969, the MPCA had given outward signs of working closely and cooperatively with Minnesota industries for the development of reasonable pollution abatement regulations for the state. The 1965 guidelines and directives issued by the Department of the Interior, however, forced the state to adopt more stringent standards and regulations. Interestingly, the MPCA had just three months earlier published a staff report, (2) which, in essence, concluded that Reserve's discharge had no significant impact upon water quality of Lake Superior. Though the causes for MPCA's change in attitude toward Reserve are not completely clear, it is safe to speculate that public and political pressures were involved. The so-called Stoddard Report, which was leaked to the press in January, 1969, stimulated a dramatic change in public sentiment toward Reserve during 1969 and precipitated the "Federal Enforcement Conference" in May 1969.

Prior to the trial of the merits of the case, various preliminary motions were made by the parties. Hearings were held before the court on each motion before the court issued its final orders. The judge of the Lake County District Court (Sixth District) handling the case was the Honorable C. Luther Eckman.

The first motion filed was a request by the MPCA for a change of venue from Lake County to Hennepin County. The Lake County district is in Two Harbors, an old port town on Lake Superior, approximately 30 miles from the Reserve plant at Silver Bay. Hennepin County Court is in Minneapolis. The MPCA stated its grounds in support of its request for the change of venue as:

1 / the MPCA's official residence is Hennepin County (Minneapolis);

2 / the alleged cause of action arose entirely in Hennepin County; and

3 / the convenience of witnesses and the ends of justice would be promoted by transferring the case.

Although not specified in the motion, it would appear that the state agency had other motives for seeking a change in trial location. The Lake County region was dominated by residents whose livelihood depended upon mining and ore processing interests. By contrast, the Hennepin County region was well-populated with environmentalists. These stated and unstated reasons proved insufficient to sway the court. On February 3, Judge Eckman denied the motion for change in venue.

The state then moved to dismiss the suit on grounds that the notice of appeal failed to state a claim upon which relief could be granted and that the court lacked jurisdiction over the subject matter because Reserve failed to comply with the requirements of Minnesota Statutes 115.15, Subd. 3 with respect to time for service of its notice of appeal. The court also denied this motion.

Finally, on a motion of Reserve, the court issued an order restraining and enjoining the MPCA and the Minnesota commissioner of conservation from holding hearings on revocation of Reserve's permits insofar as the proceedings were premised upon an alleged violation of WPC 15. The court further prohibited the Minnesota agencies from otherwise seeking to resolve the issues until a determination was made by the court.

The restraining order had far-reaching implications. It was issued after and superseded an order that had already been issued in another state district court. For on September 17, 1969, the Sierra Club and the Minnesota Committee for Environmental Information had brought suit in the Fourth District Court in Hennepin County to compel the MPCA to hold hearings to consider the alleged violations of Reserve's 1947 permit. This suit alleged that Reserve violated terms of the permit by discharging tailings outside the permit area, resulting in material clouding and discoloration of the waters of Lake Superior. In this case the state had not been willing to hold hearings on the permit and argued that it could not be compelled to hold hearings because hearings are discretionary. Furthermore, the MPCA argued that the complaining organizations had no standing to sue in the district court because their rights had not been violated. However, the judge of the fourth district, Judge Donald Barbeau, thought otherwise and ruled that a writ of mandamus was appropriate because the parties were seeking only to compel hearings and not to compel any particular finding. A further reason was that the parties were entitled to sue because a public right had been created that could be enforced by the public. And so by court order dated November 12, 1969, the MPCA and the

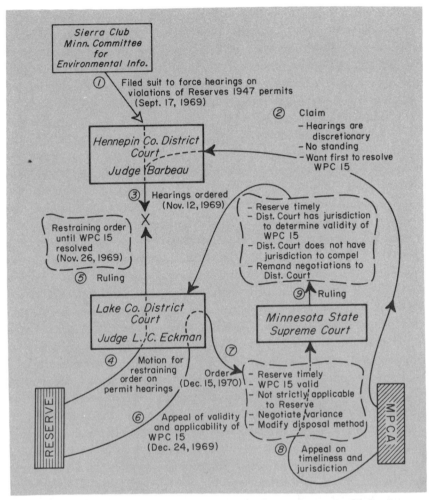

FIGURE 13   Sequence and disposition of proceedings in state court.

Department of Conservation were required by the Fourth District Court to hold public hearings before May 30, 1970.

Judge Eckman's ruling in Lake County Court blocked this order for hearing on the 1947 permit until Reserve's appeal of WPC 15 had been decided. Secretary Hickel had approved Minnesota's water quality standards two weeks after Judge Barbeau issued his order compelling hearings on the alleged permit violations. From Reserve's standpoint, it was a duplication of effort to determine basically the same issues in two different judicial forums. Reserve was severely condemned by critics for selecting this course of action and not meeting the charge of polluting Lake Superior in the proposed administrative hearings. It was also argued that the permit hearings were called because they concerned violations of Reserve's permit and were not limited to violations of WPC 15.

The statutory authority for the pollution control power of the MPCA comes from Minnesota Statute No. 115.42, which provides: "It is the policy of the state to provide for the prevention, control, and abatement of pollution of all waters of the state. . . ." Undoubtedly, the legislature intended that administrative agencies determine the question of pollution. Recourse to the court system would occur only if there was dissatisfaction with the administrative decision. In this case, the MPCA itself had decided that administrative hearings should be eliminated, as evidenced by the filing of the counterclaim, bringing the issue of pollution directly before the court. Also, a letter dated February 13, 1970, from the chairman of the MPCA to the state's Assistant Attorney General, described the filing of the counterclaim as a "good procedural move" by the MPCA, which "might have the effect of bringing the matter of Reserve Mining Company's problem into the courts much more quickly than we could accomplish by an independent hearing of our own. Finally, such a procedure might even negate the necessity of our holding an independent hearing on the matter."

Judge Eckman believed that the court should resolve the conflict, because to proceed by way of administrative hearings would have involved a lengthy and involved proceeding, probably resulting in any case in an appeal to district court for a final determination. The court pointed out that, if at a hearing the findings were adverse to Reserve, the company would have been forced to

1 / oppose the allegations and contest the issues,

2 / apply to the agencies for a rehearing, and/or

3 / appeal any adverse decision of the MPCA or the commissioner to the district court.

Another factor in bypassing the administrative hearing stage was the consideration that to proceed by way of permit revocation hearings assumed that the portions of WPC 15 involved were reasonable, and not arbitrary and capricious as contended by Reserve. Therefore, the court believed that it should first determine whether or not WPC 15 was valid before the state agencies proceeded to act in reliance on the regulation.

> It is difficult to see [the judge observed] how the Hearing Referee could isolate and separate the portions of WPC 15 complained of in the appeal from the rest of the charges and complaints against Reserve. This could only result in confusion and delay towards an expeditious determination of the whole controversy.[1]

Judge Eckman obviously realized that more than just legal issues were involved in the controversy. In the memorandum that accompanied the order restraining the agencies from holding hearings, the judge explained:

> This Court feels that the time has come to brush aside all legal technicalities and procedures that may impede a resolution of these questions without further delay by taking the problem out of the public and political arena and into the court for a full and comprehensive judicial review, where the interests of both the public and industry can be fully explored and protected.[1]

The trial began on June 22, 1970, and became what the *Minneapolis Star* described as "the nation's hottest battle over industrial pollution." Reserve required four weeks to present its evidence, and the state took another two and a half weeks; 285 exhibits were presented and 29 witnesses testified.

The state's case was strengthened by the active cooperation of the federal government. The FWPCA (predecessor of the present EPA) provided a dozen high-level technical expert witnesses in support of the state's case. Several of those witnesses also testified at the "Federal Enforcement Conference" that had begun in May 1969 and continued intermittently through April of 1971. The state also searched the nation for additional qualified experts to testify at the trial and was successful

---

[1] "Order for Temporary Injunction and Stay of Proceedings" issued by Judge C. L. Eckman on April 30, 1970, in Minnesota (Lake County) District Court.

in bringing together a group of witnesses with outstanding credentials.

In filing its counterclaim, the state had raised the broad issue of pollution of Lake Superior. As a result, the trial was concerned with more than just the validity and application of WPC 15. Technical issues raised and argued before Judge Eckman were essentially the same as those presented in the "Federal Enforcement Conference," which proceeded concurrently with the trial. These issues included: the efficiency of the heavy density current, the distribution and fate of tailings in Lake Superior, the impact of tailings on fish and fish food organisms, eutrophication or nutrient enrichment, algal and bacterial growth stimulation, lake water chemistry, and the green water phenomenon.

Although possible violation of the permits was not a direct issue, Judge Eckman determined that this seemed inextricably related and commented on the problem in his "Findings of Fact":

> The matter of the violation and/or termination of those permits is not a direct issue in this action, but are necessarily proper evidence of the facts to be considered by the Court in the final determination herein.[2]

Therefore, the language and the effects of the permits were admitted into evidence, the court holding that the evidence was material and relevant to the positions of the parties. The court also concluded that the reasonableness of the effluent standards must be analyzed in view of the history of Reserve's operations under the provisions of the permits.

The judge pointed out that the reasonableness of the permits and compliance with the conditions therein had been reviewed many times. In 1956, and again in 1960, the permits were amended to increase the amount of water that could be appropriated from and discharged back into Lake Superior. The fact that conditions remaining in the permits were never altered could suggest that the terms were reasonable, because the amendments were adopted after extensive public hearings. However, the court speculated, "It seems highly unlikely that a similar application today for the Permit issued in 1947 would be granted. The public, in only a few short years, had been alerted and alarmed over the disastrous effects upon our environment from what appears to have

[2] "Findings of Fact," "Conclusions of Law," and "Order for Judgment" issued by Judge C. L. Eckman in Lake County District Court on December 15, 1970.

been a careless and callous disregard in the past [for] our ecological future." [3]

After explaining why the evidence on the permits was necessary, Judge Eckman discussed the procedural aspects of the adoption of WPC 15. Reserve had alleged that the requisite statutory procedure for the adoption of WPC 15 had not been complied with and that, therefore, the regulation was not enforceable. Other than to mention that the MPCA had complied with the requirements for public hearings, the court made no other comment, holding that "the requisite statutory procedure for the adoption of WPC 15 had been complied with and said Regulation per se is applicable against Appellant Reserve Mining Company." [4]

However, as to the application of WPC 15's effluent standards to Reserve, the court found the standards to be "unreasonable, arbitrary, and invalid as applied. . . ." [5] The effluent standards contained in the regulations prescribed limitations on a discharge regardless of any effect on receiving waters. The effect of applying these effluent standards would have been to prohibit Reserve's tailings discharge into Lake Superior. It should be pointed out that the effluent standard was derived from a consideration of the nominal effectiveness of secondary treatment processes used to treat *municipal sewage* and should not have been used to regulate mining operations. The court reasoned that to enforce the standards against Reserve would require (1) either the dilution of the effluent by the addition of millions of gallons of water, which would reduce or destroy the effectiveness of the heavy density current, or (2) the complete cessation of the discharge into the lake, which would require the closing of the plant for a considerable length of time until alternative disposal methods were studied and implemented. The court rejected these alternatives in the belief that the "evidence, including a tailings inventory, established the fact that after 15 years of operation and discharge by Appellant, Appellant's discharge does form a strong heavy density current. . . ." [6] The court noted at the same time, however, that a small percentage of the tailings discharge had escaped the heavy density current. Because of this, the court required Reserve to modify its operations.

Judge Eckman explained that terms of permits and public sta-

[3] Memorandum accompanying Judge Eckman's order of December 15, 1970, p. 3. (See Reference 18.)
[4] Judge Eckman's order of December 15, 1970, p. 14.
[5] Ibid., p. 15.
[6] Ibid., p. 8.

tutes requiring "material" compliance safeguard both the natural resources and industry by providing for the balancing of ecological and economic factors. He ruled, however, that variances from standards should follow "where strict enforcement would cause undue hardship" as called for in Section (a) (5) of WPC 15. Since the immediate application of WPC 15 effluent standards against Reserve were held to be unreasonable and arbitrary, the court further held that the situation "requires the granting of a variance excusing Appellant from conformity thereto until further Order of this Court, pursuant to subsequent modification in the discharge process hereinafter referred to." [7]

In considering the variance from standards, the court balanced economic and ecological factors and confessed that "the burden of striking this balance is great." Subsequently, Judge Eckman was criticized for not giving enough weight to the Minnesota Environmental Rights Act of 1971 with its charge that "Economic considerations alone shall not constitute a defense hereunder." Apparently, the fact that the court gave considerable attention to jobs, capital investment, and other economic considerations suggested that to the judge the pollution abatement to be realized was not worth the potentially disastrous economic consequences.

Concerning the anti-degradation clause as it applied to Reserve, the court concluded that Reserve's discharge is not a "disposal system or treatment works" within the meaning of WPC 15, and Reserve was therefore not exempt from the provisions of WPC 15 on that ground. However, this clause was not applicable to Reserve, because it applied only to new dischargers or those that expanded operations after the date of the adoption of the regulation, i.e., June 30, 1969. Reserve had been in operation for 15 years and had completed expansion in 1963. With respect to possible future pollution, the evidence was in such conflict that the court refrained "from indulging in such speculation."

As to the counterclaim that Reserve was polluting the lake in violation of Minnesota Statutes, Chapter 115, the court discussed at great length the meaning of *pollution*. Under the Minnesota statute:

> Pollution means the contamination of any waters of the State so as to create a nuisance or render such waters unclean, or noxious, or impure so as to be actually or potentially

[7] Ibid., p. 15.

harmful or detrimental or injurious to public health, safety or welfare, to domestic, commercial, industrial or recreational use, or to livestock, wild animals, birds, fish or other aquatic life.[8]

The court concluded that there was no substantial evidence that the discharge of tailings had "rendered the waters unclean or noxious or impure" as required by law to establish pollution.

The court further found that

after 15 years of operations and discharge of tailings into Lake Superior by the Appellant, the evidence before the Court establishes that said discharge has had no measurable adverse or deleterious effects upon the water quality or use of Lake Superior insofar as its drinking water quality, [or] any condition affecting health, affecting fish life or the reproduction thereof, or any interference with navigation.[9]

But the court found:

Appellant's discharge of tailings into Lake Superior has had a measurable effect upon Lake Superior and the use thereof in regard to:

1 / The aesthetic enjoyment of the Lake by the increase of the 'green water phenomenon' both within and without the zone of discharge as described in the permits.

2 / A decrease in the presence of Pontoporeia, commonly known as scud, in the vicinity of the zone of discharge. This fish food used primarily by smelt has had only a minimal and immaterial effect on the fish population of the Lake.[10]

In spite of these seemingly strong statements relative to the pollution of Lake Superior by Reserve's tailings, Judge Eckman refused to rule on the issue of pollution as raised by the MPCA's counterclaim. The court stated that "no conclusion is drawn as to whether or not

[8] Minnesota Statute No. 115.01, Subd. 5.
[9] Judge Eckman's order of December 15, 1970, p. 12.
[10] Ibid., pp. 12–13.

Reserve Mining Company is polluting Lake Superior." Instead, the court concluded that "the present method of discharge of tailings . . . shall be altered. . . ."[11]

While determining that "there has been no substantial or convincing evidence of deterioration to date," the judge gave great weight to testimony of numerous scientific experts who warned against the future effects of continued discharges into Lake Superior. As a result, he sought to dispel the concerns and apprehensions of the experts by ordering Reserve and the MPCA to come up with a mutually acceptable modified plan of tailings disposal that would "insure the flocculation of the fine tailings and the deposit of all the tailings by conduit to the floor of the Great Trough. . . ."[12] Nothing was mentioned in the court decision about consideration of any onland tailings disposal system.

Reserve was to submit to the MPCA its plans for approval on or before May 15, 1971. After approval, Reserve was to be given two additional years to install and begin operation of the new method of discharge. The court retained jurisdiction for the purpose of insuring good faith negotiations toward a satisfactory modification of discharge, and the court reserved the authority to render a final decision in the event that no mutual agreement could be reached between the parties.

In his memorandum of December 15th, Judge Eckman noted that the court had hoped to be an "instrument of compromise, negotiation, and settlement, but instead found itself in a strictly adversary proceeding with both parties not budging in their positions."[13]

An impressive array of scientists and experts had appeared with many educational degrees, publications, and memberships on national and international committees and government commissions together with years of experience in their respective fields. The court was still not satisfied:

> In view of this profound assistance, it would appear that the Court should have had little difficulty in arriving at a logical and determinative solution. Unfortunately, however, this was not so. Contradictions in findings and opinions in varying degrees became the role.[14]

[11] Ibid., p. 15.
[12] Judge Eckman's memorandum dated December 15, 1970, p. 8.
[13] Ibid., p. 1.
[14] Ibid., p. 2.

And so the court found itself being "completely lacking in personal expertise . . . [and] in the impossible position of being required to analyze, weigh, and choose between these controversial points of view." [15]

As could be expected, the state was dissatisfied with the district court's decision and elected to carry the pollution fight with Reserve to the Minnesota Supreme Court.

The MPCA appeal to the high court challenged only those parts of the judgment that determined Reserve's appeal timely, that determined WPC 15 (c)(6) unreasonable as applied to Reserve, and that instructed the MPCA to negotiate a variance. Thus, it was based on narrow procedural grounds, precluding the supreme court's review of the case on its merits.

The state supreme court held that "under our statutes, WPC 15, as amended, became an effective regulation on June 30, 1969, and the time for appeal commenced from that date." [16] However, the court determined that Section 115.15 (Subd. 3) must also be considered. This section provides that the 30-day period commences only after an affected party receives a copy of the order or after service of notice by registered mail, and that in the event that a copy of an order is not received within 30 days, appeals can be filed up to six months after making and filing of the order, rule, regulation, or decision. Reserve's appeal obviously fell well within this six-month filing period. The MPCA admitted that "through inadvertence Reserve did not receive a mailed notice of a copy of amended WPC 15 as filed on June 30, 1964." [17] The court concluded that because Reserve did not receive mailed notice and because the two copies that were received were not delivered with the intent to conform to the requirements of the statute, Reserve's appeal was timely.

As its second ground for appeal, the MPCA challenged the trial court's jurisdiction to determine the validity of WPC 15. The supreme court commented that "Reserve correctly points out that under Section 115.15, Subd. 10, if an appeal had not been taken, the validity of the regulation could not have been challenged in any other way." [18] There-

---

[15] Ibid., p. 7.
[16] Minnesota Supreme Court mandate dated August 29, 1972, p. 5. (See Reference 19.)
[17] Ibid.
[18] Ibid.

fore, the trial court's determination of the validity of the regulation was "entirely proper."

The supreme court reversed the trial court on the last issue on appeal, holding that the trial court in some respects had "exceeded its jurisdiction" in that it had no statutory power to compel negotiations between the MPCA and Reserve regarding the issuance of a variance. For that reason, the supreme court remanded "the matter to the district court with the instructions to remand the matter to the MPCA for proceedings under the regulations of WPC 15(a) (5) for the granting of a variance." [19]

Thus, the state court proceedings ended without a major victory for either the state agencies or the company. Unfortunately, political intervention prevented maturation of the court's directives. In January 1971, the new Minnesota governor, Wendell Anderson, took office and unofficially, though effectively, severed state negotiations with Reserve. Not coincidentally, the governor also appointed anti-Reservist Grant Merritt as MPCA director. This dramatic change in political atmosphere in Minnesota insured the impossibility of out-of-court agreement, and ultimately thrust the Reserve controversy into the federal district court.

[19] Ibid., p. 10.

Chapter 11

Federal Enforcement Conference: Second Session

On April 29, 1970, seven months after the close of the first federal-state enforcement conference, the conferees reconvened. This second session was again held at the Duluth Hotel before a standing-room-only crowd of interested and concerned observers. The session was to review the progress achieved by Reserve and, to a much lesser degree, other dischargers, in complying the recommendations of the first session. Reserve had been asked to submit a progress report to the conferees by April 1, and a full preliminary report by July 26. These dates have some significance. The April 1 date was six months from the October 1, 1969, issuance of recommendations at the first executive session. However, since Secretary of the Interior, Walter Hickel, deliberated or delayed for four months before affirming the recommendations of the conferees, i.e., on January 26, 1971, Reserve was given six months from the latter date to develop its full report.

The second session was opened by Chairman Stein of the FWQA (formerly the Federal Water Pollution Control Administration— FWPCA) in accordance with the provisions of Section 10 of the Federal Water Pollution Control Act. Since interstate pollution affecting health and welfare had not been firmly established during the first session, the conferees still lacked jurisdiction over Reserve or any other discharger in the Lake Superior basin. This meant that the recommendations of the conferees, even after approval by the Secretary of the Interior, were just recommendations and not requirements. Consequently, any response to the recommendations by Reserve was in a spirit of cooperation rather than in compliance with any binding order or pending prosecution.

Nearly the same line-up of conferees participated in the second session, including: Badalich, Tuveson, and Dr. Howard Anderson of the Minnesota PCA; Frangos and Mackie of the Wisconsin DNR; Purdy and Carlos Fetterolf of the Michigan Water Resources Commission; Francis Mayo (who had replaced Poston at the Great Lakes regional office), Bryson, and Stein of the FWQA. Stein was again designated by the Secretary of the Interior to chair the conference.

Representatives of several environmental groups were heard at the start of the second session. As at the first session, however, the groups argued as nontechnical, concerned witnesses rather than with sound scientific data.

One spokesman of particular note again was Grant Merritt, chairman of MECCA. As in previous testimony, Merritt leveled scathing accusations at Reserve and overstated many of his technical arguments. He declared, "The public is tired of the delays, the foot-dragging, and the stalling tactics of the Reserve Mining Company and the State of Minnesota." [1] Although Merritt was entitled to speak his mind on the issue, the factual basis for this accusation was not provided. Federal and state studies had shown at best only "presumptive" evidence of interstate pollution by Reserve's tailings discharge. Therefore, Reserve had no legal compulsion to change to an alternative disposal method. Furthermore, the only documented delay in the case to that date was caused by the Secretary of the Interior, not Reserve or the MPCA. Merritt emphatically urged the conferees to adopt four strong recommendations, including: "Revocation of Reserve's Federal and State permits as of December 31, 1970, the end of this year," and if Reserve

[1] Proceedings of "Federal Enforcement Conference in the Matter of Pollution of Lake Superior and Its Tributary Basin, Minnesota–Wisconsin– Michigan," Second Session, U.S.D.I.–FWQA, April 29–30, 1970, p. 18.

had commenced construction of onland disposal facilities, "permits could thereafter be issued until the construction is completed, no later than December 31, 1972." [2] He urged that no further study be undertaken.

In response to the emotional and impractical accusations and urgings of Merritt, Stein remarked: "I have said many times, we wouldn't need a panel like this [conferees] or perhaps a good lawyer like you in dealing with pollution problems if all you had to do was shut down an industry to control it. Anyone can do that. I think the challenge is to keep the industry alive if possible and control pollution." [3]

Merritt proceeded to attack Reserve's hiring of Max Edwards and Clark Clifford, former Secretary of Defense, as Washington lobbyists.

> Just last month, for example [he said], a secret meeting arranged by Secretary Clifford and attended by Reserve officials and Congressman John Blatnik, was held in Washington, DC, with General Clark, Chief of the U.S. Army Corps of Engineers. As everyone now knows, this issue of tailings pollution of Lake Superior is one of tremendous citizen concern. Yet Reserve Mining Company arranged a secret meeting in order to persuade General Clark that the federal permit issued by the Corps to Reserve shall not be revoked. [4]

Chairman Stein responded to these charges, stating "We have . . . a distressing number . . . of ad hominon arguments of respected members of the bar being indicated as holding secret meetings. Not that I was at any of these meetings, but I didn't find any of this attitude of secrecy. . . ." He went on to admonish, "Unless we all try to work this out together, I am not sure we are going to come up with an equitable solution." [5] Merritt's attempt to explain his position on the alleged meetings led Stein to counter, "Well, I think I understand your point of view. I also think it is characteristic of people who think there is a conspiratorial form of government." [6]

Following Merritt, Stoddard was called to the stand. His testimony was short and dealt mostly with a defense of the Taconite Study

[2] Ibid., p. 25.
[3] Ibid., p. 27.
[4] Proceedings of "Federal Enforcement Conference," Second Session, p. 17.
[5] Ibid., p. 29.
[6] Ibid.

Group report that he had authored. Following Stoddard's testimony, Stein directed a question that was obviously intended to refute or at least attenuate an earlier criticism from Merritt.

Stein: Well, since you were the head of that [Bureau of Land Management in the Department of the Interior], as a former top government official, I really don't see anything sinister in you taking a position on this case, do you?

Stoddard: No, I didn't. . . .

Stein: And I think you are bringing a lot to the party with your background. So I really don't see anything wrong with former top government officials such as you taking a side in any particular conservation issue and pushing it.[7]

Government witnesses then took the stand to present various reports and related testimony. Fetterolf of the Michigan WRC introduced into the conference record a document prepared by the Lake Superior Water Quality Technical Committee entitled, "Water Quality Guidelines for Lake Superior."[8] This report represented a modified version of the standards presented at the first session. The report and standards were not adopted immediately because the report had not been presented to the conferees prior to its introduction into the record. Stein gave the conferees until the next day to review the document; then it was adopted.

One of the government's key witnesses throughout the conference proceedings, Dr. Donald Mount, was recalled. He introduced into the record six technical reports that had been prepared by scientists from his laboratory. The reports contained findings and conclusions of studies conducted since the first enforcement conference a year earlier. These studies were significant since the findings were later used to show interstate pollution by Reserve's taconite tailings.[9] A brief review of these six studies follows:[10]

---

[7] Ibid., pp. 39–40.
[8] Ibid., p. 121.
[9] During an interview in October of 1974 with two of the scientists who participated in these studies, it was brought out that the studies were done hurriedly and were not meant to be conclusive!
[10] Proceedings of "Federal Enforcement Conference," Second Session, pp. 223–325.

Study No. I:

"Physical Characteristics of Green Water Along the Minnesota Shoreline" by Dr. R. Andrew and Dr. G. Glass.

Conclusions:

1 / A major cause of "green water" along the north shore is tailings suspended in water.

2 / Not all "green water" masses occurring in Lake Superior are due to tailings.

3 / Water clarity in "green water" caused by tailings is four to ten times less than clarity in clear water.

4 / The color is due to reflected light from suspended particles.

The tracer cummingtonite was used to develop these findings. Reserve's Kenneth Haley later attacked this study as based on too few samples and on cummingtonite as a tracer. The study confirmed that the green color was caused by the refraction of light and not by the presence of algae.

Study No. II:

"Distribution of Taconite Tailings in the Sediments of the Western Basin of Lake Superior" by Dr. Robert Andrew.

Conclusions:

1 / Taconite tailings from the Reserve Mining Company at Silver Bay, Minnesota, are deposited discontinuously on the surface of the lake bottom over an area of at least 1,000 square miles of the western tip of Lake Superior.

2 / The tailings are mixed in the top 5–10 cm of sediment.

3 / The percentage of cummingtonite in tributary stream sediments accurately indicates the cummingtonite content found in the subsurface bottom sediments.

4 / Tailings deposits are found in both Minnesota and Wisconsin waters. Although the sediments in Wisconsin waters contain very low percentages of taconite tailings, the tailings deposits are distinguishable quantitatively from stream sediments.

These conclusions supported the contention that Reserve's taconite tailings were being discharged into interstate waters, and this study, more than perhaps any other, was responsible for the federal government's conclusion that interstate pollution was caused by the discharge of Reserve's tailings.

Study No. III:

"Effect of Taconite on Bacterial Growth" by Dr. D. L. Herman.

Conclusions:

1 /   Tailings are biologically active at concentrations of approximately 1 mg/l . . . a concentration expected to occur over a significant area of the lake.

2 /   The reduced die away or enhanced growth is displayed by indicators of fecal contamination, as well as a pathogenic bacterium.

The scientific methodology and relative significance of this study is subject to question and criticism. Haley noted that all tests were performed at a temperature of 6°C. He contended that Reserve's tailings discharge did not contribute these bacteria and that tailings, like any other suspended solid, provide only a surface for protection. He also pointed to the observation that there had been no demonstrable increase in turbidity in the western part of the lake over the 14 years of Reserve's operation.

Study No. IV:

"Taconite Bioassays" by Dr. A. E. Lemke.

Conclusion:

Direct toxic effects of tailings on lake organisms were found at concentrations that were expected to occur only in local areas of the lake.

The significance of this *conclusion* should be examined more closely in light of Lemke's actual findings during his study. Lemke tested eight different species or age groups of organisms for test periods extending from 21 to as long as 128 days on taconite tailings ranging in concentration from 0.2 mg/l to 200 mg/l solids (100% effluent was 200 mg/l solids). His results showed that in four of the eight tests, at least 50% of the test organisms died under *control conditions* (i.e., in lake water without tailings) and in three other tests 25–45% of the controls died. In *six of the eight* tests, organisms in 10% tailings suspension showed equal or higher survival than those in "pure" lake water. Only in the 100% tailings (i.e., effluent directly from the launder) was there evidence of toxicity. Lemke acknowledged this in his discussion when he stated, "Since only *Daphnia* have been used in previous tests, the problems of testing new and delicate animals resulted in lower control survival and reduced precision. Considering the data as a whole, the 100 percent (200 mg/l) seems to have a consistent adverse effect on all species." He also stated, "*Daphnia*, one of the most sensitive organisms to heavy metals, appeared to be little affected by tailings."[11]

One is prompted to reread and attempt to justify the single conclusion offered by Lemke. In the opinion of this author, his results should have been totally disregarded and should not have been admitted into the conference record.

The questionable validity of the Lemke report and its conclusions was compounded during the testimony of Mount, Lemke's boss. Though he had introduced the study, he explained: "The statement I am going to give has been carefully worked over by myself and our staff in order to try to present what we believe to be the key points that have been raised in past conferences, what the data really show, and particularly the results of the additional studies which we were instructed to do by the commissioner of FWPCA."[12] Regarding the "direct toxic effects of tailings on lake animals," Mount acknowledged,

Concentrations less than 10 percent, which would be equivalent to 20 parts per million of suspended solids, less than 2 microns, had *no direct effect* on the eggs of brook trout, lake trout or lake herring, *nor were there significant effects*[13] on the reproduction of important plankton organisms such as *Daphnia*. The data for *Mysis*[13] and *Pontophoria*,[13] two of the other important invertebrate food organisms in the lake, *are*

[11] Ibid., p. 292.
[12] Ibid., p. 325.
[13] Emphasis provided by author.

inconclusive,[13] but suggestive that there may have been effects at lesser concentrations. [He went on] Mortality in control tanks was higher than is normally acceptable for bioassays of this type, and so *no significance* [13] can be attributed to the mortalities of these two invertibrates. [Mount continued] Bioassay data clearly suggest that *direct adverse effects* [13] of the tailings on fishes and fish food organisms *will not occur*[13] at concentrations expected in the lake, except for local areas near the discharge and in the heavy density current.[14]

These statements by Mount rebut the findings and conclusions of his staff member, Lemke, and not only cast doubt on the validity of this study but also prompted doubts regarding other work by the laboratory. Why did Mount permit this report to be entered into the record? The conferees, conservationists, and the press all failed to seize upon this statement by Mount to set the record straight regarding the alleged toxicity of tailings. News of this type is generally no news. But that doesn't justify the failure of the conferees to raise the question.

Study No. V:

"Effect of Taconite Tailings on Algal Growth" by Dr. Andrew and Dr. Glass.

Conclusions:

1 / Algal growth rate was higher in 10% (16 mg/l particles < 2 microns) taconite tailings suspensions.

2 / Increased growth rates are related to increases in soluble silica from the tailings and possible subsequent utilization by diatoms.

Andrew and Glass failed to admit that their study also showed the same or higher growth rate of algae in "pure" lake water as in lake water contaminated with 0.1% or 1% tailings. These latter two concentrations are found more frequently outside of the discharge zone than the higher concentrations used in the study. The 10% level would likely be found only near the heavy density current. Again a study's conclusions were incomplete and its significance was misleading.

[14] Proceedings of "Federal Enforcement Conference," Second Session, p. 333.

Reserve's Haley, moreover, pointed out that the tailings were heated to 140° F (60° C) for pasteurization. He asserted that some silica would have gone into solution during this laboratory step, a condition that would not occur in the natural lake environment.

Study No. VI:

"The Dissolution of Taconite Tailings in Lake Superior" by Dr. Glass.

Conclusions:

1 / In addition to the increase of soluble salts as the ore is processed, taconite tailings show continuous solution after leaving the plant.

2 / The rates of dissolution increase with decreasing concentrations of particles/unit volume of water and with increasing temperature.

3 / After 332 days, increases in soluble components from tailings in Lake Superior water under simulated lake conditions were:

COMPONENT	INCREASE IN MG/KG TOTAL TAILINGS
SiO_2	331
Na	37
K	70
Ca	282
Mg	11
SS	61
TDS	1,110

Again it appears that Glass elected to limit his conclusions to only those factors that reflected negatively on Reserve's discharge. Note the absence in his conclusion of the key nutrients responsible for eutrophication, i.e., phosphorus (P) and nitrogen (N). Also note the absence of *any* heavy metals or toxic elements such as copper (Cu), Zinc (Zn), chromium (Chr), or cadmium (Cd). These toxic metal ions were reported earlier by the government to be present in the tailings. Apparently, Reserve witnesses Lee and Bright had been correct in their evaluation at the May 1969 conference that these elements do not readily leach from the particulate matter and, hence, are not biologically active. Glass' omission of these elements in his table was probably not an oversight but rather the inability of his testing apparatus to detect measurable quantities of these substances. Although omitted in his conclusions, he did report in the body of his study, "Sodium, iron, copper, manganese, zinc, and cadmium showed little or no increase in concentration." [15] The absence of these nutrients and toxic elements becomes more significant in view of the 330-day contact period used by Glass in his laboratory experiments.

The weakness of these FWQA reports and the bias in reporting conclusions is clear. One might similarly, and possibly fairly, accuse Reserve of presenting only "partial truths" in company reports and memoranda. But there is a difference—a major difference. In one instance, the conferees (all state or federal government officials), anti-Reserve groups, and the concerned public very likely viewed Reserve's reports and presentations, like those of most respondents in adversary situations, with at least a degree of self-serving bias. This is not to suggest that Reserve's reports were not factual or truthful, but rather to state a fact of life with regard to expected defense tactics. The conferees and the concerned public, however, are justified in expecting total objectivity in the findings of federal scientists and federally sponsored reports. This would seem logical, because the federal effort, especially from a research laboratory, is expected to be one of fact-finding and investigation, not advocacy. Federal scientists should be compelled to present the whole truth on technical issues. Even though the whole of the information was often contained in the federal reports, the findings were not wholly presented in the conclusions. Such omissions are critical since most of the non-technical or non-scientific readers of a technical report tend to review only the conclusions and recommendations.

Mount, leader of the contingent of federal scientists, concluded his presentation, summarizing the key points and factors of concern regarding the discharge of tailings in Lake Superior. He then stated, "*In my judgment the effect of Reserve's discharge should be assessed in terms of altering the lake's appearance rather than the toxic effects on fish and fish food organisms or endangering water supplies.*" [16] He further concluded, "the effects of present discharges are small, but they are in the direction of degradation, mostly because the materials being added are persistent and the flushing rate of the lake is very slow. Their effects are

[15] Ibid., p. 313.
[16] Emphasis supplied by author.

irreversible and cumulative." His final remark was one of great significance, "Should our plan of action protect for 50 years or 500 years or
more?" [17] Finally, the conferees had an honest assessment by a responsible government official.

Mount's frank and perceptive statement opened the door to numerous questions from the conferees. The key question dealt with interstate pollution and whether the conference could assume jurisdiction over
Reserve's discharge. Mount reiterated the findings of his laboratory regarding the presence of tailings in Wisconsin waters of Lake Superior,
but refused to go the next giant step and conclude that these tailings
affected the health or welfare of Wisconsin residents.

Badalich of the Minnesota PCA reported on the second day of
the conference on Minnesota's progress in relation to the recommendations of the first conference, as endorsed by Secretary Hickel. His report
concluded with these observations:

"The discharge of tailings has been kept under surveillance to
the extent permitted by our resources. We have no new findings to report." [18]

"The company is proceeding with these studies [on reducing tailings discharge] and on April 13 provided a working progress report." [19]

The afternoon session of the second day of the conference was
devoted almost entirely to statements by Reserve witnesses Fride, the
company's attorney, and Dr. Haley. Fride introduced a prepared statement that dealt primarily with Reserve's reaction to the conduct and
conclusions at the executive session of the first conference session. He
noted that the purpose of the executive session was to analyze the record
of the May conference and not to hear new evidence. He complained
that new evidence was presented by the FWPCA and that Reserve was
not given an opportunity to review the information and prepare a rebuttal. Indeed, Badalich of the MPCA also had objected to the introduction of this new evidence, noting that neither he nor anyone else at
the session had been given the opportunity to review and digest it.

Fride also responded to accusations that Reserve failed to meet
the April 1, 1970, deadline recommended by Secretary Hickel for a
progress report. He stated, "In accordance with that recommendation,

[17] Proceedings of "Federal Enforcement Conference," Second Session, p.
343.
[18] Proceedings of "Federal Enforcement Conference," Second Session, p.
572.
[19] Ibid.

Reserve Mining Company supplied the staff of the MPCA with a working copy of its progress report prior to April 1." [20] This working document was submitted to the MPCA prior to April 1 but was returned to *Reserve* for some revisions prior to a presentation of the report before a regularly scheduled MPCA meeting on April 13, 1970.

Fride then introduced the "Engineering Task Force Progress Report." [21] This document included a presentation and brief evaluation of 19 different possibilities for reducing the amount or impact of tailings discharged into Lake Superior.

Some dramatic changes in Reserve's position on the technical issues in the controversy were stated by Fride. For the first time, Reserve acknowledged that green water sometimes may come from taconite tailings. He, however, sought to put this admission in perspective by declaring that this was true only in the area of tailings discharge and that "long before this plant commenced operation, there were areas of green water in Lake Superior." [22]

A debate between Fride and Stein was touched off on the issue of interstate pollution. Here again for the first time, Fride acknowledged interstate movement of tailings by stating, "I could not reasonably suggest that some of those particles (tailings) may not on occasion get into Wisconsin waters." [23] He further acknowledged that Reserve had found cummingtonite in Wisconsin waters and had reported this finding to the federal agency.

Reserve's Vice President, Haley, then presented a detailed critique of the NWQL technical studies presented the day before. Many of Haley's criticisms were valid, but he didn't strengthen his position when he attempted to persuade the conferees that the 67,000 tons of tailings had no effect whatsoever on Lake Superior. This prompted Stein to paraphrase Winston Churchill, "Never has the discharge of so much done so little." [24]

In summing up the second session, Stein expressed concern for the lack of a definite decision regarding the abatement of pollution in the Lake Superior basin. But he noted that substantial progress had been made during the seven months since the executive session. He stated, "In this case, and I say this for all participants here . . . the

[20] Ibid., p. 756.
[21] Ibid., pp. 681–734.
[22] Ibid., p. 769.
[23] Ibid., p. 777.
[24] Ibid., p. 790.

citizens, the alleged dischargers and the conferees . . . I think all have approached this really in good faith." He warned, however, that "Come early August [1970] we are going to make a decision one way or the other, and I hope the company will be with us on the decision." [25] Thus, the second session also closed without finding that interstate pollution affected the health or well-being of citizens in states other than Minnesota. Consequently, the conference adjourned without any change in jurisdictional status.

RECONVENED SECOND SESSION
(August 12–13, 1970)

On August 12, 1970, for the third time in 16 months, the Duluth Hotel became the arena for the "Federal Enforcement Conference." This meeting was officially designated as the "Reconvened Second Session," in other words, a continuation of the conference meeting held three months earlier. The line-up of conferees remained essentially unchanged. Chairman Stein opened the meeting with his usual recital of the authorization for the conference under the Federal Water Pollution Act, affirming that states have the primary responsibility for taking action to abate pollution and declaring that the conference call was initiated by the federal government under the presumption of possible interstate pollution.

The parade of witnesses began with testimony from several conservation groups, including the Izaak Walton League, Save Lake Superior Association, and the Northern Environmental Council. The testimony by representatives of these groups was mostly repetitive of prior conference sessions and again was based more on emotion and inherent concern than on scientific evidence. Their persistence and obvious sincerity could not have gone unnoticed, however, by the conferees.

Michigan's Purdy attempted to get quickly to the question of jurisdiction and interstate pollution. He stated, "I, for one, would not like the record to stand that as conferees we are waiting for a dead body [26] to be floating in Wisconsin waters. As a conferee, though, I am waiting for some good solid information to show that an injury to the

---

25 Ibid., p. 875.

26 This reference to a "dead body" occurred long before allegations of health hazards resulting from asbestiform fibers in Reserve's tailings.

health and welfare of a person in a state other than [the one] in which the discharge is originating is occurring." [27] In referring to the NWQL studies on bacterial growth, he commented, "I am not talking about laboratory conditions, I want to know what is taking place in the lake. As soon as we have that information, I, for one, as a conferee, am ready to act." [28]

Stein shared Purdy's concern and appetite for definitive information and went on to explain that the problem was not one of proving tailings in interstate waters but rather proving that they endanger "health and welfare." He then proceeded with his interpretation of the legal meaning of the term *health and welfare,* presenting a list of legitimate uses of watercourses that should not be endangered. These were public health; public water supplies; propagation of fish, wildlife, and aquatic life; recreation; industrial uses; and agricultural uses. He then declared, "If a discharger endangers any one of these uses, it is subject to abatement here." [29]

A brief progress report was made by Badalich. He then introduced Lane Friedell, Assistant Attorney General of the state of Minnesota. Friedell informed the conferees of the status of Reserve's lawsuit against the MPCA. This court battle, discussed in Chapter 10, proceeded concurrently with the "Federal Enforcement Conference." Friedell noted that the Attorney General of Minnesota had not been an active participant in the conference prior to this point but had been deeply involved with the issue of pollution abatement in the Lake Superior basin. Friedell briefly summarized the state's position on the MPC 15 issue at the Lake County trial. He noted that on behalf of the state of Minnesota, the Attorney General and the MPCA "went across the country to obtain the best scientific people available to show that Reserve Mining was in fact polluting Lake Superior." [30] Among those retained by the state were Dr. Charles Goldman,[31] Dr. Alfred Beeton [32] and Dr.

[27] Proceedings of "Federal Enforcement Conference in the Matter of Pollution of Lake Superior and Its Tributary Basin, Minnesota–Wisconsin–Michigan," Reconvened Second Session, U.S.D.I.–FWQA, August 12–13, 1970, p. 49.
[28] Ibid.
[29] Ibid., p. 50.
[30] Ibid., p. 203.
[31] Dr. Charles Goldman: Professor of zoology at the University of California, Davis.
[32] Dr. Alfred Beeton: Professor of zoology at the University of Wisconsin, Milwaukee.

Theodore Olson.[33] Friedell explained that the Attorney General's position was, "If the trial court [Lake County] says that we in Minnesota are incompetent to deal with our problems, then the Attorney General will recommend to the Governor to seek Federal assistance." Friedell added that if the state won its court suit against Reserve, "as soon as the trial is over, the State will commence the hearing on the 1947 permit."[34]

(Lake County Court Judge Eckman was to hand down his decision in the case on December 15, 1970. The decision went against the state.)

The first state witness at the reconvened conference, Dr. Joseph Shapiro, presented his findings on the growth of algae in taconite tailings. Shapiro was a professor in the Department of Geology and the Department of Geography at the University of Minnesota and certainly was well qualified to address this issue. Shapiro summarized his findings by stating that "in inshore waters of Lake Superior phosphorus alone seems to be a limiting factor in the sense that addition of phosphorus stimulates the growth of algae." Also in offshore waters "both phosphorus and manganese can stimulate growth of algae." He pointed out that the water quality standards did not mention manganese, but should. Shapiro also found that, "Taconite tailings . . . do stimulate the growth of algae and not necessarily in a linear fashion with regard to concentration. Taconite tailings do contain manganese [and] phosphorus. I cannot say which of these components in the tailings are doing the stimulating."[35]

Recall that at the first executive session, Bartsch, the FWPCA eutrophication expert, stated that Reserve was not a significant contributor of phosphorus. Later, in the April 1970 conference, laboratory test data presented by Glass had failed to show any phosphorus release and only a very slight release of manganese. In good scientific demeanor, Shapiro was unwilling to develop premature and weak conclusions from his preliminary findings but rather described what he found in a factual manner.

Friedell also introduced Dr. Glenn Berryman, of the University of Minnesota, as a witness for the state. Berryman proceeded to analyze

[33] Dr. Theodore Olson: Professor, School of Public Health, University of Minnesota.
[34] Proceedings of "Federal Enforcement Conference," Reconvened Second Session, August 1970, p. 201.
[35] Ibid., p. 262.

the economic impact on the company if it were forced to curtail intake tailings disposal. He found that Reserve's theoretical profit would be reduced from $1.58 to $.63 per ton. Though Berryman admitted that this was a "considerable decline, to be sure," [36] profit based on sales, he said, would decline only from 5.6 to 5.0 percent. On a rate-of-return basis, Reserve's operation would remain profitable at just under a 20% return. Berryman explained that if Reserve were to close down its operation, parent companies would be faced with an expenditure of approximately $82 million to cover outstanding mortgage-type bonds.

The significance of Berryman's testimony does not lie in the specific values shown related to profit and loss but more importantly that Reserve would not experience economic hardship by implementing an onland tailings disposal system, if such were necessary. The Federal Water Pollution Control Act recognizes the importance of considering "economic feasibility" when seeking pollution abatement. Berryman's study was directed to that provision of the federal act.

"Old reliable" for the federal government, Mount, returned to the podium for yet another appearance—this was to be his most significant appearance. He opened his remarks with generalities, then reiterated his summary of technical findings holding that, "It is the combined opinion of our staff [NWQL] after evaluating all the data available that the impact and effects of present discharges in Lake Superior are mainly those of nutrient enrichment and that taconite tailings and most other wastes are not directly killing organisms." Speaking on the importance of controlling the entry of all nutrients into the lake, Mount stated, "The results of four independent laboratory studies show that tailings in parts per billion concentrations do promote algal growths *as do the effluents from sewage treatment plants and other sources.*" [37]

Before Mount was permitted to leave the stand, several conferees posed critical questions. Purdy pressed Mount for a statement relative to interstate pollution.

> *Purdy:*   In your opinion, do you believe that the discharge from Reserve Mining Company is endangering the health or welfare of persons in a state other than the state of Minnesota?
>
> *Mount:*   . . . we are dealing with a total system in Lake Superior . . . and the contributions which the Reserve dis-

[36] Ibid., p. 195.
[37] Ibid., p. 275. (Emphasis provided by author.)

charge makes are not unique. There are many other sources of these, and I have identified them. *For this reason I believe that the contribution of Reserve and these other dischargers in the form of nutrients does constitute an interstate pollution problem.*[38]

Murray Stein pursued the line of questioning and asked Mount whether, in his opinion, the Reserve discharge endangered or led to a situation of "incipient peril" of health or welfare. Mount responded, "*I think that there is clear endangerment of the use of this lake and, therefore, I think it falls under the statute.*" [39]

Frangos picked up the interrogation for clarification of whether health or welfare was endangered.

Frangos: As you see it . . . it is the welfare of the citizens in other than the originating state that are being affected.

Mount: Yes.

Frangos: And then this welfare is the fact that there is a potential for eutrophication of Lake Superior?

Mount: Yes, and with it all of the changes which we know do take place. . . .[40]

Thus, the haunting and all-important questions of interstate pollution, endangering health and welfare, and establishment of conference jurisdiction fell on one individual—Dr. Donald I. Mount. Why were the conferees or Chairman Stein so reluctant to make this critical decision? And why were the governors and regulatory agencies of Wisconsin, Michigan, and Minnesota unwilling to make it? Was this Mount's responsibility? After all he was the director of the NWQL in Duluth—with a *research* mission, not an *enforcement* mission. Was his statement consistent with his previous observations regarding the significance of the pollution of Lake Superior? These questions are subject to serious debate. Mount completed the federal portion of the testimony. Now it was Reserve's turn.

Reserve's attorney, Fride, returned to the study published by the

[38] Ibid., p. 280. (Emphasis provided by author.)
[39] Ibid., p. 282. (Emphasis provided by author.)
[40] Ibid., p. 305.

Minnesota Pollution Control Agency on November 7, 1969, entitled "Report on Investigation of Water Quality of Lake Superior in the Vicinity of Silver Bay." (2) At first, one might wonder why the Minnesota Pollution Control Agency, a designated conferee, did not introduce this report at the April 1970 session or the August 1970 session of the conference. Could the reluctance of the state to introduce its own report possibly be explained by the content and tone of the conclusions in the report? The conclusions [41] were supportive of Reserve's position!

Fride then presented testimony, mostly in the form of direct quotes from federal officials, including Mount, to refute and discredit reports cited earlier by Williams and Stoddard. Upon completion of Fride's presentation, Stein noted that the conference had expected that "Reserve Mining Company will have selected a plan, a combination of plans, or a series of alternatives, including tentative time schedules . . . which Reserve Mining believes will prevent water pollution and will satisfy the regulatory agency." These plans, which the conferees directed were to be ready for detailed engineering, were to be submitted to the conferees not later than July 26, 1970.[42]

Fride sought an additional four months extension to complete the report. He offered excuses in behalf of the company, but they didn't satisfy Stein. He admonished, "But I suggest, Mr. Fride, to you and your client that if Reserve had come up with those plans on July 26, these other questions might be moot at the present time on this interstate pollution." Fride's response was, "I am sure that there is much in what you say, Mr. Chairman." [43] Fride grasped an opening, provided by a question, to develop Reserve's arguments that there was no evidence to support the contention by Mount that the tailings discharge endangered health or welfare in Wisconsin, Michigan, or Minnesota waters. Stein acknowledged the point Fride raised, then commented that the conferees had to wrestle with this question during the next executive session.

Reserve's final witness, Dr. Lee, attacked a number of reports and statements presented by federal witnesses at this and preceding conference sessions. He questioned the significance of the cummingtonite discovery in sediments on the Wisconsin side of the lake, the bacterial growth studies, and the distribution of tailings in the lake. He discounted

[41] The four conclusions elaborated in this report are presented verbatim on p. 72.
[42] Proceedings of "Federal Enforcement Conference," Reconvened Second Session, August 1970, p. 545.
[43] Ibid., p. 548.

the scientific basis upon which Mount had earlier charged that tailings may endanger the welfare of persons in states other than Minnesota. Lee also criticized Shapiro's results as based on insufficient information, and on the fact that no replicates were run to establish data reliability. He noted that studies in his laboratory showed that algae could not use the phosphorus chemically bound in the tailings. He also noted that the manganese that does leach from tailings is rapidly oxidized to manganese oxide, precipitates, and falls to the lake bottom. The 4 ppb (parts per billion) concentration of phosphorus that Shapiro mentioned, according to Lee, was the normal concentration of phosphorus in lake waters along the north shore and was not increased by the tailings.

Pointing to the question of addition of soluble substances to the lake, Lee explained that "Reserve's discharge may increase the dissolved solids in Lake Superior in the order of 0.1 to 0.2 milligrams per liter in 50 years." [44] He suggested that this increase should be considered in relation to the natural background concentration of soluble solids of 57.5 mg/l in the vicinity of Silver Bay. He compared the 60,000 pounds of soluble solids contributed per day by Reserve with the over 1 million pounds per day added by various tributary streams in the Lake Superior basin. And he concluded that after a critical review of all information available to date, "Reserve Mining Company's discharge of taconite tailings does not have a significant deleterious effect for any beneficial use of the lake." Also, he said, "There is no evidence, in my opinion, to show the deleterious effect on water quality in the States of Wisconsin and Michigan." [45] Though a recognized expert in water chemistry, he may have exceeded his expertise in criticizing studies on biological and geological issues.

Immediately following completion of testimony at the reconvened second session, the conferees met in open executive session to develop conclusions. They concluded: [46]

"There is evidence in the record to indicate that dischargers named by the conferees in their reports to the conference, including the Reserve Mining Company, endanger the health or welfare of persons in states other than that in which such discharges originate and this pollution is subject to abatement under the provisions of the Federal Water Pollution Control Act." The "dischargers" include lakeshore communities, the Army Corps of Engineers, agricultural concerns, fed-

[44] Ibid., p. 579.
[45] Ibid., p. 581.
[46] Ibid., p. 768–83.

eral installations, and all lakeshore industries as well as Reserve. By agreeing on this conclusion, the conferees had finally established jurisdiction for federal abatement enforcement.

Then the conferees established a specific compliance schedule for Reserve. The company was required to "provide a scientific method for abating its discharge to Lake Superior, which will meet state and federal requirements, to the conferees through the state of Minnesota, by December 1, 1970." Beyond that, detailed plans and specifications were ordered by September 1, 1971.

Whereas the conclusions and recommendations of the first session were merely suggestions, the assumption of jurisdiction by the conference rendered the second session's conclusions legally enforceable if sustained. Approval of the recommendations by the Secretary of the Interior was the first step required to sustain the conferees.

RECONVENED SECOND SESSION
(January 14, 1971)

On January 14, 1971, the conference reconvened to review the preliminary design plans that Reserve was directed to prepare. Chairman Stein opened the session with a statement by William Ruckelshaus, EPA [47] administrator, dated December 31, 1970.

In it, Ruckelshaus called upon the Minnesota Pollution Control Agency to "take appropriate action under its water pollution control program and state and local laws to insure that the recommendations of the conference are carried out." He went on, "I recommend that you and the conferees seek submission of final plans by July 1, 1971, and insist on prompt submission of preliminary plans as agreed upon at the conference and recorded as Recommendation No. 4. . . . Failure to accomplish prompt planning and scheduling of corrective action for all polluters via the conference route," he warned, "must result in more stringent enforcement procedures by the federal government under appropriate federal laws." [48]

The first speaker at this session was the newly elected governor of Minnesota, the Honorable Wendell Anderson. Governor Anderson had

[47] The Federal Water Quality Administration (FWQA) was renamed the Environmental Protection Agency (EPA).
[48] Proceedings of "Federal Enforcement Conference in the Matter of Pollution of Lake Superior and Its Tributary Basin, Minnesota–Wisconsin–Michigan," Reconvened Second Session, EPA, January 14–15, 1971, p. 3.

taken a hard line against Reserve during his campaign so the substance of his statement could have been predicted. His first official act after taking the oath of office only nine days prior to the meeting had been to officially join the state of Minnesota in the conference. During his brief presentation, the governor urged the conferees to require Reserve to provide appropriate onland facilities for tailings disposal.

Wisconsin's new governor, the Honorable Patrick J. Lucey, was next to speak. He, like Governor Anderson, immediately committed his state as a full participating member of the conference. "I regret," he said, "the notion that a discharge must be proved damaging to the environment and a danger to public health before it is altered or stopped altogether. With Lake Superior, it is not an academic question." [49]

The third governor involved in the Reserve controversy was the Honorable W. G. Milliken of Michigan. Unable to attend, he sent a telegram, which stated that "Michigan will be a full party and participating member of the conference." [50]

Other telegrams from prominent politicians supporting the vigorous actions by the conference poured in and were read into the record. These came from U.S. Senators Hart, Nelson, Mondale, Humphrey, Proxmire, Griffin, and Congressmen Blatnik and Ruppe. The conference, therefore, had not only legal jurisdiction on the basis of interstate polluion, but also a mandate from three states, the federal government, and leading congressmen of the states involved.

Then the conferees heard from representatives of the federal government and states of Michigan and Wisconsin, with little new evidence presented. When it was Minnesota's turn, MPCA head Badalich brought the conferees up to date on progress made on the recommendations presented at the first session and those elaborated at the second session. "The Agency," he stated, "is implementing the recommendations made concerning standards for the open waters of Lake Superior." [51] Badalich then noted that Reserve had not yet filed a final report on waste disposal improvements that was due on December 1, 1970. This report was originally due on July 26, 1970, but an extension had been granted. The results of the Lake County trial were then summarized by Badalich: "Although the court held that the effluent standard of Minnesota, Regulation WPC 15, is invalid in regard to Reserve, at the same time the court ordered Reserve to flocculate the fines and convey all of

[49] Ibid., p. 8.
[50] Ibid., p. 13.
[51] Ibid., p. 70.

the tailings by pipeline to the floor of Lake Superior to thus eliminate the green water effect. Plans to accomplish this task were ordered to be submitted by May 14 [1971] to the agency for approval, and the agency was directed to grant a variance from the regulation until this is done. The Attorney General has stated that an appeal will be filed." [52]

The partial Reserve victory against the Minnesota PCA won the company no points with state agency officials. And at this session of the enforcement conference, the MPCA, for the first time, took a noticeably harder line on the Reserve issue. Most specifically, the attitude of Badalich, the executive secretary of the agency, hardened, and he was noticeably less conciliatory toward the company.

The man soon to replace Badalich, MECCA's Grant Merritt, was next to testify. He immediately demanded onshore or onland disposal of tailings, just as he had in his days of private advocacy. Stein objected to the concept of onland disposal until appropriate environmental studies could assess the potential impact on the land resource. He challenged Merritt, "Why do you think onshore disposal would be less damaging to the ecology. . . ?" [53] Merritt replied, "If we adopt an onshore disposal plan, there will be no further dumping in Lake Superior, and as the Governor has pointed out—this will solve the problem." Stein countered, "We never substitute, for example, an air pollution problem for a water pollution problem. We don't intend to go with any problem [system] that is going to give us a bigger problem with the ecology." Later, Stein remarked, "We [must] come up with a method that will provide the least damage to our ecology. Shouldn't that be our goal?" [54] Stein reemphasized this position later, stating, "The issue here is: If you put this stuff on the land, whether you would be creating a greater damage to the ecology than putting it in the water; this is not a question of what it affords [costs]." [55]

A MECCA representative, Dr. Charles Carson, then presented the official position of his 3500 member group calling for onland disposal as the only acceptable alternative for tailings handling. Chairman Stein was obviously concerned that MECCA had selected a disposal method without in-depth analysis of potential environmental impacts. He established through a series of questions to Carson that MECCA would not consider the flocculation and underwater disposal method advocated by

[52] Ibid., p. 71.
[53] Ibid., p. 118.
[54] Ibid., p. 119.
[55] Ibid., p. 126.

Judge Eckman in the state court case and later accepted by Reserve. Carson commented, "Well, we are willing to give Reserve a hearing [on the recently proposed underwater plan], but we still call for onland disposal." "You know," Stein commented sarcastically, "that comes very close to the motto of the old west, 'Hang'em first and try'em afterwards.' " [56] Stein became visibly perturbed when Carson and Merritt were unable or unwilling to grasp this concept.

Later Reserve took the stand. As in past sessions, Reserve was represented by Ed Fride. He reflected briefly on the state court's *Findings of Fact and Conclusions of Law*, interpreting Judge Eckman's ruling as a court order and directive "to both the Minnesota Pollution Control Agency and the Reserve Mining Company to—agree upon a plan which will meet the major concerns expressed by the court. . . ." [57] Badalich of the MPCA agreed with Fride's interpretation.

A major turn in Reserve's attitude toward the controversy came in a message by Reserve's President Furness. He informed the conferees that company representatives would soon present a plan for "altering" its disposal tailings. The plan would cost some $14 million in capital costs and would "represent a financial commitment by Reserve over the next 20 years of nearly $49 million, about one-seventh of the total cost of our mining and processing facilities at both Babbitt and Silver Bay." [58] Furness went on to say that these new facilities would not improve product yield and would be implemented solely for environmental protection. He stressed the significance of the Lake County District Court trial, which explored the entire question of possible effects of tailings on the waters of Lake Superior.

Furness then reminded the conferees that Judge Eckman ordered "a modification of the present method of tailings discharge to provide for the flocculation of the tailings and their transportation by a form of conduit to the lake bottom where they present no ecological concern." [59] He further explained that the plans were based upon reports and recommendations from several nationally known engineering firms including: the Bechtel Corporation; Engineering Science, Inc.; Arthur D. Little, Inc.; Parsons-Jurden Corporation; and Trygve Hoff and Associates. He noted that the Parsons-Jurden Corporation, of New York, had earned a reputation for the design of tailings handling systems

56 Ibid., pp. 141–42.
57 Ibid., p. 225.
58 Ibid., p. 229.
59 Ibid., p. 229a.

in foreign countries and in the United States (including systems in Minnesota).

Stein obviously was impressed with the apparent change in attitude of Reserve as expressed by its president. Stein declared, "This is without prejudging anything [the proposed plan] but in a sense I think this is really a landmark . . . because for the first time I think we have from the company of Reserve here a proposal to go forward with a plan." [60] Stein later added, "I think we may have gotten over an essential hurdle here, and I am grateful." [61]

But more hurdles stood in the way, and Stein was aware of most of them. He recognized that one faction, including Governor Anderson, MECCA, and other conservation groups were calling for onland disposal whereas the "court had ordered disposal in the lake bottom."

"I don't know if we can put these together. . . ," [62] Stein observed.

To overcome the dilemma, he urged that, "the only thing we could do in the federal conference is keep all options open and entertain a method which will protect the ecology of the lake and not substitute one form of pollution for another." [63]

Fride further explained Reserve's commitment, stating "we have a plan that we believe is sound and will meet the concerns raised, and as soon as approval is forthcoming from the appropriate agencies, this plan will be completely designed, constructed, and made operational within two years." [64] He went on, "If we had the approval of the MPCA and this conference, we would go forward." [65]

Stein uncovered another possible hurdle that could block the plan. He referred to a recent change in the posture and responsibilities of the U.S. Army Corps of Engineers. The Army Corps had just begun to consider the effects of discharges on water quality in the issuance or revalidation of its permits. Thus, the deep lake disposal plan offered by Reserve and ordered by Judge Eckman would require a separate permit from the Army Corps. The onland disposal option, of course, would not require Army Corps approval.

The Reserve report, entitled "Plan to Modify Tailings Discharge

[60] Ibid., p. 230.
[61] Ibid., p. 231.
[62] Ibid., p. 233.
[63] Ibid., p. 234.
[64] Ibid., p. 236.
[65] Ibid., p. 237

System," [66] was put into the record by Fride. Although put in final form by Reserve's own engineering staff, it represented the ideas and concepts of some of the nation's most prestigious consulting firms. Reserve asked Charles Skinker, vice president of Parsons-Jurden, to make the technical presentation to the conference.

Essentially, the plan called for tailings thickening by use of chemical flocculents (chemical settling agents) and hydro-separator units. Clarified flow from the separators would be mixed with power plant cooling water and returned directly to the lake. The flow from the units would contain most of the tailings solids in thick, slurry form. This slurry would then be pumped through pipelines fanning out across the existing delta and then down the slope of the lake bottom to a point 140 feet beneath the surface. From there the pipelines would extend further horizontally on the lake bottom to their discharge points while the lake bottom continues its down slope.[67]

Reserve then called Dr. Leon Weinberger, a technical consultant and former assistant FWPCA commissioner for research and development, to evaluate the Reserve plan from an ecological perspective. He based much of his defense of the plan on the summary statement made earlier by Mount: "In my judgment the effect of Reserve's discharge should be assessed in terms of altering the lake's appearance rather than the toxic effects on fish and fish food organisms, or endangering water supplies." [68] Mount, however, had subsequently clarified this statement to extend his concern to nutrient enrichment that would result in algal growth, and hence indirectly affect the appearance of the lake. In other words, Mount was not just concerned about the green water phenomenon.

Weinberger stated that the "physical filling or deposition of solids is not a significant factor and indeed the rapid settling . . . of fine materials in the depths of the lake would be preferable" to the current method. He also noted that the proposed plan would "overcome the aesthetic objections and greatly reduce the migration of fine particles." [69]

During the ensuing questioning of the Reserve witnesses, Mount reaffirmed his position regarding concern not only for green water but

[66] Ibid., pp. 259–85.
[67] Ibid., p. 294.
[68] Ibid., p. 303.
[69] Ibid., p. 304.

for nutrient enrichment. He felt that "the primary criticism that I would have of this proposal [is] in regard to the soluble materials." [70] Mount expressed the opinion that recycle of clarified process water was essential to reduce the discharge of soluble solids to the lake.

Badalich raised the question of type and biological impact of chemical flocculents that were to be used. Weinberger acknowledged justification for this concern and stated that the company was experimenting with different types of flocculents. He said Reserve would work with appropriate state and federal agencies to arrive at a safe, effective flocculent.

The questioning reverted to a possible onland disposal approach. Fride explained why Reserve located its beneficiating plant at Silver Bay rather than at the Babbitt mine site, citing lack of water availability and lack of suitable land for tailings disposal.

Mount joined in the discussion of onland disposal, criticizing the attitude expressed the day before by Merritt and Carson of MECCA and others. He stated, "One thing that did disturb me yesterday was the apparent feeling that just putting these things [tailings] on land is enough. It isn't possible to evaluate right now an onland disposal system." [71] He listed several inherent disadvantages of onland disposal that had to be carefully considered, including: the dust problem, loss of possible recreation area, and seepage through the ground. He remarked, "There is no assurance that just pumping it on the land is going to keep the water out of the lake."

"This water is going to go somewhere," he said. "It is either going to go into the lake or it is going to go into a river, and I do not subscribe that we should take it out of Lake Superior and send it to another river. I think this is burying your head in the sand." [72]

Stein ended the open testimony portion of this session of the conference with further commendation for the company's change in position on tailings disposal. "The company," he complimented, "has come forward with a proposal or a proposition which reflects an attitude on its part which leads me to believe that there may be a chance that this case may be solved by negotiation rather than confrontation. I believe if they say they are ready to sign a commitment. . . , we don't have a smoke screen or a delaying tactic." [73]

[70] Ibid., p. 318.
[71] Ibid., p. 363.
[72] Ibid., p. 364.
[73] Ibid., p. 373.

The conferees agreed to form an ad hoc committee consisting of representatives of state and federal agencies and Reserve to evaluate the underwater plan in detail and report back to the conferees in 45 days. Afterward, a conference would be called to discuss the findings and recommendations.

Chapter 12

Federal Enforcement Conference: Third Session

Nearly two years after the start of the Federal Enforcement Conference, conferees met for what was to be their final session. This session was convened in Duluth on April 22, 1971, before a large gallery of observers. There were some notable changes in the line-up of conferees. David Dominick, acting commissioner of EPA's Water Quality office, returned to chair the conference. Stein, chairman of most of the previous sessions, was relegated to the role of vice-chairman. Two new state representatives also joined the conferees. Minnesota was represented by its new MPCA executive director, Grant Merritt—the same Merritt who had led the opposition attack against Reserve the past two years as chairman of MECCA, an active Minnesota environmental group. Merritt had been appointed a month earlier by the new Minnesota governor, Wendell Anderson, to replace Badalich.

In his opening statement, Chairman Dominick declared that the purpose of this session was to hear the report of the Technical Committee, which had been assigned the task, at the January 14–15, 1971 reconvened second session, of evaluating Reserve's new plan for the disposal of tailings in Lake Superior.

The Technical Committee reported four basic concerns about the modified discharge system. It feared that the proposed system—

1 / would not eliminate green water,

2 / would not materially reduce dissolved solids discharged to the lake,

3 / would not materially reduce suspended solids discharged to the lake, and

4 / would employ flocculents which would be discharged to the lake and which would have unknown ecological impact.[1]

The committee concluded that the plan "is an unacceptable method of disposal," then stated that "It is the responsibility of the appropriate regulatory agencies to provide guidance to the discharger— as to the acceptability of a method of disposal and, if unacceptable, to provide guidance as to the modifications necessary to become acceptable." [2] The committee further recommended that Reserve be instructed to develop a disposal method that would relieve the committee's concerns.

Reserve's attorney, Fride, given an opportunity to comment upon the committee's report, first launched an attack on Merritt, stating, "I suppose it isn't always the case where the principal civilian antagonist of a company ends up purporting to act in judgment of the views he had long expressed." Fride charged Merritt with attempting "to frustrate an honest, technical evaluation of Reserve's plan." [3] Merritt had indeed appeared before the technical committee in his new official capacity as MPCA executive director and had served notice that any plan that failed to include *total* onland deposition of Reserve's tailing would be unacceptable.

---

[1] Proceedings of "Federal Enforcement Conference in the Matter of Pollution of Lake Superior and Its Tributary Basin, Minnesota–Wisconsin–Michigan," Third Session, EPA, April 22–23, 1971, p. 19.
[2] Ibid., p. 27.
[3] Ibid., p. 40.

Merritt, defending his new role as an administrative "judge," explained that he did not visit with the technical committee until its last session and only after a draft of the committee's report had been prepared. He denied attempting to frustrate the committee, but did not deny his long-standing conviction that onland disposal was the only acceptable approach.

Fride continued his presentation by introducing numerous reports and documents including a summary of Judge Eckman's recent decision in the state court. Fride noted that many scientists of national reputation had testified before Judge Eckman in behalf of the MPCA, including a dozen federal scientists. Yet this impressive parade of expert witnesses was unable to demonstrate to the judge's satisfaction that Reserve's tailings were seriously polluting Lake Superior. The judge had expressed concern, however, over the green water effect and the decrease of scud in the vicinity of the zone of discharge.

Fride argued that Reserve had acted in good faith in response to Judge Eckman's decision and came forth with a modified tailings disposal plan similar in concept to that envisioned by the judge.

On the morning of the second day of the session, several private citizens and representatives of environmental groups appeared before the conferees, offering little new information. Following the testimony of all participants, Chairman Dominick dropped a bombshell. He informed the conferees:

> After due deliberation on evidence presented at the conference yesterday and after reviewing the history and the progress of the Lake Superior Enforcement Conference, *I have reached a conclusion* [4] in my capacity as Acting Commissioner of the Water Quality Office of the Environmental Protection Agency. *I have concluded* [4] that the proper course of action to follow with respect to the continuing discharge of taconite tailings by Reserve Mining Company into interstate waters of Lake Superior is to recommend to the Administrator of the Environmental Protection Agency, William D. Ruckelshaus, that he initiate proceedings under Section 10(c)(5) of the Federal Water Pollution Control Act, as amended, against the Reserve Mining Company at Silver Bay, Minnesota.[5]

[4] Emphasis provided by author.
[5] Proceedings of "Federal Enforcement Conference," Third Session, p. 442.

He went on to note that *"I can only conclude* [6] that the time for direct and immediate Federal action is at hand." [7] Section 10(c)(5) of the FWPCA would require Reserve to "propose a plan for pollution abatement which is acceptable to the United States Environmental Protection Agency within 180 days or be subject to suit by the United States. . . ." [8] By this action, Dominick, a lawyer with little or no training or expertise in environmental quality matters and who had attended only one other session of the enforcement conference, wrested authority and responsibility in the matter not only from the conferees but also from the states as well.

This final act or statement by the federal convening authority, Dominick, was in marked contrast to the opening statement at the first conference session by Carl Klein, Assistant Secretary of the Interior. Klein had stated at the May 13, 1969, session,

> Both the State and Federal Governments have responsibilities in dealing with water pollution control problems. The Federal Water Pollution Control Act declares that the States have primary rights and responsibilities for taking action to abate and control pollution. Consistent with this, we are charged by law to encourage the States in these activities. [9]

Dominick based his summary recommendation on the lack of definitive action by Reserve to correct its discharge problem, Reserve's failure to meet two report deadlines, evidence of interstate pollution, the urgings of governors of Minnesota and Wisconsin, and the lack of action by the MPCA to assist Reserve in the development of a mutually satisfactory disposal plan.

Fride argued that Reserve and the MPCA had acted cooperatively and in good faith in response to Judge Eckman's directives. He also noted that Reserve came forward with its alternative tailings disposal plan well in advance of the deadline specified by the judge. Fride further asserted that if the commissioner's recommendation were followed, "this conference has taken a giant step backward." He charged

[6] Emphasis provided by author.
[7] Proceedings of "Federal Enforcement Conference," Third Session, p. 444.
[8] Ibid., p. 445.
[9] Proceedings of "Federal Enforcement Conference," First Session, p. 7.

Commissioner Dominick with ignoring Judge Eckman's findings and directives because he (Dominick) "apparently has reached some preconceived notion of a solution to this problem." [10] Fride concluded his critique by proclaiming, "make no mistake about it, if this recommendation is followed it is not the Reserve Mining Company that has forced this issue into lengthy federal court litigation. It will be the recommendation to invoke Section 10(c)(5) of the Federal Water Pollution Control Act which will have that result."

Dominick allowed the conferees the noon recess to consider his recommendation. Immediately after lunch, the conferees met in open executive session to discuss the recommendation and to vote.

Conferee Frangos of the Wisconsin DNR commented, "I am somewhat disappointed in the manner in which the Chair made this announcement. Certainly it is contrary to procedures and practices that we States have experienced in other conferences . . . I think it is regrettable that we have not had an opportunity to discuss what has transpired here for the last two days and [be] given an opportunity to evaluate the situation among all conferees." [11] However, Frangos added that he did not disagree with the substance of the recommendation, and would in fact support it.

As expected, Merritt strongly supported Dominick's recommendation, calling it "a giant step forward."

After brief discussion, all three states voted to support Dominick's recommendation. It became the official recommendation of the conference. That action, in effect, transferred jurisdiction for the *Reserve* case directly to the Environmental Protection Agency.

After two long, arduous years, the "Federal Enforcement Conference in the Matter of Pollution of Lake Superior and Its Tributary Basin, Minnesota–Wisconsin–Michigan" had come to an abrupt end.

[10] Proceedings of "Federal Enforcement Conference," Third Session. p. 448.
[11] Ibid., p. 452.

Chapter 13

In Federal District Court: A Summary of Happenings

ORIGIN OF THE CASE

EPA administrator Ruckelshaus notified Reserve on April 28, 1971, that based upon the recommendation of the "Federal Enforcement Conference" and pursuant to Section 10(c) of the Federal Water Pollution Control Act, the company was in violation of federal–state water quality standards. The company was given 180 days to effect compliance with these standards or be subject to suit by the federal government. In the absence of any satisfactory expression of compliance on the part of Reserve, the EPA fulfilled its threat on February 2, 1972, and, through the Department of Justice, filed suit against Reserve in U.S. District Court, District of Minnesota. The presiding judge who would become involved in this complicated, landmark legal battle was the Honorable Miles W. Lord.

Long a highly visible and vocal activist in the state's Democratic Farm Labor party, Lord had become known as a controversial judge with a propensity for driving for the jugular in a manner not always condoned by the courts above. His reputation as a champion of environmental causes soon was to be recognized throughout the nation. But in the process he was to bring down upon himself and his court words of admonishment only infrequently uttered by a United States Court of Appeals.

During the prolonged trial at which he was to preside, opinion divided sharply as to the role he played: to some he was "judicial god-father to the troubled environment"; to others he was something less. One observer saw him as a "Patton in black robes"; clearly he enjoyed the battle.

His preparation for judicial life was not restricted to law school, politics, and the courts. The *Minneapolis Star* summed up the background from which his judicial temperament derived. "His Honor," the paper commented, "was an alley fighter. He was also a bellhop, a cat skinner and a fry cook." [1]

The federal government charged Reserve with violation of WPC 15 (the federal–state water quality standards), the Refuse Act of 1899, and federal common law nuisance standards. Altogether there were 48 specific scientific charges, dealing primarily with the pollution issues argued earlier at the "Federal Enforcement Conference" and in Judge Eckman's state court.

It was immediately apparent that the decision rendered in this federal case would have a tremendous impact on thousands of persons, numerous organizations, the states bordering Lake Superior, and possibly even the national economy as a whole. As a result, the states of Wisconsin and Michigan moved to intervene as plaintiffs, as did the Minnesota Environmental Law Institute, Northern Environmental Council, Save Lake Superior Association, and Michigan Environmental Confederation.

Originally, Reserve was alone as defendant in the case. But several groups soon came to Reserve's assistance, intervening on behalf of the company and alleging a general or specific economic interest in Reserve's continued operation. These interveners included the village of Silver Bay, village of Beaver Bay, Silver Bay Chamber of Commerce, village of Babbitt, Range League Municipalities and Civic Associations,

[1] *Minneapolis Star*, Dec. 8, 1974.

Northeastern Minnesota Development Association, Duluth Area Chamber of Commerce, St. Louis County, Lake County, and Lax Lake Property Owners Association.

Later, other parties moved to intervene or were ordered by the court to be joined as parties to the case.

A NEW CASE EMERGES—
ASBESTOS DISCOVERED!

On June 15, 1973, some 15 months after the suit was filed but before the trial started, the course of the case changed significantly. Newspapers in cities surrounding Lake Superior and throughout the nation broke out dramatic banner headlines announcing that asbestos-related minerals or fibers had been found in Lake Superior, the source of supply of drinking water for area residents. This, the headlines warned, was an immediate cancer threat. Near panic ensued as city and town officials cautioned residents against drinking their tap water.

The genesis of the asbestos issue was more revelation than profound scientific discovery. A Duluth environmentalist, Mrs. Arlene Lehto, founder of the "Save the Lake" movement, had heard about the potential dangers of asbestos-like substances in waters at an International Joint Commission hearing in Duluth in late 1972. She urged the MPCA to investigate this potential problem in Lake Superior. MPCA followed up, hiring Steven Burrell, a geology professor at the University of Wisconsin, River Falls, to investigate the possible problem. A few months later, in May 1973, Glass, the EPA scientist with the Duluth National Water Quality Laboratory, had a dream—a bad dream. He awoke with a fear of drinking water from Lake Superior. The next day, Glass explained his vision to Dr. Phillip Cook, a colleague at the NWQL. Cook, prompted by this vision and the alarm sounded by Mrs. Lehto, initiated a search for asbestos in Duluth's water supply. He found it. Without the usual scientific verification of Cook's sudden discovery, representatives of the EPA raced to Lord with a new charge against Reserve—creating a potential health hazard to north shore residents. On June 14, Judge Lord abruptly summoned parties to the case and representatives of the EPA and MPCA to his chambers. MPCA consultant Burrell informed the judge that he had found that fibers emitted from Reserve's smokestacks and discharged in its tailings were "in every way identical to the amphibole minerals amosite and actionolite (i.e., asbestos-like fibers). . . ."

(*20*) Asbestos, when inhaled in close occupational environments, was known to cause cancer years after exposure.

The timing of the new discoveries was extremely important because the trial of the federal case against Reserve was about to begin—a case that up to that time rested completely on well-publicized water pollution issues not related to human health. With the introduction of the new allegations, emphasis quickly shifted to the public health danger in Reserve's air and water discharges. The original charges were all but forgotten in and out of court in the ensuing months.

The public's alarm was not relieved by the EPA pronouncement:

> While there is no conclusive evidence to show that the present drinking water supply . . . is unfit for human consumption, the agency feels that prudence dictates that alternative sources of drinking water be found for very young children. (*21*)

This created a health hazard of its own—unwarranted fear and apprehension. People scrambled for alternative sources of drinking water. Stores immediately sold out bottled water stocks and grocers sent out frantic orders for emergency shipments. As the demand skyrocketed and supplies dwindled, prices for bottled water soared to over 60¢ per gallon. The city of Duluth enacted emergency measures.

Every public official in the area felt compelled to issue a public statement:

> **Duluth Mayor Ben Boo** cautioned that "rumor can be as damaging as fact and we must immediately dispel or prove the statements put forth on this issue. . . . Until the alleged dangers are proved or disproved by experts, we must retain objectivity and not react to emotional alarm." (*22*)

> **Governor Wendell Anderson,** in a press conference, said he had "no comment" when asked if he would seek the shutdown of Reserve Mining Company. He said he would issue no other statement on the water situation until all the facts were in.

> **Dr. Warren Lawson,** executive director of the state Department of Health, acknowledged that federal water studies of Duluth's water supply had revealed the presence of minerals that are chemically related to asbestos, but he added, "I guess

everybody is trying to decide what the significance is. . . . The fact is that nobody knows what the significance is." (22)

U.S. Representative John Blatnik and Minnesota Senators Walter Mondale and Hubert Humphrey urged the Nixon administration to immediately mobilize all federal resources in an effort to determine what hazard is posed by the presence of asbestos-like fibers in the water supplies.

James R. Coleman, assistant director of the Division of Environmental Health for the Minnesota Department of Health was critical of the EPA for not consulting with local and state officials *before* the issue was made public.

Edward Schmid, assistant to the president of Reserve, charged that "It is unfortunate that this unfounded charge has been made public without testing its validity." (23)

Judge Lord, who would soon be presiding over the Reserve case, announced that he had asked doctors from the University of Minnesota and the Mayo Clinic for their expert judgments.

The EPA announced that it had contracted with Dr. Irving Selikoff, an authority on asbestos at Mt. Sinai Hospital in New York, to determine the accumulation of fibers in the tissue of deceased Duluth-area residents. Selikoff was well known as a campaigner against asbestos exposure.

Both **U.S. Senator Robert Griffin,** R.-Michigan, and **U.S. Representative David Obey,** D.-Wisconsin, immediately sought injunctions to halt Reserve's operation.

U.S. Justice Department officials announced that it was too soon to say what kind of response they would make to requests for injunctions.

Dr. Mount, NWQL director, revealed that the presence of the asbestos material had been known for at least five years. He explained the long delay in announcing the presence of the fibers this way: "we are not medical doctors and our people did not recognize the significance of the material until very recently." (*21*) Mount stated that for six months his colleagues at the lab had been photographing fibers, and "as if out of the blue," they saw a similarity in the structure of the fibers in the lake water and those fibers thought to be a cause of cancer if air-borne. These findings were taken to EPA headquarters in Washington, D.C., where the information was given to Dr. Selikoff for study. Selikoff quickly concluded that the levels of amosite fibers found in the Duluth water supply "were 1,000 times higher than found in any other samples so far studied" by his laboratory. (*21*)

The public anxiously awaited the results of Selikoff's study, undertaken to determine whether people who drank water from Lake Superior retained these fibers in their tissues—and if so, whether it was cancer inducing. However, many did not wait for the results of the new studies before reaching their own conclusions. The *Duluth Herald* reported on June 21 that "Duluthians are scared and dismayed—but at least not panicky—over the condition of their water." Twenty-five families, selected at random, were polled by telephone for their opinions of the latest health warnings. Reactions varied:

— "this has been in the water for some time, and we have been fine."

— "it's polluting what was once the freshest body of water."

— "the news media have caused sort of a panic."

— "I am concerned about it and scared of cancer."

— "we should wait a while longer to see how serious this really is."

— "I think they should shut that plant down immediately and should have done it a long time ago."

PRE-TRIAL HAPPENINGS

Meanwhile, back at the Minneapolis Federal Courthouse, Judge Lord decided that the trial should commence in six weeks, on August 1, 1973. Now that the health issue had been added to the pollution issue, Lord outlined the trial procedure:

"The first order of business" will be to determine if—

1 / the water supplies contain asbestos fibers, and

2 / if so, are fibers present in the tissue of deceased residents? and

3 / if so, do the fibers cause cancer? and

4 / if so, are tailings the source of the problem? and

5 / if so, then what are the alternate ways of handling the wastes or restricting the plant's activity?

The original pollution issues were relegated to later consideration.

Attorneys for the mining company requested that the case be tried in Duluth, close to Silver Bay. Judge Lord denied that request, saying that the case should be tried in Minneapolis. He noted that a trial in Duluth might become too sensational. At the pre-trial hearing, which lasted approximately five hours, 15 attorneys appeared for the various parties. The judge commended the attorneys for their cooperation in planning for the necessary scientific studies, then cautioned that public officials exercise "a little more restraint" in publicly commenting about the case. A sterner admonition enjoined comment by Reserve or its attorneys.

Many public officials honored Judge Lord's plea for restraint. Others, however, less obliged to restrict comment on the sensational new development in the *Reserve* case, continued to speak out. Newspapers featured editorials and related news stories daily. Water supplies and filter systems became the topic of studies, reports, and controversy. Public officials hurled charges at one another, even as they scurried about trying to determine if there was a problem to remedy. Public agencies disagreed with each other. For instance, an EPA study revealed the presence of "high concentrations" of asbestos fibers in Duluth tap water; however, preliminary studies of the water samples taken by the Minnesota Department of Health indicated that the number of asbestos fibers "reasonably compared" with those in other communities in the United States. Assistant Health Director Coleman, bearing direct local responsibility, revealed that he was disturbed at the failure of the EPA to provide the State Health Division with the data on which the federal agency based its decision to advise the public that alternative drinking water supplies be found.

Citizen reaction culminated in the circulation of a petition by the Save Lake Superior Association, which eventually acquired approximately 11,000 signatures. The petition requested the Duluth City Council to (1) urge an end to tailings disposal in the lake, (2) publicize information on Duluth's water problem and sources of pure water, and

(3) require restaurants and motels to have bottled water on hand for tourists and children under five years old.

On June 20, President Nixon, in response to requests to mobilize government resources, announced the appointment of Russell Train, a top government environmental official, to coordinate interagency efforts in the matter. The announcement of the appointment was echoed by Congressman Blatnik, who was among those requesting action. At the same time, Blatnik announced that the U.S. Army Corps of Engineers would immediately fly a special water treatment unit to Duluth to begin preliminary water purification tests.

On June 22, EPA announced a five-pronged study of Duluth water: (1) medical research on tissues of deceased residents, (2) water sampling to determine the extent of contamination, (3) filtration methods, (4) alternative water supplies in a cooperative team effort with local, state, and federal agencies, and (5) air sampling to determine the extent of fibers in the atmosphere. (24)

On June 30, Dr. Robert H. Harris, a representative of consumer advocate Ralph Nader, pronounced the Lake Superior problem "the environmental disaster of the century." He criticized Dr. Harold Leppink, executive health officer of St. Louis and Lake Counties, for saying that the presence of asbestos fibers was "a chronic situation and not an emergency." The Nader advocate argued that Leppink's statement was the "same as saying the disease is fatal but not serious." (25) Harris is an environmental engineer—not a physician. Later, in August, Ralph Nader invoked his national leadership role to tell newsmen that the *Reserve* case represented "the most demonstrable eco-catastrophe in the country." [2]

On the same day the Federal Office of Economic Opportunity announced that a $100,000 grant had been awarded Duluth to purchase bottled water for children under age five of low income families as recommended by the EPA.

On July 1, residents of Duluth's twin city, Superior, Wisconsin, were asked to make voluntary efforts to conserve water during the summer because of added demands on the city's water wells; officials warned that there might not be enough to go around.

On July 8, M. M. Swetonic, executive secretary of the Asbestos Association of North America, referring to the purported air problem, said:

[2] *Duluth News-Tribune*, August 11, 1973.

Some physicians, politicians, and environmentalists will not accept this absence of evidence as proof of the harmlessness of asbestos in the community air. Instead, they ask that it be proven that asbestos is not harmful. That is a most difficult thing to do, since it amounts to proving a negative. (26)

On July 10, Coleman reported that preliminary studies conducted by the Minnesota Department of Health showed that no asbestos fibers were being absorbed by fish inhabiting Lake Superior. Regarding public health he stated: "From the information we now have there does not appear to be an emergency. . . ." (27)

Much later, upon resigning his post in July 1975, Coleman was to reveal that in March of the previous year Lord had called him into the judge's chambers and ordered him to stop downplaying the health risk posed by Reserve's discharge into Lake Superior.

Many environmental groups meanwhile pressured the MCPA to use its emergency powers to immediately close the plant at Silver Bay. However, a few months earlier, on April 30, 1973, Judge Lord had joined the state of Minnesota and the MPCA as parties to the suit against Reserve. This action foreclosed their taking any independent out-of-court action in the case. As a result, the MPCA board voted at its July 10 meeting to continue opposition to Reserve's methods of discharge—but only through the U.S. District Court and not by exercising independent jurisdiction. The board, however, voted to have air-quality samples analyzed and to hold a special meeting to determine its recourse if the results of the tests revealed harmful levels of asbestos fibers.

LEGAL CLAIMS AGAINST RESERVE

A day before the trial was to begin, Lord, by oral order, allowed the Environmental Defense Fund to join the already numerous plaintiffs in the case.

The United States had originally petitioned the court for a permanent injunction against only the daily and continuous discharge of taconite tailings into Lake Superior.

The United States asserted five independent bases for its claim for injunctive relief: [3]

[3] Supplemental memorandum issued by Judge Miles W. Lord on May 11, 1974, re: USA v. Reserve Mining Company, pp. 6–14. (See Reference 7.)

(I)   That Reserve's discharge is subject to abatement pursuant to the FWPCA, Section 10(c)(5), which provides in part:

> The discharge of matter into such interstate waters or portions thereof, which reduces the quality of such waters below the water quality standards established under this subsection . . . is subject to abatement. . . .

Subsection 10(g)(2) provides that the secretary (now administrator of the EPA)

> in the case of pollution of waters which is endangering the health and welfare of persons only in the State in which the discharge . . . originates, may, with the written consent of the Governor of such State request the Attorney General to bring a suit to secure abatement of the pollution.

It was also claimed that Reserve violated three provisions of interstate water quality standards for the waters of Lake Superior known as Minnesota Regulation WPC 15:

a / WPC 15 (a)(4), which contains a non-degradation regulation requiring that the waters of a quality better than the established standards be maintained at high quality;

b / WPC 15(c)(2), which prohibits industrial discharges causing nuisance conditions; and

c / WPC 15(c)(6), which requires that secondary treatment or its equivalent be applied to all non-biodegradable industrial wastes. (Secondary treatment facilities are further defined as works that will produce an effluent having a total suspended solids concentration of no more than 30 milligrams per liter, turbidity of 25 units, and five-day biochemical oxygen demand of 25 milligrams per liter.)

(II)   That Reserve's discharge constitutes interstate pollution and endangers the health and welfare of persons in the states of Michigan and Wisconsin and is therefore subject to abatement pursuant to the FWPCA, 33 U.S.C. 1160(c)(5) and 33 U.S.C. 1160(g)(1). Under these provisions, the Attorney General of the United States was requested by the administrator of the Water Pollution Control Agency to bring a suit to secure the abatement of pollution.

(III)   Violation of 33 U.S.C. 407 ("Refuse Act"), which provides that it shall be unlawful to discharge any refuse matter of any kind or description whatever other than that flowing from streets and sewers and passing therefrom in a liquid state . . . unless a permit is first obtained.

(IV)   A common law nuisance in that the discharge of tailings contains substantial quantities of amphibole fibers, many in the cumming-tonite-amosite-grunerite series and identical or similar to amosite asbestos fibers, which constitutes a public health hazard to persons depending upon the lake for drinking water. It was further alleged that the discharge stimulates the growth of algae and bacteria, creates substantial increases in turbidity, impairs the ecological balance of the lake, accelerates the eutrophication of the lake, causes the green water phenomenon, and substantially detracts from the natural scenic beauty and aesthetic enjoyment and use of Lake Superior.

(V)   A common law nuisance for the reason that the substantial quantities of amphibole fibers released in the air endanger the health of all those people who breathe the contaminated air.

RESERVE DEFENDS AND COUNTERCLAIMS

The fact that significant amounts of tailings were being discharged into Lake Superior and dust was being discharged into the atmosphere by Reserve was not in dispute. The company, however, vigorously contested the precise nature of the discharge, its biological effects, and the ultimate destination of the tailings discharged. It denied that its discharges presented a serious health threat, claiming that the commingtonite-grunerite did not have a fibrous form and was otherwise distinguishable from amosite asbestos, the known human carcinogen when inhaled. In any event, Reserve maintained that tailings largely settle to the bottom of the lake in the Great Trough within close range of the plant.

Reserve then requested damages, based on the counterclaim that since Reserve had valid permits and licenses, any restriction, limitation, or termination of its rights would constitute the taking of defendant's property wthout just compensation in violation of the Fifth Amendment of the U.S. Constitution.

Reserve then requested damages, based on the counterclaim that permits, asked compensation for impairment of its contractual rights in violation of the constitutions of the United States and Minnesota.

THE TRIAL

Although the outcome of this case would have monumental local, state, and national significance, the trial itself was at times explosively dramatic and at times tedious. It required 134 days over a nine month period, ending with Judge Lord's injunction order on April 20, 1974.[4] Over 100 witnesses appeared during the trial. There were over 18,000 pages of testimony. In addition, over 1600 exhibits were introduced. Lord did not rely solely upon experts presented by plaintiffs and defendants. Instead, he appointed prominent experts as impartial witnesses to advise the Court on technical and public health issues.

Several weeks before issuing his injunction order on April 20, the judge made known his conclusion that Reserve's discharge did pose a serious threat to public health. At that point, however, he had not heard all testimony on this issue; nor had he even received the results of an important tissue study which *he* had ordered.

RESERVE IRKS THE COURT

On January 4, 1974, the Court ordered that Republic and Armco, the parent companies of Reserve, be joined as party defendants. They promptly appealed the order. Subsequently, the Circuit Court of Appeals ruled that it was an "abuse of discretion" to join Armco and Republic at that time. This matter, the appellate court said, could be resubmitted after resolution of the public health and liability aspects of the litigation. The plaintiffs then subpoenaed various officials of Armco and Republic

---

[4] Litigation in district court did not officially terminate until October 18, 1974, when Judge Lord issued a final order closing the record. The court of appeals later sent it back to district court for certain limited purposes.

along with any documents they might have relating to Reserve's operations and plans.

Responding to repeated requests by Lord during the trial for onland disposal plans, Reserve maintained that no such plans existed. However, when the parent company officials appeared in court on March 1 with their foot-high stack of subpoenaed documents, it was apparent that several onland disposal proposals had been considered. Ward Browning, head of Armco's engineering department, explained that the company did not have "a specific plan in the event it's required to dispose of [the wastes] on land." Lord glared at the witness. "I can't see how you can have $300 million or so hanging in the air with the Court having pronounced that it regards this thing as a serious health hazard. And you haven't made a plan yet!" Lord exclaimed.

The judge then ordered cost comparison figures on building a new plant at Babbitt or closing down the Silver Bay plant. The implication was as clear as Lord intended it to be. When Browning replied that producing those figures would be difficult, Lord replied, "I am not concerned about difficulty. We're talking about thousands of jobs and hundreds of millions of dollars, and digging through a few files won't cost you much."

Lord's anger exploded at the March 1 session when he learned that the proposal presented by Reserve three weeks earlier at his insistence had been rejected two years before by one of Reserve's parent firms. The *deep pipe* plan, by which wastes would be deposited through several large pipes 150 feet down in Lake Superior, had been described to the court in February by Reserve Vice President Haley as the plan that the company felt would be the best method for disposal of tailings. It was substantially the plan ordered by Judge Eckman but rejected by the state. Upon learning that the proposed plan had also been rejected by the company, Lord pronounced in disgust: "Do you realize that this Court spent three days considering a plan which your company put forward as something that was feasible and possible and that they wanted to do and that you had rejected in 1972?"

The judge's aggravation was not yet complete. The subpoenaed records brought into evidence on March 1 further showed that just a week earlier Armco representatives had contacted federal government officials in an apparent effort to discuss an out-of-court settlement. At this point the trial was seven months old. With this revelation Lord taunted Republic officials in the courtroom, asking if the companies were waiting for him to force them to go to onland disposal and thereby provide the companies with the opportunity to seek state and federal funds for a new disposal system and processing facility. Regardless, Lord ordered both Armco and Republic to produce memos, files, and records of any meetings with representatives of their companies and federal officials. These were later to be the subject of one of the tensest sessions of the trial, providing a dramatic, but perhaps meaningless confrontation between Lord and company officials.

BABBITT PLAN

On March 15, 1974, Reserve presented the onland disposal data ordered by Judge Lord two weeks earlier. It included a cost estimate of $452 million for moving the entire Silver Bay processing plant on the shore of Lake Superior to Babbitt, which is the mining site 40 miles inland. Moreover, if this solution were adopted, most of Silver Bay's 2000 employees and their families would be forced to move to Babbitt. Ore from the company's open-pit mines near Babbitt would be processed nearby, and the taconite pellets would be transported over Reserve's existing railroad to Silver Bay for shipment.

Although Reserve submitted this as a contingency plan, the company said it "will never be carried out" because it would be impractical and economically unfeasible. The following day Ed Schmid, assistant to the president of Reserve, attempted to reassert the company's cooperative posture, publicly stating that "we will give full, objective consideration to any plan or concept located in any area, including Babbitt." (28)

Reserve President Furness later explained why the Babbitt disposal study had not been produced earlier. "I understood the Judge wanted approved plans we could and would do," he said. (29)

Lord was not satisfied with the information contained in the Babbitt contingency plan and requested more information—specifically the price of taconite and the cost of capitalization. On March 26, when given additional cost figures, Lord angrily denounced the Babbitt plan as a "cruel hoax." "These figures," he charged, "are so outrageously inflated they strain the credulity."

The same day Lord threatened to fine Reserve $60,000 a day, beginning Friday, March 29, if certain documents were not produced. The penalty was figured to be equal to Reserve's daily profit. The documents Lord wanted included additional plans for onland disposal and records of task force meetings to discuss any such plans.

The dates were important because Reserve witness Haley had repeatedly testified that Reserve had no plans to change to onland disposal. Lord warned: "Bear in mind where we are . . . this gets to be a serious matter. The Court may impose appropriate sanction if it feels material is being deliberately withheld. . . ."

JUDGE OR POLICYMAKER?

Not content with simply conducting the trial, Lord called for a public meeting to be held in Duluth on March 22 to discuss water filtration systems. He apparently was angered that the north shore communities did not share his sense of urgency in correcting what he had already judged to be a "substantial public health menace." He explained that he intended to halt the Reserve discharge—the only major unresolved question being when. So the speed with which a filtration system could be installed in Duluth could have a bearing on how much time he gave the mining company.

In response to Lord's summons for cost estimates, local, state, and federal task forces responded that it would cost about $10 million to provide minimum interim asbestos-free drinking water to five Lake Superior communities and to construct permanent filtration systems. This figure was later revised to $16 million. Early in May 1973, the Army Corps of Engineers had been ordered by Lord to supply the communities with asbestos-free drinking water. This order was subsequently appealed by the government to the Circuit Court of Appeals.

Enmeshed in the technical problems associated with providing satisfactory filter systems was the question of who would pay the bill. Citizens argued that Reserve should pay the bill since it was the company's discharge that was creating the alleged hazard. Reserve supporters argued that there were other industries and community sources discharging, too, so Reserve should not be solely responsible. Mayors contended that the taxpayers should not bear the financial burden since it was "not the fault of the citizens."

On March 26 the Redwing (Minn.) *Republican Eagle* observed editorially:

We had thought that this public policymaking on pollution, this balancing of the conflicting interests in protecting the environment, was to be the assignment of Minnesota's PCA with its representative citizen board rather than a lone federal judge.

The paper also quoted Lord: "I am the man who knows the answers, and the answer is filters."

LAST DAYS OF MARCH

On March 29, 1974, the parent companies were rejoined by Lord as parties to the action. And in an unrelated move, the federal government declared in effect that it had "had enough," filing a motion for an immediate injunction.

The same day Reserve submitted a 32-page memorandum further justifying its early failure to produce documents demanded by the court. The memorandum referred to documents that Reserve had consistently and tenaciously argued were covered as "proprietary and trade secrets" under a protective order issued by Lord on April 24, 1973.[5] Through this memo, Reserve attempted to vindicate the company's position and that of company officials regarding the availability of plans for onland disposal of tailings. The memo stated:

> Throughout the litigation Reserve has believed, and continues to believe, that it is appropriate to investigate and evaluate numerous concepts which could potentially lead to an offer of settlement by Reserve. . . . The documents and data developed through such investigations of possible settlement offers have been considered by Reserve to be privileged under the doctrine of work product and the attorney-client privilege.

The memo further pointed out the extremely competitive nature of the iron mining and steel industry, and said that if another mining firm were to get these trade secrets, it could immediately put them into effect and save themselves years of research and millions of dollars in development costs.

Reserve Vice President Merlyn Woodle, who was later to succeed Furness as president, attempted to clear up the issue of prior re-

---

[5] A protective order was granted by Lord prior to the beginning of the trial to insure that proprietary information and trade secrets not relevant to the case would not be divulged in open court.

jection of the deep pipe plan by the parent companies. He explained that the earlier statements on the lack of feasibility of the deep pipe plan were issued by staff engineers and did not reflect or constitute company policy.

Woodle testified that minutes of meetings of company engineers in 1973 and 1974 did not exist, although there were some records of earlier meetings. One of the plaintiff's attorneys pressed him for details. He was particularly interested in knowing if Haley had been present. It was stated that he had been at some but not all of the meetings.

POLITICAL IMPROPRIETIES?

In early April, a document produced in court again outraged Judge Lord and caused him to order Armco and Republic to produce records of all their political contributions of any nature for the last five years. He also wanted to see all documents pertaining to meetings with government officials concerning the Reserve case. The document in question was a two-page agenda of a company meeting held in 1971 to plan the strategy for handling the Reserve problem. Various cryptic comments and observations were penciled in the margins about several government officials and steps necessary to expedite the case. Judge Lord, obviously disturbed by some of the notations, fumed as he told the trial participants:

> If what is represented in this document is taking place every day in the lives of the corporations of our country, I fear for our country. This document seeks to undermine the work, the position and the . . . very jobs of anyone who stood up to Reserve. . . . And I tell you that when I felt ill, it was in my heart, not in my stomach.

The agenda notations also raised the suspicion of financial arrangements between the parent firms and the Committee to Reelect the President, the "CREEP" of the Watergate case.

Later, C. William Verity, Jr., chairman of the Board of Armco, and Harry Holiday, Jr., were questioned in Court about the memorandum and notations. Holiday appeared and testified on May 1, the day he replaced Verity as president of Armco. The cryptic comments that appeared to be conspiratorial and calculated to undermine the judicial process apparently were explained to the court's satisfaction, or at least sufficiently for the judge to drop the entire matter.

LORD, "NEGOTIATE."

On April 10, Lord called the parties together for a report on out-of-court negotiations that had been under way for a month at his direction. The meeting began in open court, but quickly moved to chambers when attorneys were reluctant to talk about negotiations with reporters present. The judge was disturbed by the lack of progress in the negotiations. He pointed out it had been a month and a half since he had determined that there was a health threat; "unless there is an agreement by the time the Court is ready to issue its judgment," he warned, "it may be a judgment that will have a substantial impact." (30) The issues under negotiation were:

1 / alternate methods of disposal,

2 / timetable for implementation, and

3 / possibility of fines up to $70 million against Reserve for violation of various state pollution laws.

Plaintiffs' attorneys asked Lord to impose a fine of $960,000 on Reserve and assess the additional daily penalty of $60,000 which Lord previously had threatened if the company continued to withhold vital documents. Plaintiffs also requested that the court charge Reserve with the entire legal costs of the trial. This could be millions of dollars.

Finally, the judge warned that he wouldn't delay his judgment and decree "one day" to wait for progress in negotiations. Time had run out.

"ARMCO STATES POSITION"

April 20 was both a fateful and an intense day in Judge Lord's court. Verity, chairman of the Board of Armco, was on the stand and under intense interrogation by Judge Lord and counsel for the state of Wisconsin as to the parent company's intention if the court were to order a shutdown of Reserve.

At one point, apparently angered and frustrated at Mr. Verity's refusal to accept the court's assessment of Reserve's daily profit, Lord squared off at the Armco chairman:

I am going to give you and your associate about one hour now to determine whether or not it is possible for you to

meet the requirements of Air Pollution Control Regulation No.
17, which will cost you about 19 million dollars, whether you
can meet the requirements that there be complete on-land disposal, and whether or not you can meet the requirements of
the State Department of Natural Resources insofar as the place
and the manner of disposal of tailings is concerned.

I am going to give you about an hour or an hour and
a half. We will come back at 1:00 o'clock, and you tell me
whether or not you can meet all of the laws and regulations
as regards pollution.

The time is running short. It started running about
three months ago. . . .

The associate to whom the judge referred, who was also in the
court, was William J. DeLancey, president and chief executive officer
of Republic Steel.

An hour later the court reconvened.

Verity stated,

Your Honor, we have done as you asked, and I have come
back to the courtroom to report to you the decision we have
reached. I have these in writing, and I would like to read
to you what we have written. I hope that I will be permitted
to read these remarks in full before being asked to respond to
questions concerning them.

I should also like to state that it is our desire to enter
these remarks as an exhibit in this case.

Responsive to the Court's inquiry the morning of April
20, 1974, I, as Chairman of the Board of Reserve Mining Company, make the following statement in connection with the
litigation between the United States, et al., vs. Reserve Mining
Company, et al.:

"It is our considered judgment that Reserve's discharges do not constitute a health hazard and they are not
in violation of the State and Federal permits granted to Reserve as a basis for which an investment presently exceeding
$350,000,000 has been made. It is further our judgment that
these discharges are not in violation of any applicable rules,
regulations or legal standards.

"We sincerely desire to continue Reserve's operation
in Minnesota and are mindful of the impact that a cessation of

operations would have on Reserve's 3,000 employees, its neighbors, the tax base of the municipal subdivision and the State, as well as the impact that such a cessation could have on Armco with its 50,000 employees and Republic with its 43,000 employees and on shareholders and customers of those companies and the communities where they operate. Important to our consideration is the contribution of Reserve to the vitality and security of the United States.

"On March 4, 1974, representatives of Reserve, Armco and Republic were authorized to change our underwater proposal and participate in settlement negotiations for on-land deposition, hopefully looking toward an amicable resolution. While we pursued these discussions in good faith, agreement was not reached. Without waiving the usual rule that offers of settlement are privileged and confidential, we are faced with a situation in which some publication of various positions has heretofore been made and also we wish to indicate to the Court, to the Plaintiffs and to the public our fervent desire to continue operations in Minnesota. Therefore, with no concession of liability, Reserve and its shareholders are prepared to authorize commencement of engineering on April 22, 1974, and to recommend to the respective Boards of Directors the construction of facilities which would eliminate the discharge of taconite tailings to Lake Superior and place those tailings in a total on-land system in the Palisade Creek area as modified near Silver Bay with a closed circuit water recirculation system and full compliance with applicable ambient air and APC 5 air quality standards.

"We question the application of APC 17 to this operation and also its implementation in this plant poses substantial technical and economic problems. The new facilities will be so designed as to provide for some improvement in the finished pellets in an effort to make the pellets competitive and improve Reserve's posture among similar producers.

"The Palisade Creek total tailings plan and compliance with APC 5 is estimated to cost approximately $172,000,000 at current interest rates. The expenditure of such sums would substantially reduce the rate of return on the Reserve investment to the shareholders far below that of Reserve's competitors.

"This additional large investment would not result in any economic benefit to the shareholders even taking into consideration product improvement."

Mr. Verity then detailed the conditions under which the new system could get under way. In response to questions from the judge, he estimated that the tailings could be completely out of the lake within five years.

Republic's DeLancey next took the stand and endorsed the Armco statement.

Lord was obviously unmoved by the conditioned assurances of Armco and Republic. Furthermore, he apparently had his lengthy injunction ordered prepared prior to hearing the companies' position.

LORD'S DECISION TO STOP
THE DISCHARGE

On the afternoon of April 20, Lord solemnly ordered that Reserve stop dumping tailings into Lake Superior (and end air emissions as well) as of one minute after midnight the following day, Sunday, April 21. He promised that an in-depth memorandum explaining his reasons would follow later. But several weeks would be required before a detailed version of the findings of fact and conclusions of law could be prepared. Lord explained that he was compelled to move rapidly because of the public health issues involved. Meanwhile, he handed down his findings in an abbreviated form. He found that:

1 / Reserve Mining Company is set up and run for the sole benefit of its owners, Armco Steel Corporation (Armco) and Republic Steel Corporation (Republic), and acts as a mere instrumentality or agent of its parent corporations. Reserve is run in such a manner as to pass all its profits to the parents.

2 / Reserve, acting as an instrumentality and agent for Armco and Republic, discharges large amounts of minute amphibole fibers into Lake Superior and into the air of Silver Bay daily.

3 / The particles when deposited into the water are dispersed throughout Lake Superior and into Wisconsin and Michigan.

4 / The currents in the lake, which are largely influenced by the discharge, carry many of the fibers in a southwesterly direction toward Duluth and are found in substantial quantities in the Duluth drinking water.

5 / Many of these fibers are morphologically and chemically identical to amosite asbestos and an even larger number are similar to amosite asbestos.

6 /   Exposure to these fibers can produce asbestosis, mesothelioma, and cancer of the lung, gastrointestinal tract, and larynx.

7 /   Most of the studies dealing with this problem are concerned with the inhalation of fibers; however, the available evidence indicates that the fibers pose a risk when ingested as well as when inhaled.

8 /   The fibers emitted by the defendant into Lake Superior have the potential for causing great harm to the health of those exposed to them.

9 /   The discharge into the air substantially endangers the health of the people of Silver Bay and surrounding communities as far away as the eastern shore of Wisconsin.

10 /   The discharge into the water substantially endangers the health of the people who procure their drinking water from the western arm of Lake Superior including the communities of Beaver Bay, Two Harbors, Cloquet, Duluth, and Superior, Wisconsin.

11 /   The present and future industrial standard for a safe level of asbestos fibers in the air is based on the experience related to asbestosis and not to cancer. In addition its formulation was influenced more by technological limitations than health considerations.

12 /   The exposure of a non-worker populace cannot be equated with industrial exposure if for no other reason than the environmental exposure, as contrasted to a working exposure, is for every hour of every day.

13 /   While there is a dose-response relationship associated with the adverse effects of asbestos exposure and may be therefore a threshhold exposure value below which no increase in cancer would be found, this exposure threshhold is not now known.

The court's more detailed, 109-page supplemental memorandum was filed on May 11, 1974. In it, Lord discussed several significant elements of the case which were peripheral to the technical issues but important to the final judgment. He listed the various plaintiffs, defendants, and interveners and mentioned that the day before the injunction order was issued, the court granted the motions of Duluth[6] and Superior to

---

[6] This position by the city of Duluth is in sharp contrast to that taken by the Duluth Area Chamber of Commerce, which had joined the case a year earlier as an intervener for defendant Reserve.

intervene as plaintiffs. The cities requested to join the suit after it became apparent that the presence of fibers in the water supplies would necessitate expensive filter systems. They sought an injunction to halt the discharge and also compensation from Reserve for the installation of the filtration systems. The cities also claimed against the United States alleging that, according to law, the U.S. Army Corps of Engineers must provide these communities with safe drinking water.

The judge explained at length the factors that caused him to disregard the corporate entity of Reserve, finding that Reserve was merely an agent of Armco and Republic. With that conclusion, the joinder of the parent corporations was then necessary or else "Armco and Republic would be free to take the benefits of these violations without being accountable for any fines, penalties, or liabilities that attach to such conduct." The judge concluded that the parent companies were using Reserve as a shield to protect themselves from the consequences of their illegal acts, since the evidence clearly indicated that Reserve makes no "profit" and so would be unable by itself to meet any and all obligations imposed upon it. The judge even mentioned that he was quite aware that the "corporate parents were kept well informed of this case and were briefed frequently during the trial on what was happening in Court,"stating "This Court has no doubt that Armco and Republic were fully apprised of the situation and assisted Reserve in its presentation of the case."

CONCLUSIONS OF LAW

The court found that Reserve was in violation of the following statutes:

1 / *Minnesota WPC 15.*

a / Section (c) (6), which limits the allowable suspended solids concentration in an effluent to 30 mg/l.

b / Section (c) (2), which deals with nuisance conditions. The court maintained that the green water phenomenon and the public health impact of tailings constituted a public nuisance.

c / Section (a) (4), which restricts discharges that degrade the high quality of waters such as Lake Superior.

2 / Minnesota Air Emission Law: APC 1, 5, 6, and 17.

The court also concluded that since Reserve's discharge polluted the "waters of Lake Superior as to endanger the health and welfare of persons in Minnesota, Wisconsin and Michigan . . . the discharge is subject to abatement pursuant to FWPCA 33 U.S.C. 1160 (c) (5) and (g) (i)." It noted that federal law required the court to "not only consider the practicability, physical and economic feasibility of securing abatement of the pollution but also to consider the public interest and the equities involved in the case."

The court further found that a common law nuisance was created under federal common law, common law of the state, and the applicable state laws of nuisance. When a public nuisance is found, the propriety of an injunction depends upon a showing of *substantial* injury to the public. The court supported its finding of the need for an injunction by relying on a case wherein such an alleged injury is a type of public nuisance that endangers public health [*Board of Commissions* v. *Elm Grove Mining Co.*, 122 W.V. 442, 452, 9 S.E. 2d 813, 817 (1940)]. The court went on to say that the harm caused by the nuisance must be of "an overwhelming magnitude" to warrant an injunction. Obviously, the court believed that the equities of the case demanded that further discharge to Lake Superior be prohibited.

The issue of whether or not Reserve's discharge was in violation of the Refuse Act was taken under advisement by the court, to be considered after more testimony and argument. The court did not permit Reserve to bring forth witnesses on this subject due to the pressing public health issues. Other violations of Minnesota statutes on discharge were also taken under advisement.

The court pointed out that a condition in Reserve's original permit was that the terms of the permit "shall not be construed as estopping or limiting any legal claims against the permitee . . . for any damage or injury to any person or property or to any public water supply resulting from such operations." Therefore, the state permits were not allowed to serve as defenses to the claims brought by the federal government, Wisconsin, Michigan, and Minnesota. Further, the court found that the terms of the permits were being violated, i.e., the discharge was not confined to the nine-mile zone of discharge, the discharge caused discoloration of the surface water outside the zone, it caused an increase in turbidity, and it adversely affected the public water supplies of several communities, all of which are prohibited by the permits.

The judge also included a significant discussion involving the economic and technological feasibility of abatement. He had looked at what modifications could be made, how much they would cost, and whether or not Reserve could afford such expenditures. It was at this time that Lord became disgusted with Reserve and charged the company with acting in bad faith in misrepresenting facts, producing studies and reports with obvious built-in bias, and intentionally evading the submission of its fully engineered plans for alternative means of tailings disposal.

In the last analysis, the Judge found that the "company can afford to abate the health threat, has the technological ability to abate the health threat, yet refuses to do so. . . ." The court realized that the work force of Reserve would suffer immensely if the plant were shut down, but believed that Reserve was using the work force as "hostages" to continue its present mode of operations. Finally, Lord concluded, "this Court cannot honor profit over human life and therefore has no other choice but abate the discharge."

Chapter 14

In Federal
District Court:
Technical Issues

The Reserve trial, in addition to other distinctions, was the longest and most technically complex environmental case in history. Over 100 witnesses, most of them technical experts, had testified. After detailed testimony from such an impressive array of MDs, engineers, multi-disciplined scientists, economists, and others, facts in the case presumably would be established and the final verdict would be clear-cut. Actually the reverse happened.

There were essentially three major issues in the trial:

1 / the quantity, composition, and fate of taconite tailings discharged into Lake Superior;

2 / the public health significance of the tailings and air emissions from the Reserve plant; and

3 /   the impact of tailings on the ecology, appearance, and overall quality of Lake Superior.

Each of these issues warrants examination.

QUANTITY, COMPOSITION, AND DISTRIBUTION OF TAILINGS

MINERALOGY

Dr. James Gunderson,[1] reported that cummingtonite-grunerite [2] is the most abundant silicate that occurs in almost all of the submembers of Reserve's metamorphosed iron formation. In many parts, this mineral commonly exceeds 60% of the rock. Reserve conceded that approximately 26% of the deposit in its pit is amphibole [3] mineral in the cummingtonite-grunerite series. One of the issues in the case was whether or not these mined amphibole minerals were "identical to" or "similar to" amosite [4] asbestos.[5] Reserve steadfastly maintained that the silicate mineral in its mine was totally unlike amosite asbestos.

The court personally studied a great number of electron microscope photographs and described itself as "knowledgeable on the subject of distinction based on morphology alone, and no one, to the Court's satisfaction could point to any distinguishing characteristics." On the basis of the electron diffraction patterns, the court concluded that amosite and

---

[1] Dr. James Gunderson: Chairman and professor of geology at Wichita State University.

[2] Cummingtonite-grunerite: A general name for a series or group of amphibole minerals that are essentially identical except for the relative quantities of iron and magnesium in them. The more iron-rich members are sometimes referred to as grunerites, although the word cummingtonite is all inclusive and refers to the entire series.

[3] **Amphiboles:** Denotes the mineral family made up by silicates of calcium and magnesium and, usually, one or more other metals such as iron or manganese.

[4] Amosite: A trade name and non-mineralogical term used to identify certain commercially important fibrous minerals in the cummingtonite-grunerite chemical series. The name is derived from a certain asbestos mine in South Africa.

[5] Asbestos: A generic term for a number of hydrated sillicates that, when crushed or processed, separate into flexible fibers made up of fibrils.

cummingtonite-grunerite were indistinguishable, at least in terms of crystallography.

The court concluded that chemical evidence was quite clear that amosite asbestos fell within a sub-range of the broad category of silicate amphiboles in the cummingtonite series. Consequently, the court found that a portion of the cummingtonite-grunerite in Reserve's taconite ore would undoubtedly contain substances with a chemistry "similar to" or "identical to" amosite. The court noted

> Scientists for both sides have found that cummingtonite-grunerite and amosite have in most instances similar morphology, crystallography, and chemistry and are, therefore, indistinguishable.

Reserve pointed to some conflicting testimony indicating that significant and distinguishing differences were apparent. Dr. Cornelius Hurlbut,[6] a witness for Reserve, testified that the two minerals, or groups of minerals, were similar chemically but have distinguishing optical properties, i.e., refractive index and angle of extinction. The court acknowledged this testimony but noted that Dr. Hurlbut's analysis dealt with groups of crystals and that individual crystals would have optical properties similar to amosite. Another witness for Reserve, Dr. Jack Zussman,[7] testified that the physical structures of amosite and cummingtonite-grunerite were clearly distinguishable. He contended that fibers of amosite split apart readily, whereas cummingtonite fibers are brittle and resist separation.

The court was satisfied that cummingtonite-grunerite and amosite are similar and in some cases identical. The next question was whether some portion of the *tailings* is "similar to" or "identical to" amosite fibers. The court found that "there are fibers [in the discharge] that have the identical morphology, crystallography, and chemistry as amosite asbestos, a known human carcinogen," but interestingly the judge acknowledged that he could make "no finding as to the relative abundance of cummingtonite-grunerite and amosite in the air and water discharges of Reserve Mining Company."

[6] Dr. Cornelius Hurlbut: Professor Emeritus of mineralogy at Harvard University.

[7] Dr. Jack Zussman: Professor and head of the Department of Geology at the University of Manchester, England. He is a co-author of the five-volume standard geological text, *Rock Forming Minerals*.

CUMMINGTONITE AS A TRACER

The court was convinced that the 67,000 tons of tailings "dumped" into Lake Superior each day were not as completely deposited into the Great Trough as claimed by Reserve. The migration and distribution of tailings in the lake became the subject of heated debate. Plaintiffs argued that tailings could be effectively and reliably traced by the presence of cummingtonite, a common constituent of Reserve's tailings discharge but an uncommon constituent of natural sediment loads. They explained that samples of lake water and/or bottom sediments were collected and analyzed by X-ray diffraction analysis for the presence of cummingtonite. Then, by quantifying the amount of cummingtonite present, it was claimed that the relative quantity of tailings in the sample could be reliably estimated. Reserve argued that this type of analysis was unreliable as a tracer of Reserve's discharge because cummingtonite enters the lake from a variety of natural sources. The court dismissed this argument, stating

> The conclusion is clear that cummingtonite-grunerite in detectable quantities is generally not deposited into Lake Superior from natural sources. The Court finds that where cummingtonite-grunerite is found in the Western Arm of Lake Superior in detectable quantities, it can be traced to Reserve's discharge.

In making this determination, the court rejected testimony of a Reserve expert witness who claimed that his studies showed the presence of cummingtonite-grunerite in 60 tributaries emptying into the lake. The court believed that "the criteria used for identifying cummingtonite-grunerite in this study were highly subjective with bias entering into the determination."

Prior to the trial, Reserve had undertaken an extensive "inventory" to try to account for solids discharged. This inventory, commended by government witness Dr. Robert Dill, of the National Oceanic and Atmospheric Administration, revealed that approximately 85% of Reserve's tailings were deposited on the delta or on the lake bottom in the immediate vicinity of the discharge. Most of the remaining solids were distributed on the lake bottom over an area of some 1058 square miles. Based on this inventory, Reserve was able to account for all but 0.4% of its tailings. Dr. Dill later testified that Reserve's inventory, though well conceived and executed, had an inherent margin of error of plus or minus 10%. Dr. William Normarc, an oceanographer employed by Reserve to oversee the inventory measurement techniques, testified that there were insufficient data upon which to base an accurate estimate of error.

Government witnesses Baumgartner and Dill revealed that some of the tailings solids are stripped from the density current during periods of thermal stratification in the lake and spread along the thermocline layer. These solids can then move vertically or horizontally with prevailing lake currents, wind action, upwelling, and other turbulent phenomena in the lake. Baumgartner did concede, however, that once particles reached a depth of 150 feet, deep lake currents were insufficient to resuspend settled solids.

The court finally concluded that a large number of particles not caught up by the density current remain in suspension, or are deposited and resuspended—totally discrediting Reserve's density current theory:

> It is the finding of this Court that although the existence of the heavy density current is a fact, there are a number of physical phenomena working both on the density current and the tailings after they escape the force of the current that precludes it from being effective. The following is a list of those phenomena: prevailing currents, the presence of thermoclines, deep currents, wind action, interval wave action, upwelling, wave action, slumping, and vertical mixing.

Fibers in Water Supplies and Atmosphere

Witnesses for the plaintiffs attempted to prove, using cummingtonite-grunerite as a unique tracer, that taconite could be found in surface waters throughout the western arm of Lake Superior and in the water supply intakes of several north shore communities. EPA's Dr. Cook, a stalwart witness for the government throughout the trial, testified that he found detectable quantities of cummingtonite-grunerite in every sample of tap water taken at Beaver Bay, Two Harbors, and Silver Bay. He further testified that there was absolutely no doubt in his mind that Reserve's tailings discharge is the source of amphibole fibers in the Duluth water supply.

Drinking water samples from several communities were analyzed in seven different laboratories to establish a reliable estimate of amphibole fibers present. Results from these laboratories showed highly divergent fiber counts between laboratories and for replicate samples tested within a given laboratory. As much as a tenfold increase or decrease was not uncommon. Much of the counting inconsistency can be traced to the lack of a standard counting procedure that could be used by all investigators. Some used light microscopy, which is limited in resolution to particles one micron or larger; others used electron microscopy, which offered far greater magnification.

The court recognized the gross inconsistency in amphibole fiber counts but came forward with the following mean estimates for community water supplies:

Duluth	12.5	million	fibers/liter[8]
Two Harbors	21.1	million	fibers/liter
Beaver Bay	63.0	million	fibers/liter
Silver Bay	0.45	million	fibers/liter
Superior, Wisc.	4.0	million	fibers/liter

Cook reported fiber counts in the Duluth public water supply ranging from 60 to 220 million fibers per liter, with a mean value of 84 million. His results were clearly a factor of 10-or-more higher than the values accepted by the court.

Reserve argued that these high fiber counts did not reflect amphibole substances but rather silica shells from diatoms [9] and mineral fibers other than cummingtonite-grunerite. They pointed to testimony by court-appointed witness Dr. Frederick Pooley [10] who stated that the true amphibole fiber content of the water samples in most cases was "negligible," i.e., "below the detection limit as imposed by the counting procedure." [11]

Pooley analyzed a sample of Duluth water obtained by the Army Corps of Engineers and found 160,000 fibers per liter. He said, however, that "no fibers were found corresponding in morphology [shape] and chemistry to Reserve's tailings." [12] Ian Stewart, manager of Electron Optics Group and also a consultant to the government, testified that "most of the fibrous material observed by light microscopy is dia-

---

[8] One liter is approximately ⅘ of a quart.

[9] Diatoms: Microscopic aquatic organisms encased in a silica shell.

[10] Dr. Frederick Pooley: A world-renowned scientist from Cardiff, Wales, and an expert in identifying physical and chemical properties of asbestos and asbestos-like fibers.

[11] Federal trial transcript, p. 17,732.

[12] Ibid., p. 17,738.

tomaceous [silica shells of diatoms]. . . ." [13] Samples collected for the Court and analyzed under a protocol established by court-appointed experts showed that there were many non-amphibole fibers found in lake water, which could not have been introduced by Reserve's discharge.

Reserve was charged with contributing asbestos fibers not only to the waters of Lake Superior, but also to the ambient air in Silver Bay as well. Government's witness Dr. Nicholson [14] testified that air emissions from the Reserve beneficiation process resulted in air-borne fiber concentrations ranging from 400,000 to 6.5 million amphibole fibers per cubic meter. [15] The court noted that Nicholson's values represented the "worst case" situation, since he always collected samples directly under the smoke plume at the Reserve plant—not a normal way of measuring air pollution.

Witnesses for Reserve cited test results that showed much lower fiber counts, i.e., 6000 to 320,000 fibers per cubic meter. The court criticized these air counts, declaring that they failed to include small fibers.

Finally Judge Lord ordered an air count study of his own; this, too, was beset with problems. The court explained that "there were many deficiencies" in its study, pointing out that the court was "extremely pressed for time by the substantial public health threat." [16] The court's study was by its own admission "limited by the capabilities of the laboratories involved, and limited by the very state of the [sampling] art. . . ."

From a scientific standpoint the entire issue of fiber counts in lake water, tap water, and the atmosphere was clouded by gross inconsistency in test results and by widely divergent opinions of expert witnesses. Court-appointed witness Dr. Arnold Brown [17] summed up the significance of the fiber count issue in several passages excerpted from testimony:

[13] Ibid., p. 3,932.
[14] Dr. William Nicholson: Associate professor of community medicine at the Mt. Sinai School of Medicine in New York City—an associate of Dr. Selikoff.
[15] One cubic meter has an equivalent volume of 35.31 cubic feet.
[16] Author's note: If reliable data were not available, how could the court be so sure that a serious health threat existed?
[17] Dr. Arnold Brown: Chairman of the Department of Pathology and Anatomy at the Mayo Clinic in Rochester, Minnesota. He served the court both as a court-appointed technical advisor and as an impartial witness.

It is reasonable to assume an error in the counts of fibers in both water and air of at least nine times on the high side to one-ninth on the low side.

Well, in my thinking, Your Honor, as far as using the information that is supplied to the Court on counts, in view of the incredibly large errors associated with this procedure, I would have to assume virtually only a qualitative base for what is being reported. In other words, Your Honor, I do not recall having been exposed to a procedure with an error this large, and [to] which people have seriously proposed a number based on this very poor procedure.

It has become, at least in my thinking, the kind of soft underbelly, if you will, of all of the research, much of the research, I should say, of the work that has been reported on asbestos in patients and in experimental animals." (8)

Despite the hazy shadow cast by Dr. Brown on the value of the widely divergent test results, Lord concluded that "there is a significant concentration of asbestos-like fibers in the ambient air" and "millions of asbestos fibers [in] every quarter of water drunk by every citizen of Duluth, Two Harbors, Beaver Bay, and Superior, Wisconsin."

PUBLIC HEALTH SIGNIFICANCE

ADVERSE IMPACT

The government alleged that the asbestos-like fibers present in drinking water of north shore communities and in the ambient air above Silver Bay were "similar to" or "identical to" the cummingtonite-grunerite found in Reserve's tailings and air emissions. It further argued that since these fibers were similar to those that are known human carcinogens under other circumstances, the lives of north shore residents were endangered.

Reserve countered that tailings solids settled to the bottom of Lake Superior and therefore had no impact on downstream water supplies. Reserve also argued that the fibers contained in their tailings and air emissions were different from those that had been associated elsewhere with human cancer when inhaled occupationally and that the level of exposure was insufficient to create any health problems.

To refute this claim, the court pointed out that in 1971 the National Academy of Sciences convened a distinguished panel to study asbestos contamination. The panel reported that "no type of asbestos can be regarded as free from hazard." The court attached great significance to the report's conclusion and its relationship to the trial stating:

> This conclusion was buttressed by the testimony in the trial and the Court adopts it as a finding of fact.

The court also relied heavily upon the testimony of government witness Selikoff on matters relating to asbestos and human health. Selikoff is responsible for much of the epidemiological work that has demonstrated that workers exposed to occupational (high) levels of air-borne asbestos show an abnormally high incidence of lung cancer or mesothelioma.[18] During the trial, Selikoff explained to the court that other epidemiological studies also had shown an increased incidence of *gastrointestinal* cancer among occupationally exposed persons.

Reserve pointed to the testimony of court-appointed expert Dr. Brown. He had been charged by Lord to undertake a comprehensive review of all literature and all court testimony that reflected on the asbestos-related health issue. (The court had previously identified Brown as the person who presumably knew more about this subject than anyone in the world.) According to Brown, there were many known carcinogens in our environment including coal tar, benzidine, tobacco, vinyl chloride, X-rays, and sunshine. Regarding the health hazard of asbestos-like substances, Brown informed the court:

> It seems to me, Your Honor, that the precise scientific answer to many of the questions that are being raised in this court in this case, that these answers will not be available to us for some time. . . .[19]

Brown further testified that in his opinion asbestos can cause several kinds of cancer including lung cancer, mesothelioma, and gastrointestinal cancer. He went on to explain that

[18] Mesothelioma: A rare but particularly lethal cancer, frequently associated with asbestos exposure.
[19] Federal trial transcript, p. 18,399.

the evidence is probably good enough for me to draw the conclusion that it is likely that one could expect an increased incidence of cancer of the gastrointestinal tract in *occupationally exposed people.*[20, 21]

Dr. Brown's differentiation between environmental and occupational exposure should not have gone unnoticed by the court.

Reserve, moreover, pointed to opinions of several other experts including Dr. Selikoff himself, Dr. William E. Smith,[22] Dr. John Davis,[23] and Dr. Paul Gross,[24] who unanimously testified that there was no *known evidence* that asbestos fibers ingested with drinking water would produce cancer or any other health hazard.

FIBER LENGTH

Reserve maintained that the fibers in its discharge could not be compared with commercial amosite, because the average length of fibers emitted by the plant operation was much shorter than the average length of fibers used in the production of commercial asbestos. This was an important consideration, since the government had presented evidence that between 98% and 99.3% of all amphibole fibers in the Duluth water supply were less than five microns in length, with the average only 0.8 micron.

The court rejected Reserve's reliance on several "animal studies" to show that adverse health history associated with amosite was due to long fibers and that the shorter fibers had not been shown to be harmful. Unimpressed, the court commented: "To begin with, there are inherent problems in relating the results in animal studies to the human experience." The court then proffered the medical opinion that "it may well be that the shorter fibers are actually more carcinogenic than the longer fibers." Selikoff had speculated in testimony that small fibers *could* have a greater pathogenic potential because of their greater surface area per unit mass.

[20] Ibid., p. 18,149.
[21] Emphasis supplied by author.
[22] Dr. Smith: Director of Health Research Institute at Fairleigh Dickenson University. Dr. Smith has spent over 35 years searching for the cause of cancer.
[23] Dr. Davis: Head of the pathology branch, Institute of Occupational Medicine, Edinburgh, Scotland.
[24] Dr. Gross: Professor of pathology at the University of North Carolina.

Reserve cited the occupational standard adopted by the Department of Labor that permits asbestos contamination in the air of up to five fibers per cubic centimeter (or five million per cubic meter), counting only those fibers that were in excess of five microns in length. The court chose not to apply the standard based on fibers longer than five microns, because it believed, on the basis of testimony given, that the standard "was established not because of health considerations but because only fibers of such size can be practically and efficiently counted" (i.e., with a standard *optical* microscope). The government's witnesses had testified that for every five micron fiber observed under an optical microscope, there would be a considerable number of smaller unobserved ones. The court reasoned that "even if the standard is sufficient to prevent asbestosis, there is no evidence that it provides protection against developing cancerous malignancies."

THRESHOLD LEVEL

Considerable testimony was elicited concerning a dose-response relationship associated with asbestos exposure. It was generally agreed that there is a level of exposure below which there is no detectable increase in asbestos-related diseases—a so-called threshold limit. Lord acknowledged that it was unfortunate that there was no authority for establishing what that safe level of exposure is.

The government's star witness, Dr. Selikoff, described to the court an epidemiological study that indicated an increased incidence of mesothelioma among residents of an area in South Africa where air is contaminated from numerous asbestos mines and mills. He cited other examples where mesothelioma and/or other asbestos-related diseases were at an abnormally high level in spite of only "neighborhood" level exposure. Selikoff cautioned that a major impediment to meaningful epidemiological studies of this type is the long period between exposure to asbestos and the development of cancer. He noted that diseases associated with asbestos exposure are often not manifested for 20 to 45 years after exposure.

Expert witnesses for Reserve cited four epidemiological studies to establish a threshold level under which exposure to asbestos will not cause cancer. The court rejected these studies because "none of these studies identifies such a threshold level." Without knowing what the safe level of exposure is, the court ascertained that "to permit the present exposure to continue is nothing more than a gamble with the hopes that the threshold level, if there is one, has not been or will not be reached." The court concluded that *"there is no known safe level of exposure."* [25]

INGESTION OF FIBERS

All major epidemiological studies that attempt to associate asbestos fibers with harm to public health are based upon inhalation of fibers by humans. Medical experts are in agreement that inhalation of massive doses of asbestos fibers can interact with body tissues, most notably the lung, and produce cancer or other disease. It is not known, however, whether ingestion of asbestos or similar fibers in drinking water could elicit a similar response in the gastrointestinal tract or other tissues.

Selikoff's epidemiological studies on workers exposed to *occupational* levels of asbestos in the air revealed not only an increased incidence of lung cancer, but a "modest" increase of gastrointestinal cancer as well. It was surmised that when asbestos workers inhale asbestos, "approximately 50% of what they inhale is coughed up or brought by ciliary action into the back of the throat; this travels to the stomach." [26]

Other witnesses for the government attempted to convince the court that asbestos fibers, once introduced into the gastrointestinal tract, have the ability to pass through membranes to other parts of the body. Dr. Volkheimer [27] testified that large particles could "transmigrate" from the gut through the mucosa and into the body. His work, however, involved the transmigration of starch particles and *no work* was done with asbestos or asbestos-like fibers.

Another study proffered by the government was that reported by Drs. Cunningham and Pontefract. (*31*) These investigators *injected* large doses of asbestos fibers through the gut wall of rats and observed that some of the fibers dispersed through the body tissues.

Transmigration experiments were also reported by several medical experts testifying on behalf of Reserve, including Drs. Gross, Davis, Smith, and Wright.[28] The court gave little weight to these studies because, in the court's view, they were limited in design and scope. The court was particularly critical of Gross, and renounced his testimony and study, stating

[25] Emphasis supplied by the court.
[26] Reference 31, p. 68.
[27] Dr. Gerhard Volkheimer: Professor of gastroenterology at the Free University, West Berlin, Germany.
[28] Dr. George Wright: A chest specialist who has examined and treated large numbers of asbestos workers.

After observing Dr. Gross and listening to his testimony for several days the Court has serious questions as to this witness' ability to report as an unbiased investigator and consequently as to his credibility.[29]

Lord similarly discredited studies submitted by four other highly qualified technical experts for the defendant. But he apparently readily accepted Volkheimer's work which was totally unrelated to asbestos. Brown recognized that there was some value in the study by Drs. Cunningham and Pontefract but elected not to put much relevance on Volkheimer's work.

Lord earlier had deprecated animal studies offered by Reserve but appeared to give considerable weight to the transmigration studies introduced by the government, even though all were based on animal experiments.

TISSUE STUDY

Lacking any direct evidence relating the ingestion of asbestos fibers to cancer (or any other disease), Lord ordered a special tissue study. The objective was to determine whether persons who drank asbestos-contaminated Lake Superior water had accumulated asbestos fibers in their body tissues or whether the fibers were simply excreted with body wastes. The court had its own court-appointed experts formulate the protocol (study plan) for the tests. It involved analysis by electron microscope of the tissues of recently deceased Duluth residents who had ingested Duluth water for at least 15 years, i.e., since Reserve began its operation at Silver Bay. As a control (basis for comparison), tissue samples were to be taken from bodies of recently deceased residents of Houston, Texas, where the water presumably was free of asbestos fibers.

Court-appointed expert Pooley of England, acknowledged by Selikoff as the "one man who has competence and knowledge in this matter," [30] was assigned the task of scientifically examining the autopsy tissues for the presence of asbestos or asbestos-like fibers.

Asked if he thought the protocol formulated by the court was sound and would yield significant information, Selikoff responded: "I think so, sir . . . I think that their study has great value and we certainly would like to see the results of it." Selikoff also acknowledged that

[29] Reference 7, p. 69.
[30] Reference 32, p. 40.

negative results likewise would possess substantial significance. He testified

> Now our feeling was that no matter what air samples show or water samples show or anything else, unless it is found that asbestos is in the tissues of people who have drunk this water . . . if we do not find it in the tissues in appreciable quantities, *then I would risk a professional opinion that there is no danger,*[31] at least up to this point, to the population no matter what air samples show or water samples.[32]

Apparently confident that the tissues would support Lord's finding of health hazard, Selikoff went further in response to a court question

> *Judge:*   And if we examine those tissues and there are not fibers there, this operation is home free as far as the health hazard goes?
>
> *Selikoff:*   I would think we should find some fibers there. We're looking for needles in a haystack, but that's all right; we should find needles in the haystack with all the difficulties of the study, the technical difficulties; if we examine sufficiently large numbers of samples in some instances we should find some fibers there.[33]

Finally the results came in from Pooley's laboratory in Wales. The study revealed the presence of only *seven* fibers that could not be explained by laboratory contamination. Two amosite fibers were found in the Duluth tissue and one in the Houston tissue. Four tremolite[34] fibers were found in Duluth tissues. Here was the crux of the health case! Lord, though, elected to discredit the study—his own study—as deficient due to "time constraints and the limitations of the state of the art. . . ." He complained that "the parts of the body that were examined were ones that the court's witnesses[35] thought would be the places where fibers would be found, not areas in which fibers had been found by other in-

---

[31] Emphasis provided by author.
[32] Reference 32, p. 41.
[33] Reference 32, p. 42.
[34] Reserve's discharge does contain some tremolite.
[35] One of these witnesses was Dr. Brown, whom Judge Lord had earlier proclaimed to be one of the most knowledgeable persons in the world on this subject.

vestigators." He rationalized that "this was the first attempt to look for fibers in a population that had only environmental exposure." [36]

He obviously was mindful that he had already publicly announced his conclusion that Reserve's discharge constituted a "substantial health hazard."

Selikoff, who earlier had supported the study and who, in behalf of the government, was given duplicate tissue samples for analysis as a "check" on Pooley's work, did not report his results. Zussman, the Reserve expert, who also received duplicate tissue samples confirmed Pooley's finding.

Brown, asked by Lord to review the tissue results, commented:

It's my conclusion, from the tissue study, that residents of Duluth have not been found to have asbestos-form fibers in their tissues when compared with Houston.[37]

Scrupulously careful to testify only to that for which there was definite scientific proof, Brown would not go beyond the statement

It does tell me that it is not an emergency situation, and that's about as far as I can go.[38]

Not even these words by the court's leading witness deterred Lord from adhering to his prior conclusion that a substantial health threat existed.

Brown was clearly not supportive of Lord's definitive conclusion. He explained with scientific precision:

The state of the scientific and medical knowledge available in this area is in its early stages and there is insufficient knowledge upon which to base an opinion as to the magnitude of the risks associated with this exposure.[39]

As a "scientist":

On the basis of the evidence that I have seen, heard [and]

[36] Reference 7, p. 65.
[37] Reference 32, p. 41.
[38] Reference 32, p. 42.
[39] Reference 8, p. 23.

read, I would be unable to predict on scientific grounds that there will be an increased incidence of cancer in the population of Duluth by virtue of their exposure to asbestos-form fibers in their water or what might be present in the air.[40]

He had a somewhat different view as a "physician" however:

I have no expectations that our environment will ever be entirely free from asbestos. But until we know what the safe limits are, as a physician who would rather see well people than sick people, I have some sort of compulsion to protect ourselves against known agents that produce cancer until we know what safe limits are.[41]

Finally, he summed up:

I can come to no conclusion . . . other than that the fibers should not be present in the drinking water of the people of Northshore. [Also] the presence of a known human carcinogen . . . is, in my view, a cause for concern, and if there are means for removing the human carcinogen from the environment, that should be done.[42]

Significantly, when the asbestos issue erupted in June 1973, the press, radio, and TV accorded the news instant and extensive daily coverage. Screaming headlines heralded the stories. Every major criticism leveled at the defendant by the court, the government, or other sectors received wide coverage. But news of negative tissue results and the courageous objective statements of Brown received minimal coverage. To the media only bad news was news!

News surfaced again, however, when Lord elected to place considerably greater weight on Selikoff's testimony than on the court's negative tissue study and the counter arguments raised of the defendants. The court found that:

1 / Exposure to asbestos fibers can and does produce significant and detrimental changes in the human body.

[40] Reference 32, p. 37.
[41] Reference 8, p. 21.
[42] Reference 32, pp. 52 and 37.

2 /   Although the heavier the exposure the more likelihood there is of contracting asbestosis, even low level exposure to asbestos fibers can and does produce detrimental changes in the human body. Frequently where there are asbestos-produced cancers, there is no indication of asbestosis.

3 /   There is no known safe limit of exposure below which it can be said that no detriment to the body will result.

4 /   The detrimental changes produced by exposure to asbestos will not be manifested in a detectable way until 20 to 30 years after initial exposure.

For icing on the cake, Lord proclaimed that Reserve is "exposing thousands to significant quantities of a known human carcinogen. . . . The Court is asked to permit the present discharge, until such time as it can be established, that it has actually resulted in death to a statistically significant number of people. The sanctity of human life is of too great value to permit such a thing!" (7)

POLLUTION ISSUES

The Environmental Protection Agency and U.S. attorney general were unwilling to accept the verdict rendered in December, 1970, by Judge Eckman in Minnesota's District Court. The judge had found that:

> The evidence before the Court establishes that said discharge has had no measurable adverse or deleterious effects upon the water quality or use of Lake Superior insofar as its drinking water quality, any conditions affecting public health, affecting fish life or the reproduction thereof, or any interference with navigation. . . .

However, the discharge of tailings does have a

> measurable effect upon Lake Superior and the use thereof in regard to: (1) aesthetic enjoyment of the lake by the increase of the "'green water phenomenon" . . . and (2) a decrease in the presence of *Pontoporeia* commonly known as scud, in the vicinity of the discharge. (3)

The government was hopeful that before the federal trial ended, further studies by the EPA and other federal and state agencies would strengthen an obviously weak technical case on pollution issues. Perhaps it was fortuitous for the successful outcome of the government's case that in June 1973, the health issue emerged and completely overshadowed the alleged water pollution problems. Judge Lord refused to receive testimony on the pollution issues until the health question had been decided. And the court finally ended the trial without ever hearing complete evidence on the pollution issues.

In April 1973, two months before the health issue emerged, the NWQL director, Mount, had submitted a report (33) to the court containing a summary of 19 recently completed EPA reports and a critique of other relevant state, federal, and company reports made available since the beginning of the Reserve controversy. To the surprise and obvious dismay of government plaintiffs, the new work by EPA offered little new *solid* evidence of pollution by Reserve's tailings discharge. The EPA had invested countless man-hours and hundreds of thousands of dollars in a seemingly fruitless effort. It is pertinent, however, to re-examine the issues that had been raised in this regard.

GREEN WATER PHENOMENON

As far back as the second session of the "Federal Enforcement Conference," in 1970, Reserve had acknowledged that its tailings were responsible for some of the so-called green water in the lake. The company quickly pointed out, however, that this was merely an aesthetic nuisance that occurred at many locations in the lake and that was not influenced by taconite tailings; also that the condition was observed in Lake Superior, as in other bodies of water, long before the Silver Bay plant opened. No data were presented by the government or the company from which a quantitative estimate could be made of the *relative increase* in green water attributable to taconite tailings.

CHEMICAL EFFECTS

Representatives of Reserve frequently described taconite tailings as "inert sand." In sharp contrast, the government's "Specification of Scientific Charges" alleged that the tailing discharge contributes more than 60,000 pounds of dissolved solids to the lake daily, including 39 soluble chemicals.

Taconite, like most other rocks, contains numerous elements in chemically bound form. Consequently, total chemical analysis of this rock has no meaning in terms of potential impact on water chemistry or biological activity.

Leaching, or solubility, studies were conducted by the government and the company. Glass of the EPA reported on leaching studies conducted in 1970. He found considerable dissolution of silica (SiO_2) and calcium but little or none of phosphorus, manganese, nitrogen, or toxic heavy metals. Reserve questioned the validity of SiO_2 data, noting that Glass had elevated the temperature of the tailings sample for sterilization, which could have accelerated SiO_2 solubility. Glass' study, referred to earlier, led him to conclude that about 160,000 pounds of dissolved solids are added to the lake each day as a result of tailings discharge. This estimate is nearly three times greater than the 60,000-pounds-per-day figure claimed later by the government in its "Specification of Scientific Charges." Dr. Lee, a consultant for Reserve, compared the 60,000 pounds of soluble substances in the tailings discharge to the estimated 1 million pounds contributed daily by tributary streams.

Plumb, a Reserve consultant, found in independent leaching studies that 0.8% to 1.0% tailings solids dissolved in 500 days contact with lake water. By comparison, only 0.1% to 0.7% of natural sediments dissolve in comparable tests.

Though evidence is now quite clear that taconite solids are not completely inert, the solids release chemicals only at a very slow rate in an aquatic environment. Furthermore, the toxic heavy metals and the algal nutrient, phosphorus (P), present in taconite rock are not released in significant or measurable quantities. The environmental significance of adding 60,000 pounds/day of non-toxic soluble chemicals to Lake Superior has not been established. This impact would have to be compared with the potential environmental impact of discharging tailings onland.

Biological Effects

Early in the Reserve controversy, the government, based upon the work of EPA's Herman, charged that taconite tailings significantly enhanced the growth of bacteria including fecal coliforms and pathogenic bacteria. In 1972 another EPA scientist, Dr. Victor Cabelli, repeated Herman's earlier experiments and found that neither type of bacteria multiplied as earlier reported. Other bacteria (of a non-harmful variety) did show some growth enhancement in the presence of tailings.

Other investigators, including Dr. Vennes of the University of North Dakota and a consultant to Reserve, reported that taconite in suspension provided a "platform" that tended to enhance the growth of some bacteria present in the lake. Vennes noted, however, that a similar situation developed with natural sediment and glass particles.

Thus, it appears that the physical platform effect of tailings and not the dissolution of a stimulating chemical from the solids particles promotes bacterial growth. Moreover, this stimulating effect was observed only under laboratory conditions. EPA field studies in 1972 revealed that bacterial densities were not higher in waters contaminated with taconite tailings. In fact, there were many test samples that showed a decrease in bacterial count in the presence of tailings.

Numerous laboratory and field investigations were conducted by the EPA and Reserve to determine the impact of tailings on the growth of phytoplankton and periphyton. These two groups of algal organisms are important in the fish food chain. Their presence in lake waters reflects the nutritional characteristics of the lake. Phytoplankton is a group of algae that grows suspended in water, whereas periphyton attach to the lake bottom or submerged objects. However, the studies were so inconsistent that conclusive findings as to whether tailings were stimulatory or inhibitory to these organisms could not be made.

Additional studies were undertaken on benthic organisms,[43] most notably *Pontoporeia*, a minute fresh water shrimp. This organism serves as a primary food source for smelt and other fishes at certain stages of their life cycle. In 1968, the Minnesota Department of Conservation conducted a field study to determine the extent of reduction of *Pontoporeia* in near-shore areas contaminated by tailings. They found fewer *Pontoporeia* south (down current) of the tailings discharge; but the total production of all organisms was greater than north of the discharge. They estimated a possible reduction in annual fish catch of 5% in the near-shore areas affected by tailings deposits (i.e., for up to 15 miles south of the discharge). Subsequent studies reported by Reserve showed the reduction of *Pontoporeia* to be insignificant.

In his summary of pollution issues, Mount stated,

---

[43] Benthic organisms: Invertebrates that live on the bottom of the water body.

It is only common sense that there would be reductions of benthic organisms immediately under the outfall, in view of the daily rain of such tonnage onto the bottom. So it is not a question of whether there is reduction of *Pontoporeia,* but rather how much occurs and over what area.

This same common sense applied to onland disposal of tailings suggests that some wildlife would inevitably be destroyed or displaced, regardless of where the tailings are ultimately placed. To date, there has been no conclusive study providing a reliable quantitative estimate of the overall reduction of *Pontoporeia* (or any other benthic organisms) attributable to taconite tailings. But reports by the U.S. Bureau of Sports and Commercial Fisheries and the Minnesota Department of Conservation show commercial fishing in the Silver Bay region to be comparable to, and often more productive than, other regions of Lake Superior.

During the "Federal Enforcement Conference," numerous claims were made by environmentalists and some government scientists that taconite tailings were directly toxic to fish. Studies by the government as well as those by Reserve [44] have shown tailings to be toxic to only the most sensitive aquatic organisms and only at high concentrations, i.e., concentrations well above those expected outside of the immediate discharge zone. After reviewing all available information on the toxicity of tailings, Mount concluded that direct toxicity "does not appear to be a problem. . . ." [45]

There were interesting contradictions in the charges and allegations presented by the government in this regard. For example, it had been charged that tailings contain toxic substances that *inhibit* growth of fish food-chain organisms. This is bad! However, there are other charges that tailings *accelerate* the growth of fish-food organisms, such as algae. This, too, is bad! Then the charge has been made that tailings solids increase the turbidity of surface waters in the lake, thereby reducing light penetration and hence *restricting* the growth of photosynthetic organisms. That is bad! The same scientists complain that these solids also provide a "platform" that *enhances* the growth of algae. That is bad, too!

EPA's Cabelli attempted to explain inconsistent field data relating to bacterial growth, stating

[44] Reserve Mining Company breeds and stores lake trout in a pond constructed exclusively of tailings.
[45] Reference 33, p. 19.

where the concentration of launder effluent material is high, there is an inhibition of the growth of the bacteria. Extending outward from this area, there is a zone of stimulation for bacterial growth followed by a zone of "no detectable effect." (34)

Contradictory findings and charges such as these suggest that the EPA and other governmental agencies were uncertain about what is beneficial and what is deleterious to water quality and aquatic life. Recall Mount's analysis during the "Federal Enforcement Conference" which sheds light on their apparent dilemma:

I think we have a tendency at times to close our eyes to the multiple-use concept of water . . . I don't really think that we want a distilled water basin in Lake Superior . . . We have to have some phosphorus in the water in order to provide nutrients for the necessary amount of algal growth that must take place in the lake in order to sustain a commercial fish crop. I am thankful that I am not in the shoes of you conferees of having to decide where you draw the line between clarity in the water and good fish production; but a line will have to be drawn. . . .

The point I am making is that our goal is not zero phosphorus but some appropriate value which will permit sufficient plant growth and still maintain the aesthetic appearance of the lake.

There is a tendency to think that anything in this water is bad beyond H_2O and this is clearly not the case . . . So we must shoot for some compromise. . . .[46]

[46] Proceedings of "Federal Enforcement Conference in the Matter of Pollution of Lake Superior and Its Tributary Basin, Minnesota–Wisconsin–Michigan," First (Executive) Session, U.S.D.I.–FWPCA, September 30, 1969, p. 118.

Chapter 15

In Circuit Court
of Appeals

Judge Lord issued his injunction immediately halting the taconite operation at Silver Bay on April 20, 1974. Within hours, Reserve was able to convince a three judge panel of U.S. Circuit Court of Appeals (8th Circuit) to hear Reserve's emergency appeal. The panel sat in a Springfield, Missouri, motel room at 9:30 in the evening while attending a judicial institute. After reviewing Lord's opinion and the written motion presented by Reserve and after hearing oral arguments by counsel for both sides, the judges ordered a stay of the injunction pending a hearing before the court on May 15. The decision came as anti-Reserve forces geared up for their victory celebration. On April 22 Reserve reopened and Silver Bay was given a reprieve. The company quickly resumed its prominent role in the production of iron.

Later on May 15, after hearing arguments on the appeal, the court extended the stay of Judge Lord's injunction for another 70 days subject to certain conditions. It noted in its formal decision on the stay filed June 4, that the case originally was a water pollution abatement case, but after the discovery of asbestos-type fibers in Lake Superior the "focus of the controversy shifted to the public health impact of Reserve's discharge of asbestiform particles into the air and water." The court was not convinced that adequate evidence was available to constitute "proof" of a "substantial health hazard" as charged by Lord. The court stated

> The proof of a health hazard requires more than the mere fact of discharge; the discharge of an agent hazardous in one circumstance must be linked to some present or future likelihood of disease under the prevailing circumstances.[1]

The court reviewed the testimony of Dr. Selikoff, the government's chief medical witness, and concluded that "this evidence does not support a finding of substantial danger and that, indeed, the testimony indicates that such a finding should not be made."[2] In order to apply Selikoff's findings to the exposure resulting from Reserve's air discharges, the appeals court noted that "it must be shown either that the circumstances of exposure are at least comparable to those in occupational settings,"[3] or, alternatively, that the principles may be applied to predicting the occurrence of such diseases in altered circumstances. Lord had refused to consider the five-fibers-per-cubic-centimeter standard for permissible occupational level exposure. However, the appeals court cited the standard "as evidence that the level of exposure in the air of Silver Bay, even at its upper range, is far below the legally permissible level for occupational settings, and thus obviously below those levels typically associated with environmental exposure."[4]

Since studies dealing with occupational levels of exposure cannot be used to determine the likelihood of disease at lower levels of exposure, the court addressed two questions: (1) how to determine, with some precision, what the lower level of exposure is, and (2) whether that level, once established, is safe or unsafe. Dr. Brown testified during the trial that the levels of fibers present in the air cannot be accurately measured, and that fact was verified by the widely divergent sample counts received by the lower court. Consequently, the testimony and studies did not indicate more than the presence of "some" fibers in the air.

As to the risk posed by the presence of these fibers, the court of appeals did not agree with Lord that a "substantial" health hazard existed. The tissue study conducted at the request of the district court and designed and directed by court-appointed experts measured the

[1] Reference 8, p. 6.
[2] Ibid., p. 9.
[3] Ibid., p. 10.
[4] Ibid., p. 11.

hazard to Duluth residents of ingesting fiber-contaminated water. Lord's expert witness, Dr. Pooley, explained the study results, indicating that the tissues of Duluth residents were "virtually free" of any fibers that could be attributed to the Reserve discharge. Lord refused to accept the negative results of this tissue study; he chose instead to base his findings of a significant health hazard on the "months of epidemiological testimony by the world's leading experts in the field." [5] The court of appeals evaluated the tissue study differently.

> On any fair reading of the circumstances of the protocol, the results of the tissue study must weigh heavily against the assessment of any demonstrated hazard to health. We think it is clear that the tissue study raises a major obstacle to the proof that ingestion of Duluth water is hazardous.[6]

The court of appeals summarized its conclusions.

1 / fiber levels are not at occupational levels,
2 / the low levels present cannot be measured and therefore cannot be expressed as a health risk,
3 / it is not known what level of exposure is safe or unsafe.

> [Therefore] although Reserve's discharge represents a possible medical danger, they have not in this case been proven to amount to a health hazard. [Also], We do not think that a bare *risk of the unknown* [7] can amount to proof in this case.[8]

The court pointedly observed that in a court of law governed by rules of proof, unknowns may not be substituted for proof of a demonstrable hazard to the public health. It, therefore, believed that Lord "carried his analysis one step beyond the evidence" [9] in taking the position that all uncertainties should be resolved in favor of health safety.

[5] Reference 7, p. 66.
[6] Reference 8, p. 19.
[7] Emphasis provided by author.
[8] Reference 8, p. 23.
[9] Ibid., p. 24.

The district court's determination to resolve all doubts in favor of health safety represents a legislative policy judgment, not a judicial one.[9]

In considering the issue of pollution of Lake Superior, the court of appeals described the original decision to permit the discharge of tailings into the lake as a "monumental environmental mistake." Determined to abate continued pollution of Lake Superior, the court conditioned its stay of the injunction upon "Reserve taking prompt steps to abate its discharges into air and water."[10] The court ruled:

1 / Reserve's plans for onland disposal and control of air emissions shall be submitted to plaintiffs for review and recommendations within 25 days of this order.

2 / Plaintiff shall be given an additional 20 days to file their comments on such plan.

3 / The district court (Judge Lord) shall consider Reserve's plans and accompanying recommendations, and then report its recommendations to the Court of Appeals within 15 days.

In a footnote to its order the circuit court observed

We note that the trial court has characterized Reserve's approach to abatement as one of "intransigence" and seems to have considered this a factor in closing down the plant. . . . The crucial court-designated medical and scientific witnesses were yet to be heard; the results of tissue studies were yet to be fully evaluated and explained. . . .[11]

The appeals court went a step further to exonerate Reserve of bad faith charges leveled by Lord:

To us there are neither heroes nor villains among the present participants in this lawsuit, nor among their predecessors in government, business, and society who were once allies in

[10] Ibid., p. 26.
[11] Ibid., p. 27.

encouraging and creating a taconite industry in northern Minnesota.[12]

Finally the court offered soothing words:

We think settlement of this kind of case represents a necessary and desirable goal, and the matter should be pursued in the district court. One possible approach is the use of mediation techniques in resolving disputes on technical matters by utilizing experts from business and science who can assist the parties in reaching a settlement or can advise the parties in reaching a settlement or can advise the district court on technical matters in his consideration of Reserve's plan.[13]

The state of Minnesota, pressured by environmentalists not to accept the circuit court's June 4 ruling, on July 5 asked the U.S. Supreme Court to vacate the stay. Four days later the Supreme Court denied this application.

LORD REJECTS RESERVE PLAN

Reserve's engineering staff and consultants rapidly put together a plan for disposing of tailings on land. Their new plan turned out to be only a modified version of the so-called Palisades Plan which the MPCA and Lord had rejected three months earlier. Per remand instructions set out in June by the appeals court, Lord reviewed the new Reserve disposal plan and quickly rejected it as unreasonable. He recommended that the appeals court vacate its stay.

UNRESOLVED ISSUES

Lord also informed the higher court that several other issues in the case, including the biological effect of Reserve's discharge on the lake, remained unresolved and under advisement. This prompted Appellate Judges Bright and Ross (Judge Webster joined a few days later) to convene a conference on August 9 to —

[12] Ibid., p. 26.
[13] Ibid., p. 29.

inquire into consolidation, clarification and simplification of issues pending on appeal and to advise this Court of the time necessary to submit unresolved issues pending before the district court.[14]

Upon noting the large number of pending issues before the district court, the appeals court on August 9 granted the government's request for an "en banc"[15] hearing, stating:

But one of the reasons for this conference is that the Court is concerned that if there should be an in bank consideration in the case, that the Court ought to have the whole case before it. This case already has been, at least in preliminary posture, before our Court. It's been before the Supreme Court and contrary to our impression, after receiving Judge Lord's recent opinion, we note that there are several unresolved issues in the case.[16]

The court continued:

Now, this case has been just about like a yo-yo, back and forth between the Court of Appeals and the District Court. Now, it seems to me it's time to get the case decided in the District Court and then up here.[16]

The following week, on August 16, the court of appeals remanded the case back to district court with instructions to "expedite the disposition of the unresolved issues. . . ." The defendants had told the court of appeals that these undecided matters could be dealt with by documentary evidence plus "a day or two of testimony." The government argued, however, that one or two months of additional testimony would be necessary to complete the trial. Lord elected another path. He called for a concluding hearing on August 23 to dispose of unresolved issues, then declared "The evidence . . . will be closed . . ." and ". . . I will be prepared in a few days to enter a final judgment on all other aspects

[14] Reference 32, p. 14.
[15] "In bank" or *en banc*: Full contingent of court judges.
[16] Transcript of court of appeals preliminary hearing held on August 9, 1974.

of the case." The heavy workload in Minnesota's 8th District Court caused Lord to extend the "few days" to a few weeks. His final decision was rendered on October 18, 1974. This decision included the following rulings:

1 / Reserve's discharge into the water constitutes a violation of the Refuse Act (33 U.S.C. §407;E);

2 / Reserve's counterclaims should be dismissed;

3 / Reserve's air emissions violate Minnesota air pollution control regulation (APC 3) and Minn. Stat. Ann. §116.081(1), which requires that permits be obtained for the operation of certain emission facilities;

4 / Reserve's discharge of waste into the Dunka and Partridge Rivers of Minnesota violates Minn. Stat. Ann. §115.07(1), which requires a permit for the operation of a disposal system;

5 / Reserve's discharge of pilot plant effluent into Lake Superior also violates Minn. Stat. Ann. §115.07(1);

6 / Evidence is insufficient to justify liability under Minn. Stat. Ann. §105.41, which makes it unlawful to appropriate water without a permit; and

7 / the state of Wisconsin could not assert the states' "public trust doctrine" as an affirmative cause of action against Reserve's discharge into Lake Superior.

This still left some matters unresolved, Lord warned, including the question of fines and penalties and the liability of the defendants for water filtration systems for north shore communities.

ALTERNATE DISPOSAL SITE
CONSIDERED

The court of appeals, at its August 5 conference session, had requested that the state of Minnesota suggest a feasible onland tailings disposal site located "closer to Silver Bay [than Babbitt] which might be an appropriate site. . . ." The site obviously in the mind of the court was the Lax Lake area. Minnesota Governor Wendell Anderson responded to this invitation by letter, dated August 16, 1974. The governor identified a possible site in the Lax Lake area provided

1 /   that dam safety would be assured;

2 /   that perpetual maintenance of the impoundment be provided for; and

3 /   that Reserve's mining operation be limited to the projected forty-year mining plan.

On August 27, Reserve formally advised the court that the company would agree to the Lax Lake site (Milepost 7) [17] even though the total cost would be $252 million including the installation of stack scrubbers to reduce air emissions. This would be by far the largest expenditure for environmental control by a single company in U.S. history.

The following day, August 28, the three-judge appeals court panel entered an order continuing the stay while the final appeal was pending. The panel concluded:

1 /   The representations of counsel at the hearing on August 27, 1974, satisfy us that significant progress has been achieved by parties in seeking agreement for the on-land disposal site and method for abatement of Reserve's discharge into Lake Superior, [and]

2 /   No substantial reason has been advanced why the stay order should not be continued pending such appeal other than the argument of imminent health hazard, which this court, for purposes of the stay pending appeal, has already determined adversely to appellees.

ANOTHER SUPREME COURT REJECTION

Plaintiffs [18] in the case, with the exception of the lead plaintiff, i.e., the U.S. government, applied to the U.S. Supreme Court for a second time

---

[17] Reserve prefers to designate the Lax Lake disposal area as the "Milepost 7" site.

[18] Plaintiffs submitting application included: States of Minnesota, Wisconsin, and Michigan; MPCA; and the private environmental groups.

on September 30, 1974, to vacate the stay order of the court of appeals. On October 11, the Supreme Court, by a vote of four to one denied the applications. Mr. Justice Douglas cast the dissenting vote, commenting,

> If equal justice is the federal standard, we should be as alert to protect people and their rights as the Court of Appeals was to protect 'maximizing profits.' If, as the Court of Appeals indicates, there is doubt, it should be resolved in favor of humanity, lest in the end our judicial system be part and parcel of a regime that makes people, the sovereign power in this Nation, the victims of the great god Progress. . . .

APPEALS COURT *EN BANC* HEARING

The court of appeals, on October 7, 1974, called for an *en banc* hearing in early December, assuming that the district court would be out of the case by then. Lord rendered his final decision October 18. The appeals court also established an accelerated briefing schedule, calling for all briefs and reply briefs by December 9.

The brief filed by the state of Minnesota and the MPCA reflected the level of their dissatisfaction:

> If "dead bodies" are to be required, and if all "uncertainties" in proof are to be decided against protection of public health, we will be condemning untold numbers of people to death.

The "dead body" issue had been raised earlier by Merritt, Senator Hart, and others in protesting the May 15, 1974, court of appeals stay.

On December 6, the government took a deposition from Dr. Brown, the district court's chief impartial witness. Both parties in the case stipulated that this testimony could be considered by the court of appeals. Brown testified that little new relevant information had emerged since his testimony in April and reiterated that there was no immediate health hazard. Persisting, the government attorney asked

> Is there any question in your mind that the people living on

the North Shore are being exposed to a human carcinogen in the air and water? [19]

[*Dr. Brown*]:   Court studies demonstrated to my satisfaction that similar [asbestiform] fibers are present in the air of Silver Bay and since I am convinced that asbestiform fibers are carcinogenic for humans, my answer to your question would be yes.[20]

Brown added:

I took some pains to also say that it was my medical opinion that the presence of a human carcinogen in the air and water was not to be taken lightly. . . . Until I know what the safe level is I therefore could not, as a physician, consider with equanimity the fact that they are being exposed to a human carcinogen.[20]

The full hearing before a five-member panel of the court of appeals was conducted on December 9. Four hours of argument were heard. There were several appeals pending before the court at that time, including:

1 / Defendant Reserve's appeal that WPC 15 is arbitrary and unreasonable;

2 / Reserve's appeal from the April 20, 1974, injunction order;

3 / U.S. government's appeal from the district court order of April 19, 1974, directing that the U.S. Corps of Engineers provide filtered water to north shore residents at government expense;

4 / Reserve's appeal from Lord's judgment of October 18, 1974;

5 / State of Wisconsin's appeal from Lord's judgment of October 18, 1974. Wisconsin later abandoned this appeal.

With the start of the new year, two new appeals were filed by the plaintiffs. These appeals were by the state of Michigan and the

[19] Reference 32, p. 38.
[20] Ibid.

Minnesota Environmental Law Institute (a private plaintiff) and dealt with Lord's decision to "sever" the biological pollution issue from his final judgment. The late filing of these appeals *by the plaintiffs* and the necessity for allowing time for a briefing schedule (through February 4), precluded the circuit court's issuance of any decision by the January 31, 1975, deadline earlier set by the Supreme Court.

Though responsible for some of the delays in the court of appeals hearings, these plaintiffs on March 4, 1975, renewed their application to the Supreme Court to vacate the stay order on the ground that the court of appeals had not issued an opinion on or before January 31st. Shortly thereafter, on March 14, the court of appeals handed down its final opinion in a 107-page document, with a summary of key rulings:

1 / The United States and other plaintiffs have established that Reserve's discharges into the air and water give rise to a potential threat to public health. The risk to public health is of sufficient gravity to be legally cognizable and calls for an abatement order on reasonable terms.

2 / The United States and Minnesota have shown that Reserve's discharges violate federal and state laws and state pollution control regulations, also justifying injunctive relief on reasonable grounds.

3 / No harm to the public has been shown to have occurred to this date and the danger to health is not imminent. The evidence calls for preventative and precautionary steps. No reason exists which requires that Reserve terminate its operations at once.

4 / Reserve, with its parent companies Armco Steel and Republic Steel, is entitled to a reasonable opportunity and a reasonable time period to convert its Minnesota taconite operations to on-land disposal of taconite tailings and to restrict air emissions at its Silver Bay plant, or to close its existing Minnesota taconite-pelletizing operations. The parties are required to expedite consideration and resolution of these alternatives.

5 / The evidence suggests that the threat to public health from the air emissions is more significant than that from the water discharge. Consequently, Reserve must take reasonable immediate steps to reduce its air emissions.[21]

[21] Reference 32, p. 2–3.

Several specific comments offered by the appellate court are noteworthy:

the evidence demonstrates that the medical and scientific conclusions here in dispute clearly lie 'on the frontiers of scientific knowledge'.

we find no evidence of any interstate health hazard, and no testimony from medical witnesses indicating any substantial concern over the health of any citizens exposed to Reserve's air discharge other than those residing in the Silver Bay, Minnesota, area.

On specific charges dealing with air pollution, the court:

— *rejected* "the federal common law of nuisance as basis for relief."
— *affirmed* "the district court's finding that Reserve, by its air emission, is violating APC 1, 3 and 5 and Minn. Stat. Ann. 116.081(1) [and] 'may be enjoined as a public nuisance.'"

On water pollution charges, the court:

— *sustained* "the district court's determination that Reserve's discharges into Lake Superior constitutes pollution of waters 'endangering the health and welfare of persons' within the terms of . . . the Federal Water Pollution Control Act and is subject to abatement."
— *agreed with* "the district court that Reserve's discharges in the future are subject to abatement under the Refuse Act. . . ."
— *deemed unnecessary and unwise* "to also rely on federal nuisance law."

The court also dealt with the numerous subsidiary appeals as follows:

— *dismissed* Reserve's appeal relating to the appropriateness and applicability of Minnesota Standards WPC 15;
— *dismissed* appeals from Michigan and environmental plaintiffs regarding ecological questions;
— *dismissed* appeal of the United States that dealt with the district

court's order for the Army Corps of Engineers to provide water to north shore residents. (The court of appeals noted that the district court's order obviously applied only to the existing allocation of federal funds for this purpose.)

In the "Remedy" section of the court of appeals' opinion, the court stated:

> We believe that on this record *the district court abused its discretion* [22] by immediately closing this major industrial plant. In this case, the risk of harm to the public is potential, not imminent or certain, and Reserve says it earnestly seeks a practical way to abate the pollution. A remedy should be fashioned which will serve the ultimate public weal by ensuring clean air, clear water, and continued jobs in an industry vital to the nation's welfare.

Although the court acknowledged difficulty in precisely estimating what constituted a "reasonable time," it did provide some guidelines. It suggested that "with expedited procedures a final administrative decision [on the disposal site] should be reached within one year after a final appellate decision in this case." The court then suggested that Reserve be given a reasonable turn-around time to complete construction of an onland disposal facility once the state permit was granted. It was further opined by the court that should both parties be unable to agree on an onland disposal site within this reasonable period, "Reserve, Armco and Republic Steel must be given a reasonable time [one year] to phase out of the Silver Bay facility."

Reserve was also ordered by the court to comply with Minnesota air pollution regulations APC 1 and 5, which would reduce the asbestos fiber count in the ambient air at Silver Bay to "below a medically significant level."

The final statement in the court of appeals' written opinion was an order remanding the case back to Judge Lord in district court to ensure that the appellate decree was fully carried out.

LORD OVERREACTS

On Saturday, March 15, 1975, the day following the court of appeals' final order, Judge Lord hastily called a meeting of parties to the case,

[22] Emphasis provided by author.

stating, "I called this meeting in a burst of enthusiasm that we might finally resolve this case." He then added, somewhat defeatedly, "I was overenthusiastic. . . . That became clear as I read the Eighth Circuit opinion. We must now be within seven to 10 years of the end of this case." (35)

Then Lord challenged Governor Anderson to take charge and make a political decision to locate a land disposal site and halt the Reserve discharge. He also urged the Minnesota legislature to get involved in choosing an acceptable onland site, ordered a 30-day schedule for the state and Reserve to file motions on resolving the air and water pollution at Silver Bay, and ordered state officials to furnish, by the following Friday, a detailed schedule of events and deadlines that would lead to the issuance of a permit to Reserve for onland disposal of tailings.

On April 8, 1975, an angry Circuit Court of Appeals issued an almost unprecedented special order that rapped Lord for judicial indiscretions. The appeals court noted that Lord called parties together *before* the issuance of a mandate by the appeals court and characterized the proceedings of that meeting as "irregular." The appeals court ruled that the various directives issued by Lord, such as suggestions to the governor of Minnesota, the Minnesota legislature, and members of Congress, are "a complete nullity."

"The judge [Lord] initiated steps which appear to be in conflict with the express language of this court's opinion of March 14, 1975. . . ," the upper court observed sharply. "Neither the District Court nor any party is free to ignore our determinations. . . ." As a finale to its public reprimand of Lord, the court of appeals ordered that "the District Court judge should not interfere in matters concerning the parties which lie outside his jurisdiction in these cases."

SUPREME COURT DECISION

On March 31, 1975, the U.S. Supreme Court rejected the application of Minnesota, Wisconsin, Michigan, and several environmental groups to vacate the stay order of the court of appeals. It also refused an alternative request by these groups to set a two-year deadline for an end to pollution of Lake Superior by Reserve.

The U.S. Department of Justice announced on March 24 that it would not appeal the court of appeals March 14 decision to the Supreme Court. Thus litigation in the federal courts apparently had come to an end.

CHRONOLOGY OF IMPORTANT EVENTS
IN THE FEDERAL COURTS

February 17, 1972	U.S. filed suit against Reserve
August 1, 1973	Trial began in federal district court
April 20, 1974	Judge Lord issued injunction
April 22	Court of appeals stayed injunction (temporary stay until full hearing)
May 11	Judge Lord filed supplemental memorandum supporting stay order
May 15	Court of appeals held hearing — parties agreed to settle if possible — court indicated it wanted *entire* case to review
June 4	Court of appeals extended stay for 70 days with condition that Reserve submit good faith "plan"
July 5	Appeal to U.S. Supreme Court to vacate stay order
July 9	Supreme Court denied application
throughout July	District court held hearings to discuss Reserve's plans
August 3	District court rejected Reserve's Palisade plan and made report to court of appeals as required by order of June 4. Report listed trial issues unresolved
August 5	Court of appeals issued "Order for Pre-hearing Conference" to resolve issues (immediate response to Judge Lord's report of numerous issues unresolved)
August 9	Court of appeals conference to determine issues — Lax Lake suggested (by court) — en banc hearing approved for future
August 12	Order from court of appeals directing parties to appear to determine status of stay order (hearing August 20) — This date ended the 70-day period of the original stay order, so stay extended.
August 16	Letter from Governor Anderson recommending the Lax Lake site with certain conditions
August 16	Court of appeals remanded case to district court for "prompt" resolution of undecided matters

August 20	Court of appeals held hearing to determine whether or not the stay order should be extended — Lax Lake (Milepost 7) idea explored
August 23	District court held hearing to discuss and dispose of the remaining unresolved issues. Closed the record.
August 27	Hearing before court of appeals to consider an extension of the stay order
August 27	Reserve advised the court of appeals that the company would agree to the Lax Lake site
August 28	Court of appeals extended stay order pending appeal
September 30	Application to U.S. Supreme Court by all plaintiffs except the U.S. government to vacate or modify stay order of court of appeals — also requested directive that court of appeals decide case this year
October 7	Court of appeals called for an *en banc* hearing of the case in early December. Briefs due December 9.
October 11	Supreme Court denied application to vacate the stay. Ordered case to be decided by court of appeals by January 31, 1975.
October 18	Lord issues final order charging numerous pollution violations by Reserve and dismissing Reserve's counterclaim
late November	Reserve submitted permit request to state for development of Milepost 7 area for tailings disposal
December 7	State rejected Reserve's permit request
December 9	Full hearings before five-member panel of court of appeals
March 4, 1975	Plaintiffs renew appeal to U.S. Supreme Court to vacate stay order. Claimed that January 31, 1975, deadline had been exceeded.
March 14	Court of appeals renders opinion and order. — found Reserve's discharge to endanger health safety—danger not imminent — call for abatement on "reasonable grounds"

March 15   Lord calls meeting of parties to case to expedite selection of onland disposal site

March 24   EPA announced that it would not appeal court of appeals decision to Supreme Court

March 31   U.S. Supreme Court rejected plaintiffs application to vacate the court of appeals stay order

April 8   Court of appeals criticized Lord for several irregularities in handling the remand order

PART III

ALTERNATIVES

Once denied the use of Lake Superior as a repository for tailings, Reserve had the option of onland disposal or closing shop.

Chapter 16

Disposal Alternatives

"We are going to have to put it [residue] somewhere." This simple yet profound statement by EPA's Murray Stein in 1971 cuts at the heart of the Reserve controversy. By the very nature of the iron beneficiation process, vast quantities of residues are inevitably produced, i.e., nearly two tons for every ton of product. These residues cannot remain suspended in space; they must come to rest in some natural repository or sink. They are not produced frivolously; they are the by-products of an acknowledged national need. The basic issue in the *Reserve* case then was which natural sink to use for tailings disposal.

In the mid-1940s, when Reserve was developing plans for plant construction, an onland tailings disposal facility near the Babbitt mine site appeared at first to be the logical answer. Most other mining operations nationwide had developed processing facilities as close to

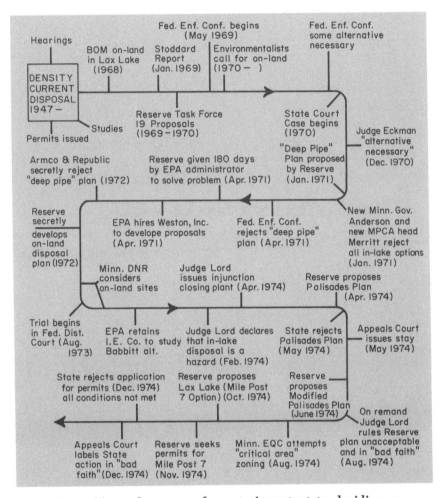

FIGURE 14   Sequence of events important to deciding on an alternative tailings disposal method.

the mine as possible to reduce costs of materials transport. This consideration had to be weighed by Reserve, too. But the situation at Babbitt was somewhat different, at least in the eyes of Reserve officials. The company ruled out the Babbitt location for three essential reasons: first, there appeared to be inadequate water available to satisfy the huge demands of the beneficiation process; second, land near the Babbitt site was relatively flat and would have required tremendous acreage for tailing ponds; and third, economics. The company found that conveying unprocessed ore 47 miles by rail to Silver Bay and disposing of tailings in Lake Superior would be less costly than processing at the Babbitt site. Since economic considerations held higher priorities than environmental considerations in the 1940s, Reserve's proposal seemed acceptable and in the best interest not only of the company but of the region and the state, as well.

However, more than two decades later, after the release of the "Stoddard Report" in January 1969, Reserve recognized that environmentalists, regulatory agencies, and the public would soon press for an alternative to the density current tailings disposal concept. Accordingly, in April 1969, *prior to* the beginning of the "Federal Enforcement Conference," the company announced the formation of an engineering task force to consider alternative methods for tailings disposal. This task force consisted of five engineering consulting firms [1] whose professional competence and integrity were widely recognized. The task force produced 19 separate proposals ranging in concept from modified in-lake disposal to complete onland disposal in the Lax Lake area, the disposal area then advocated by environmentalists.

At the second executive session of the "Federal Enforcement Conference" in August 1970, the company's fears were realized. Reserve was instructed to "provide a specific method for abating its discharge to Lake Superior, which will meet state and federal requirements . . . by December 1, 1970." Later in state court in mid-December 1970, Judge Eckman concluded that "continuance of the present method of discharge for any substantial period of time . . . is intolerable and that substantial modifications must be put into effect." The judge ordered that "any modification must insure the flocculation of the fine tailings and the deposit of all the tailings by conduit to the floor of the Great Trough, where they will remain, eliminating thereby their dispersion to other parts of Lake Superior. . . ." (3)

Responsively, Reserve turned to its engineering staff, which, with the guidance provided by the task force proposals, developed an alternative disposal plan. In January 1971, the company submitted its "Plan to Modify Tailings Discharge System" to the conferees of the "Federal Enforcement Conference" for consideration and approval. This new plan, referred to as the *underwater reef* or *deep pipe* plan, would concentrate tailings to a thick slurry by mammoth thickeners and hydroseparators.

---

[1] Task force member firms: The Bechtel Corporation; Arthur D. Little, Inc.; Trygve Hoff and Associates; Engineering Science Inc.; and Parsons-Jurden Corporation.

The slurry would then be discharged through 14 eight-inch pipes to a water depth of approximately 150 feet, i.e., below the thermocline. This would tend to trap all solids in the poorly mixed deep waters of the lake. To minimize the loss of fine particles in overflow waters from the thickeners, flocculents were to be added. Clear water would then be returned to the lake. Implementation of the plan at that time would have cost an estimated $14 million. A description of this plan is given in Appendix B.

Reserve, committed to alter its disposal system, claimed several advantages for this plan:

1 / no tailings would be carried away by surface currents,

2 / the turbidity caused by tailings in surface waters would be reduced,

3 / the incidence of the green water phenomenon resulting from tailings would be substantially reduced, and

4 / the tailings solids would settle in the designated discharge zone or in its immediate vicinity.

After a lengthy review procedure in the spring of 1971, the federal enforcement conferees rejected Reserve's deep pipe plan, holding that it failed to meet all state and federal requirements. The conferees contended:

1 / There would be little or no reduction in dissolved solids entering the lake,

2 / taconite solids on or near the bottom could still be brought to the surface by upwelling action in the lake, and

3 / the use of chemical flocculents could endanger aquatic life.

Actually, the rejection by the conferees of Reserve's deep pipe plan had little significance—for the new executive director of the Minnesota Pollution Control Agency, Grant Merritt, and the new Minnesota governor, Wendell Anderson, had announced that no in-lake alternatives would be acceptable.

Subsequently, EPA Administrator William Ruckelshaus notified Reserve President Edward Furness that the company was in violation of state and federal water quality standards and that the company had 180 days to submit an acceptable disposal plan or face action by the EPA in accordance with Section 10(g) of the Federal Water Pollution Control Act.

Shortly thereafter the EPA itself engaged the services of Roy F. Weston, Inc. This engineering firm was asked to develop conceptual methods for treating and disposing of taconite tailings and to determine the feasibility of such alternatives. The Weston firm, one of the more prestigious environmental engineering firms in the nation, introduced the study it produced with the qualifying statement:

> Roy F. Weston, Inc., believes that the approach to this problem should be as though we were retained by the industry to develop the most economical and feasible alternative for waste water treatment and disposal consistent with the 'conference' objective for protecting the environment. (36)

The firm's final report, in October 1971, laid out five alternative plans. Two alternatives called for total onland disposal of tailings in the Lax Lake area. These had one shortcoming in common, however—the absence of a system for water recycling. The other three alternatives, to the dismay of the EPA and MPCA, involved a combination of onland and in-lake disposal. Weston estimated that the total onland alternative—if executed at that time—would require a capital investment of nearly $75 million and an annual operating cost of over $7 million.

Three years earlier, in 1968, the Bureau of Mines (BOM) had suggested disposal of tailings directly into Lax Lake as an alternative to continued disposal in Lake Superior. The cost estimate for this alternative, acknowledged by the BOM as incomplete, was $7.5 million for initial investment and $3.3 million in annual operating cost. The BOM cautioned in its report that onland tailings disposal could be fraught with several environmental problems. The Weston plan addressed one of these—it would have spared Lax Lake by creating an additional dam upstream from the lake.

The state was also preparing for a confrontation with Reserve in federal court. The Minnesota Department of Natural Resources (DNR), on its own, investigated alternative land disposal sites from Silver Bay to Babbitt. The DNR found the most promising and feasible site to be in the Lax Lake area, just below the site designated by the Weston firm.

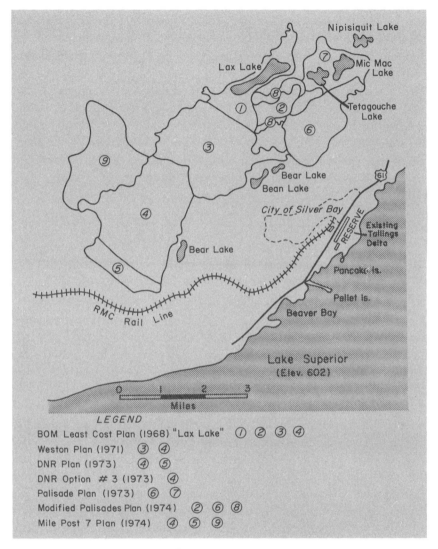

FIGURE 15   Alternative onland disposal sites.

As the federal trial got under way in mid-1973 and the public health issue surfaced, it became abundantly clear to all observers, including Reserve, that all in-lake alternatives were doomed. The company not only had lost its battle to remain in the lake, but it also had forfeited earlier opportunities to go onland near Silver Bay where the cost would have been much less.

The EPA, apparently dissatisfied with the Weston proposals, retained another consulting firm, International Engineering Company (IECO), to evaluate the feasibility of moving Reserve's beneficiating facilities up to Babbitt and disposing of tailings near the mine site. Reserve challenged the feasibility of IECO's so-called Babbitt (or Milepost 42) Plan, noting that the cost of constructing the new tailings facility at Babbitt would be dwarfed by the cost of building a new concentrating facility and employee accommodations. Reserve estimated that such a move would cost $574 million.

Faced with the spectre of having to move up to Babbitt, Reserve accelerated its effort to develop a more desirable onland alternative. The company's new proposal, the Palisades Plan introduced in April 1974, called for the construction of an impoundment in the Palisades basin, adjacent to Silver Bay, at an estimated cost of $172 million. This proposal represented a dramatic shift in the company's position regarding the economic feasibility of onland disposal and the potential environmental damage associated with such plans. Earlier Reserve had ruled out this site because of potential danger to lakeshore residents should the dam collapse.[2] Also, the company previously had cautioned —as had others—that onland disposal could lead to dust problems and possible ground and surface water contamination. Now faced with onland disposal as the inevitable alternate to cessation of operations at Silver Bay, Reserve found feasible ways to overcome these environmental and safety hazards. Some strings were attached to Reserve's Palisades offer, however. The company needed permits from all appropriate agencies assuring use of the Palisades site throughout the life of the mining operation. It also requested some form of federal government financial assistance for construction of the disposal facilities.

Though this proposal might have been enthusiastically accepted earlier, now the state soundly rejected it. The conditions, the state contended, were unrealistic, if not illegal, and the plan was environmentally unacceptable. The state evaluated this plan along with the Babbitt plan and those suggested by Weston and its own staff, using a comparative appraisal system which essentially gave equal weight to such factors as water systems, vegetation, habitat, unique natural

---

[2] There was reason for concern. A disaster of this type occurred on February 26, 1972, in the Buffalo Creek Valley of West Virginia. Several dams constructed of coal mining residue collapsed and released more than 175 million gallons of water and coal mine refuse on downstream residents. Result—118 people killed, seven missing, and 500 homes destroyed or badly damaged.

features, topography, recreation, unique cultural features, visual analysis, noise, transportation and urban systems, and ownership. Based upon this evaluation, the Palisades Plan was found to be the least desirable.

In late June, Reserve produced its second proposal, in essence the Palisades Plan with a few modifications. The company found a way to save the lakes in the Palisades basin and agreed to drop all previous conditions. The company warned that some discharge to Lake Superior would be necessary during the construction phase, however.

Governor Anderson was unenthusiastic about this plan also. He reiterated that the state's first choice, also the first choice of the environmentalists, was up near the Babbitt mine site. The DNR had given high environmental grades to two sites near Babbitt. IECO, the government's consultants, suggested that Reserve not relocate its entire beneficiation plant at Babbitt, but rather only the concentration stages. The pelleting phase would be left at Silver Bay. This, the consultants contended, would significantly reduce the overall cost of relocation.

On August 3, Lord, responding to the appeals court remand, put the final ax to the modified Palisades Plan. Also in August, the state strategically prepared to designate the north shore as an "environmentally critical" area. Such a designation by the state's Environmental Quality Council (EQC) prohibited any economic development that endangered natural resources. The EQC, not without forethought, sought to establish this critical zone to include a band extending 12 miles inland from the shore of Lake Superior from Duluth northward to the Canadian border. This zone would have included not only the Palisades area, but also the coveted Lax Lake area. Because this strategy would have further complicated the legal due process, the court of appeals urged full consideration of the Lax Lake area for the discharge basin.

It was obvious to all parties that the Lax Lake area was the logical site for compromise. Environmentalists had at one time demanded it. Dale Olsen, an Izaak Walton League representative, had stated at the "Federal Enforcement Conference" in January 1971, "We would prefer onland [disposal] even if its means filling a lake, whether it be Lax or some other inland lake. This is a state with—how many thousands do we have?" Merritt, then chairman of MECCA, was on record as at the same conference stating, "Now, by adopting onshore disposal and moving the tailings back to a stilling basin that was proposed by the Stoddard Report . . . we aren't going to destroy the ecology of Lax Lake. But suppose we did destroy the Lax Lake area or a portion of Lax Lake? There are a number of Lax Lakes in this state and in this nation, but there is only one Lake Superior. . . ." After becoming executive director of the Minnesota Pollution Control Agency and after Reserve agreed to discontinue in-lake disposal, Merritt retreated from this position and led the forces seeking to push Reserve back up to Babbitt.[3]

Recall the EPA's Weston study also recommended the Lax Lake area as a possible onland disposal location, and the DNR had previously recognized it as the best location in the Silver Bay area. Even Governor Anderson had at one time recommended this location for tailings disposal. And Reserve had also found the Lax Lake area to be the most promising site of all studied. Its engineering task force had suggested this area as early as 1970.

From that time through mid-1970, however, Reserve had expressed an unwillingness to seriously consider onland disposal in the Lax Lake area, arguing that a tailings impoundment would affect wildlife in the area, might possibly contaminate ground water, and that dam construction in the swampy terrain surrounding Lax Lake would be difficult and costly.

After the Palisades Plan was shot down by Lord and the state in August 1974, Reserve resumed its earlier favorable consideration of the Lax Lake area and agreed to restudy the site. Lord made clear that he suspected that Lax Lake was what Reserve was after all along. Of course, the same charge could have been made against the state in regard to its persistent and unrealistic demands for plant relocation at the Babbitt site.

On August 16, Governor Anderson acknowledged the Lax Lake area, subject to three conditions. Nine days later, Reserve accepted the governor's offer. By mid-November, Reserve's plans for disposal at the Milepost 7, or Lax Lake area, site were completed and submitted to the state for consideration along with a formal permit application.

The Milepost 7 option proposed by Reserve called for the development of a 25-square-mile area for tailings disposal and related operations in the Lax Lake area, approximately seven miles southwest of Silver Bay. The tailings impoundment would require about nine square miles, and Lax Lake itself would be protected from tailings con-

---

[3] An environmental coalition of 19 state environmental groups (including the Izaak Walton League of America and MECCA, which at one time had advocated the Lax Lake site) alleged in January 1975 that use of the Lax Lake site would "irrevocably destroy" natural resources and could pollute both nearby Lake Superior and the air. (See Reference 37.)

tamination by a barrier dike. Coarse solids would be used for dike construction and the smaller particles would be discharged into the resulting basin. After some of the particles had settled out, water from the tailings basin would be recirculated through the beneficiation process.

Some modification of the beneficiation process would be required, most notably the addition of dry cobbing.[4] Though necessary to facilitate onland disposal of tailings, this added process step would also enhance the quality and value of the pellet product, something Reserve had sought for a long time. Consequently, a portion of the cost incurred for tailings disposal would be recovered through product improvement. Coarse waste solids would be transported 16 miles by conveyor and rail to a three-square-miles storage site. The finer tailings would be pumped as a slurry through a 24-inch pipeline to the tailings basin.

The complete conversion from in-lake disposal to onland disposal would take an estimated 36 months. Total capital investment for the tailings disposal facilities was estimated at $243 million. The company agreed to reforest and landscape the dikes, dams, and other fill areas. Upland runoff would be diverted around the tailings basin by two large interceptor channels.

But the state rejected the Milepost 7 permit request on December 7. This action by the state both surprised and angered the appellate judges, who were hopeful of a rapid settlement on site selection. The state complained that Reserve's proposal did not fully comply with the governor's environmental and engineering conditions. The state left the door open, however, for further negotiations, and asked Reserve to provide additional information. During this same period the state also directed Reserve to provide impact data on other possible sites en route back to Babbitt.

In late December, Reserve provided the additional information requested by the state. The company gave assurances that the tailings dams would be built to "exceed conventional factors of safety"; that revegetation of the tailings site would begin in three years and continue throughout the life of the operation; that the 40-year limit in mining activity could be written into the permit; and that no other feasible alternative existed for tailings disposal. The commissioner of the Minnesota Department of National Resources, Robert Herbst, appeared satisfied with the Reserve proposal in light of the added assurances. He

---

[4] Dry cobbing: Magnetic separation of iron-bearing particles introduced into the process.

stated: "They're going about it in a responsible manner and they have supplied a considerable amount of materials on questions we raised." (38)

In mid-January, 1975, Governor Anderson was "cautiously optimistic" that the disposal site issue could be settled. He said, "Not all items at issue were resolved. But I am convinced that Reserve desires to make this site a workable alternative to Lake Superior for disposal of tailings." (39)

Shortly after the governor's conciliatory pronouncement, Byron Starns, Minnesota's chief deputy attorney general, informed the court of appeals that the governor's January 15 remarks were speculative and that the governor had since switched his stand. Now, Governor Anderson, without further explanation, informed the press on January 29 that talks with Reserve were getting "nowhere." He contended that the company "has not presently supplied adequate information as requested by the state of Minnesota [and] Reserve said it does not intend to furnish additional information in numerous problem areas." (40) It was also reported on this date that the *state of Wisconsin* was somehow "unalterably opposed" to Reserve's *onland* disposal plan *in Minnesota*.

MPCA director Merritt attempted to explain the breakdown in negotiations, noting that there were "18 problem areas" with the Milepost 7 proposal and that Reserve was unwilling to provide information to overcome them. One of Merritt's main objections was that Reserve had not adequately demonstrated that "there is no alternative to Lax Lake."

Immediately following the court of appeals decree on March 14, 1975, and on Lord's instructions, Minnesota announced its "accelerated schedule" for processing the Reserve permit application. The schedule, which was a factor in the circuit court's reprimand of Lord, included the following key deadlines:

— A directive by mid-April to the EQC (Environmental Quality Council) to begin preparation of the environmental impact statement.

— Drafting by August 12 of a statement that identifies "all prudent and feasible alternatives for tailings dump sites potentially acceptable to the state."

— Public hearings on the draft statement by September 30.

— Submission of a final statement to the EQC by October 30.

— Completion of the statements' review by the EQC by November
30.

The state explained that if all procedures, including the additional studies Merritt wanted, were conducted efficiently and without
undue delay, permits could be granted by early 1976, and Reserve could
begin construction that spring, before the 12-month court of appeals
time extension expired.

PART IV

SOCIETAL IMPLICATIONS

The *Reserve* case was a landmark in environmental and public health law. It has left in its wake many serious implications to society.

Chapter 17

Risk of the
Unknown

We do not think that a bare risk of the unknown can amount
to proof in this case—*U.S. Circuit Court of Appeals in its
May 15, 1974, opinion on the Reserve case* (8)

A few weeks earlier, District Court Judge Lord acknowledged the absence
of proof regarding the public health significance of asbestos fibers in
drinking water, but, in the words of the court of appeals, "resolve[d] all
doubts in favor of health safety. . . ."

Reserve's opponents in the case had charged that any risk regardless of magnitude was totally unacceptable and superseded any
consideration of economics, jobs, and/or the ecological impact of tailings
disposal on the terrestrial environment. Such demands for absolute elimi-

nation rather than minimization of risk can be defended only on narrow, albeit appealing, humanitarian grounds.

Most citizens would agree that the elimination of carcinogens from the environment would be a desirable goal. When more facts are gathered and more experience gained, however, it may be that this goal is tantamount to the physically impossible goal of zero environmental pollution.

Dr. Selikoff, while testifying on toxic chemicals before a congressional sub-committee in 1973, stated that "we live in a sea of carcinogens". (41) Dr. Brown, the court-appointed medical witness, testified during the trial that there are many known human carcinogens in our environment including coal tar, benzidine, tobacco, vinyl chloride, X-rays, and sunshine. Brown's list just scratches the surface of known carcinogenic and toxic substances in the environment, most added by the activities of man.

Surely man's quest for a high standard of living has resulted in the production of literally thousands of synthetic substances that ostensibly enhance the well-being of society. Unfortunately, many of these non-natural substances, including fibers, pesticides, cosmetics, drugs, detergents, and countless others, generally are resistant to rapid assimilation in natural sinks or repositories of residue. Some are, in fact, deleterious to ecological systems and public health. But before these chemicals are condemned and removed from the marketplace, and hence the environment, their relative benefits should be weighed against associated risks.

The cost-risk benefit analysis of toxic substances in wastewaters and natural systems now is receiving considerable attention. Two research scientists for the Environmental Protection Agency, Dr. Dennis Tihansky and Dr. Harold Kibby, recently reported

> As a result of rapid technological changes and industrial development, a large and increasing number of toxic and hazardous substances enters the environment or appears in consumer products each year. Because so many of these elements are generated without regulations . . . man and nature have been involuntarily exposed to their effects. Some toxic substances cause known potential hazards to human health or ecological habitats, but the majority is not understood and thus introduces uncertain risks to the environment.

They continued

> There is . . . a need for the development of methods to
> assess the cost-risk-benefit trade-offs of alternative decisions.
> [And further] Almost every decision involves elements of risk
> in addition to benefits, and their assessment is often subjective
> and based on uncertainties . . . in the protection of health
> and safety, the public is demanding more than ever that strong
> legislation be enacted . . . legislators are confronted with the
> difficult evaluation of risks and damages [both immediate and
> probable] and balancing them against social benefits of using
> toxic substances. (42)

The President's Science Advisory Committee also pointed out
the problem in a 1973 report entitled, "Chemicals and Health." (43) It
noted that the absence of quantitative information is likely to bias regulation toward the *overprotection of health and ecology*. Further, the committee acknowledged that, while risk avoidance is a necessary consideration, its value to society should be contrasted with that of products
generating or containing toxic elements. The committee also noted,
"Regulatory decisions in the name of protection of health and environmental integrity often have expensive consequences" and "Errors in
regulatory judgments can be extraordinarily expensive, in human and
monetary terms." The committee concluded: *"We must always live with
some risks both because nature forever confronts us with hazards and
also because the contribution of chemicals to human welfare are so
vital."*[1]

There are many excellent examples of substances that are both
beneficial and deleterious to public health.

The Reserve controversy focused national and international attention on the public health significance of one—asbestos. For years,
asbestos has been used in a multitude of ways to protect the health and
welfare of society. These life-saving uses have included filtration of
beverages for purification and disease control; filtration of heat-labile
medicinals; asbestos-cement pipes for conveying potable water and other
fluids (more than 200,000 miles of this pipe in the U.S.); asbestos brake
linings; fire-proofing for clothing, buildings, automobiles, etc; and many
others. Since all of these uses tend to contribute a carcinogen, asbestos,

---

[1] Emphasis added by author.

to the environment, should it be completely withdrawn from use? A cost-risk-benefit analysis similar to that proposed by Tihansky and Kibby may well show that the benefits of asbestos to human health and well-being far outweigh the potential health problems that may arise. Such an analysis should have been attempted more thoroughly in the Reserve case.

The concentration of asbestiform fibers in the Duluth water supply was vigorously contested during the federal district court trial. The issue was compounded by conflicting and inconsistent data. Dr. Cook of the EPA reported a range of values from 1–30 million fibers per liter. (*44*) Other investigators found the concentration to be less than 1 million per liter. The *Los Angeles Times,* in June 1974, reported that EPA scientists had found asbestos fibers in the water supplies of many major cities across the nation. The San Francisco water supply was reported to have over 2 million fibers per liter, more than the number originally reported for Duluth water. Since these counts were made with an optical microscope rather than an electron microscope, EPA scientists later questioned and attempted to discredit the results. In December 1974, EPA scientists published a report entitled "Asbestos Analysis by Electron Microscope."(*45*) The asbestos concentration in potable water was reported for 26 cities; however, the report failed to identify the cities involved. But of the 26 cities, 14 showed either amphibole or chrysotile fibers (or both) in their water supplies; three cities had a count of 1 million or more fibers per liter.

In March 1974, Dr. Brown advised members of the National Cancer Advisory Board (which he chaired) that asbestos fibers have been found in air, beer, wine, and ginger ale in larger concentrations than in the water at Duluth. He also noted that one of the largest cities in the country (presumably San Francisco) contained a thousand times more fibers than Duluth.(*46*)

Pesticides provide another good example of a family of substances synthesized by man to promote the health and well-being of society. They improve crop yields and are used world-wide to eradicate mosquitoes, flies, and other carriers of disease. In these instances, the use of pesticides can be credited with saving countless thousands of lives. These substances are, by definition and need, toxic and not just to harmful organisms. Unfortunately, lack of adequate controls in pesticide usage in past years resulted in some environmental and public health problems. DDT and some other chlorinated pesticides have also been shown to be *potential* human carcinogens. For these reasons, the Environmental Protection Agency banned, with a few exceptions, the use of DDT and certain other pesticides. A careful analysis of cost-risk-benefit, such as that proposed by EPA's own scientists Tihansky and Kibby, might show restricted and carefully controlled use of these pesticides to be in the overall best interest of society. In some isolated instances, such as with the tussock moth problem in Oregon, the EPA has recognized cost-benefit tradeoffs and has granted temporary variances to their ban policy.

A few years ago, Sri Lanka (formerly Ceylon), off the southern coast of India, attempted to follow America's example and cut back or discontinued the use of chlorinated pesticides like DDT. It soon found, however, that alternatives such as organophosphates were ineffective for mosquito control. As the incidence of malaria began to rise, Sri Lanka quickly returned to the use of DDT. (47) It was further found that the organophosphates, when improperly used, were considerably more hazardous to human health.

Chlorine is another example of a substance used by man to protect public health. This chemical has been used in the United States since 1908 to disinfect drinking water supplies and in more recent years to disinfect domestic waste discharges. Chlorine can be credited with preventing the spread of water-borne diseases and with saving millions of lives in this nation and throughout the world. Yet there appear to be serious public health problems associated with chlorine also. Recently, EPA scientists have found that chlorine can react with substances in water to form chloroform, chlorinated derivatives, and other substances that are known carcinogens. Will chlorination be discontinued because it produces known (not potential) carcinogens?

Cancer-causing substances are not just restricted to asbestos fibers and synthetic chemicals. Many other substances in popular use by society have also been associated with cancer. Dr. James E. Enstrom, of the University of California School of Public Health, has reported that *beer* drinkers may suffer intestinal cancer more frequently than those who abstain from the brew. (48) His study did not prove that cancer is caused by beer consumption but rather that a strong correlation was found between beer consumption and cancer of the large intestine and rectum of both males and females.

Eating *red meats* has also been associated with increased incidence of cancer. For a number of years, cattle have been fed the synthetic hormone diethylstilbestrol, or DES, to stimulate growth and thus provide more and better beef. This same hormone, sometimes used as a human medicine, has been shown to cause cancer in laboratory animals. Another chemical (USDA approved) additive, sodium nitrite, has been used behind the meat counter for nearly half a century to impart a fresh, red color to hot dogs and other processed meats. Animal experiments around the world have shown conclusively that nitrites can induce cancer. (49)

Of course the classic popular cause of cancer is *cigarette smoking*. Dr. George P. Rosemond, president of the American Cancer Society, told the ACS Science Writers Seminar in March 1975, that in the next 10 years lung cancer alone, if present rates continue to increase, will cost about 1 million lives. He went on to explain that "lung cancer, the one major cancer we know the cause of and could reduce by about 80 percent by preventative measures, is the site that statistically keeps cancer death rates increasing. Without lung cancer, cancer death rates show a steady decline over the years." He called cigarettes "the major carcinogenic threat of our modern world."(50)

Two U.S. senators, Nelson of Wisconsin and Hart of Michigan, are legislatively attempting to halt perils to health. They have introduced a bill in Congress that attacks industrial discharges but sidesteps critical health problems like cigarette smoking. Motivation for this bill can be directly linked to frustrations these two senators experienced during the Reserve controversy. Both were outspoken critics of Reserve since the early days of the controversy and felt that existing laws were inadequate to deal with such cases. So on August 19, 1974, they sponsored an amendment to a solid waste bill (S 1104) introduced earlier by Hart. According to Nelson,

> The purpose of this amendment is to protect individuals threatened by various kinds of conduct which cause very serious potential health hazards. It would come under the category of environmental health legislation.

Also,

> In these highly urgent circumstances the amendment would *shift the burden of proof to the party creating the grave risk* [2] to health and require that party to prove either that *no* [2] threat to health exists, that the threat is negligible or that other considerations outweigh the health threat.

Several serious implications and shortcomings characterize this proposed amendment. Current legislation charges the government with

[2] Emphasis provided by author.

proving that a serious health hazard *does* exist. This is in accord with the "innocent until proven guilty" dictum of law. Although shifting the burden of proof may seem to be a relatively simple legislative maneuver, the concept will prove in application to be ineffective and totally unworkable.

Proving that a substance *is* a health hazard is less difficult by several orders of magnitude than *proving* that a substance constitutes *no* health hazard, i.e., proving a negative. In the first instance, an elaboration of toxicity or other deleterious response to a test organism in a carefully controlled laboratory experiment can be accepted as evidence of a possible health hazard. Failure to observe toxicity, i.e., a negative finding, cannot be interpreted as proof of no health hazard, because it could be argued that the test conditions were not proper, or different test organisms should have been used, or different responses should have been observed, or the effect is likely chronic rather than acute and would be observable only after years rather than hours of exposure. During the *Reserve* trial, Lord threw out numerous studies proffered by Reserve's witnesses, charging that negative findings were invalid. He even discredited the court's own tissue study when it yielded only negative results. EPA's Dr. Cook, one of the government's stalwart technical witnesses, cited Dr. Gross's study as a prime example of *how negative results must not be considered as positive results.* (51)

Shifting the burden of proof to the discharger presents still other problems. The public, environmental groups, the press, and the court generally accept at face value findings reported by government scientists and their expert witnesses. Yet these same groups often are reluctant to accept reports submitted by industry even if the work is by qualified and recognized experts. This was demonstrated all too often in the Reserve case in the Federal District Court. Because of this credibility gap, scientific proof developed by or sponsored by industry labors under a cloud, and is often given little weight. How then could industry prove its process or product innocent?

Still another factor mitigating against the success of the seemingly simple Hart-Nelson shift in burden of proof is the necessity of using animal studies to prove potential health hazards where it is suspected rather than manifested in humans. Lord, in his May 11, 1974, memorandum, placed heavy emphasis on this:

. . . there are inherent problems in relating the results in animal studies to the human experience. Some substances

cause cancer in man which, when given to animals, induce
little or no response.

The Hart-Nelson amendment, like other simplistic solutions, is
fraught with technical shortcomings and obvious bias against dischargers
—in this instance, the Reserve Mining Company. It represents yet another
example of a congressional attempt to disregard scientific possibility and
to legislate the impossible. If adopted, the amendment would complicate,
not clarify, the legal process in dealing with environmental and public
health issues. Fortunately, the amendment failed to be enacted by the
93rd Congress. Future Congresses may recognize its shallow base and
give it no support.

This does not suggest a relaxation of vigilance. Indeed, there
can be no excess of intelligent, objective caution. For with the growing
number of health hazards in our environment, living itself has become
our most dangerous occupation. Yet it will become increasingly difficult
for most Americans to accept a lifestyle that requires meatless meals;
beerless busts; super-charcoal filtered (and tasteless) water; abstention
from smoking; insect infestation of the home, the farm, and the forest;
and a return to horse and buggy transportation. All of these are the
"safe" alternatives to known and suspected health hazards.

Even sex may have to be banned to be completely safe! Dr.
Ellen Borenfreund of the Sloan-Kettering Institute recently told the
American Cancer Society's "Science Writers' Seminar"(52) that sperm
may play a key role in cervical cancer in women and prostate cancer in
men. She explained that it has long been known that eunuchs (castrated
males) have a low rate of prostate cancer and nuns seldom develop
cervical cancer.

But while life is revealed to be growing more dangerous with
each passing day, the average life span of Americans has increased
nearly 20 years since 1900. Perhaps the benefits of our industrialized
society—in health effects—outweigh some of the inherent concomitant
risks. Before these benefits are wiped out by poorly conceived legislation
and overly conservative court rulings, we had better develop effective
tools for assessing cost-risk-benefit so that they may be used for rational
decision-making.

Chapter 18

Reserve
in Perspective

THE DECISION

Litigation of the Reserve case may have come to an end, but decisions rendered in this long-drawn-out and bitterly contested court battle must now be thoughtfully weighed by responsible society. Consider the charges against Reserve: grossly polluting Lake Superior and creating a serious hazard to public health. Were either of these charges proved?

In state court in 1970, Judge C. Luther Eckman found that gross pollution was not occurring. Later, in Judge Lord's federal district court, pollution charges were never fully litigated. Though Reserve's daily discharge of 67,000 tons of tailings solids into Lake Superior definitely has some quantifiable effect on water quality, significant or material pollution has not been proved by the government in a court of law.

The alleged public health hazard, though obviously a potential problem and one to be avoided if a technically and economically feasible alternative exists, was never proved to be an *actual* hazard to north shore residents. However, the wisdom of caution in using an alternative tailings disposal system cannot be contested on humanitarian grounds.

ONLAND DISPOSAL

The court decision forcing onland disposal of tailings, though not popular with Reserve, was inevitable and was not unexpected by the company. For back in 1969, during the federal enforcement conference, environmentalists argued uncompromisingly for onland disposal. Later, in 1971, Governor Anderson, who had campaigned vigorously on the Reserve issue, called for onland disposal as the only acceptable alternative. When the governor appointed Reserve's foremost antagonist, Grant Merritt, as head of the state's pollution control agency, the handwriting was on the wall.

But what have Minnesotans bought with onland disposal? Technical experts, including several responsible government officials, wisely cautioned that onland disposal would not be without problems and risks. It was not until after the final court verdict was pronounced and both sides intensified negotiations for a mutually satisfactory onland disposal site that many of these problems and risks became apparent to "onland" advocates. It became clear that a fail-safe, problem-free disposal system was not to be had.

This author is concerned about another impact, inadequately weighed in the decision to force onland disposal. This concerns the vast amounts of additional energy that will be required to prepare and transport all of the tailings to a land storage site 600 feet above and 7 miles distant from the beneficiating plant. Then considering that environmental degradation and public health effects are inevitably associated with energy production and utilization, one should evaluate whether the more energy intensive onland disposal system is justified in view of the uncertain extent of the problems to be corrected. In other words, are we simply transferring some of the alleged pollution and public health problems of the Minnesota north shore to the coal fields of Montana or elsewhere?

CONFLICTS WITH NATURAL LAW

This case highlights conflicts between unalterable laws of nature and the less tenable laws of society. Many participants in the Reserve case were unable to comprehend or were unwilling to reconcile these conflicts.

One must accept the precept of natural law that all systems, including industrial systems and living systems, generate residues. And these residues must come to rest in some natural repository, i.e., on land or in a body of water. For the natural law "matter cannot be destroyed" cannot be altered or amended by the whims or actions of man.

Therefore, if society demands consumer goods that require a ton of iron for manufacture, then two tons of tailings must be assigned by society to some land or water repository. It follows that the only way to reduce the generation of residue, and hence pollution, is for society to attenuate consumer demands. Such action would also result in resource and energy conservation. But is the nation ready for economic contraction with all that that portends in fewer jobs, less tax revenue, and fewer conveniences?

Regrettably treatment technology is not a panacea for solving pollution problems. Treatment processes can only concentrate or disperse residues and direct their movement into a natural repository. They cannot destroy residue. Furthermore, *all technology*, including pollution abatement technology, requires the input of pollution-causing energy and often treatment chemicals as well.

ENVIRONMENTAL COURT

The Reserve controversy centered around numerous highly technical pollution and public health issues. Yet the controversy was judged in a court of law by persons without technical training or experience. In state court, Judge Eckman, an attorney by training, acknowledged that the court was "completely lacking in personal expertise . . . [and was] in the impossible position of being required to analyze, weigh and choose between controversial points of view." Higher courts found themselves in a similar position. Judge Lord evidenced his lack of personal expertise on medical questions when he appointed Dr. Brown and Dr. Pooley as impartial experts to advise the court. Regrettably,

Lord often refused to be guided by counsel from his experts and rendered opinions unsupported by scientific fact.

Solution or reconciliation of technical issues in a court of law labors under another serious shortcoming, i.e., the adversary protocol. Expert witnesses are sworn to tell the "whole truth" but are subsequently restricted in testimony to direct response to questions from counsel. Consequently, technical issues are often not explored fully and in perspective. Technical witnesses such as scientists, medical doctors, and engineers, who are or should be dedicated to the search for and expression of scientific truth, are denied the opportunity for full expression of fact and views and are forced to become aligned with parties to the case.

Perhaps a more equitable and effective means of dealing with technical environmental questions would be an environmental court comprised of a panel of highly qualified experts from diverse but pertinent specialties, including the humanistic sciences. An environmental court decision could be appealed to a court of law. However, the law court would be able to rely upon the environmental court's assessment of the technical issues in determining the validity of the appeal.

JUDGMENT RESERVED

Through 1968 the Reserve Mining Company enjoyed amicable rapport with the Minnesota Pollution Control Agency, state politicians, and most Minnesotans. Then the pollution and public health allegations, whether real or imagined, created bitter resentment toward company activities. Regrettably, this emotional trauma carried over into the courtroom where only the issues should have been considered. After reviewing the issues and testimony in the case, one must wonder whether Lord's decisions were based more on emotionalism than on sound scientific fact and legal findings.

The United States Circuit Court of Appeals evidenced a more objective and less emotional approach to the case, stating "to us there are neither heroes nor villains among the present participants in this law suit, nor among their predecessors in government, business and society who were once allies in encouraging and creating a taconite industry in northern Minnesota."

Neither were there winners or losers except perhaps the participants from the legal and technical professions who garnered many millions of dollars in fees and salaries. Environmentalists won their argument to stop the discharge of tailings into Lake Superior, but lost in their efforts to obtain immediate cessation of in-lake disposal. Politicians in opposition to Reserve might try to claim total victory. However, they, too, were frustrated by some of the Circuit Court of Appeals rulings. Reserve won its battle to continue operations but lost its preferred tailings disposal sites in Lake Superior and subsequently onland at Palisades. Whether the public won or lost remains obscure, at least for the present. Water quality in Lake Superior *may* improve when the tailings discharge ceases. However, damage to the terrestrial environment and ecology is inevitable. The public will very likely pay more for iron-containing consumer goods, since the costs for environmental protection are ultimately passed on by industry, agriculture, and other producers to the consuming public.

The crux of the Reserve controversy is whether the risk of an unknown, but possible, hazard to public health and a marginal water pollution problem justify the enormous expenditures of energy, resources, and dollars by Reserve and ultimately by society. Though a decision has been rendered, final judgment must be reserved.

The Scales of Justice

In June 1974 the 8th Circuit Court of Appeals stated "To us there are neither heroes nor villains among the present participants in this law suit, nor among their predecessors in government, business, and society who were once allies in encouraging and creating a taconite industry in northern Minnesota." Some 18 months later, however, on January 6, 1976,* the same appellate court declared that "The record demonstrates overt acts by the district judge [Judge Miles Lord] reflecting great bias against Reserve Mining Company and substantial disregard for the mandate of this court."

* Followed completion of this manuscript. Final draft was submitted to the publisher December 1, 1975.

The court of appeals continued in its January 6 order,

> Judge Lord seems to have shed the robe of the judge and to
> have assumed the mantle of the advocate. The court thus be-
> comes a lawyer, witness and judge in the same proceeding,
> and abandons the greatest virtue of a fair and conscientious
> judge—impartiality.

The court of appeals then ordered Judge Lord removed from the
Reserve case, stating, ". . . we order corrective actions *sua sponte*," and
"We request that the remaining issues be assigned to a new judge or the
Chief Judge himself, if he chooses."

Immediately following the issuance of this order, U.S. District
Judge Edward Devitt, Chief Judge for the district of Minnesota, elected
to assume responsibility himself for the Reserve Mining case.

This drastic and decisive action of the court of appeals was not a
total surprise to parties in the case. Back in mid-March of 1974, the court
of appeals ruled that Reserve Mining Company's discharges constituted
a potential health threat and should be abated as soon as practicable.
The appellate court remanded the case back to Lord to insure that their
decree was fully carried out. Instead, Lord disregarded the higher court
order and assumed an administrative and advocate role. This action led
to a stinging reprimand from the court of appeals on April 8, 1975.

Undeterred by the earlier reprimand, Lord continued to interfere
beyond his decreed authority. One such incident occurred in mid-
November of 1975 when he conducted hearings to assess damages against
Reserve. On November 14, without providing Reserve adequate notice
or the opportunity to be heard, Lord ruled,

> Reserve Mining Company, as of Monday morning at 10:00
> o'clock, shall hand to the City Treasurer of the City of Duluth,
> a check in the amount of $100,000. And there will be no stay on
> that. This is a firm and final order. That may be appealed, but I
> do not certify it for appeal because I am not at all in doubt of
> its propriety.

Lord continued,

> I have dispensed with the usual adversary proceedings here,

because I simply do not have time to spend, as I did, nine months in hearing, six months of which was wasted by what I find now, and did find in my opinions, to be misrepresentations by Reserve Mining Company.

Reserve did appeal this order for deposit of $100,000 on December 18, 1975. Reserve further sought in its petition "to recuse the district judge from further proceedings in this case."

Upon review of the record of Judge Lord's actions the court of appeals found,

Ordinarily, when unfair judicial procedures result in a denial of due process, this court could simply find error, reverse and remand the matter. Recusal would be altogether inappropriate. However, the record in this case demonstrates more serious problems. The denial of fair procedures here was due not to good faith mistakes of judgment or misapplication of the proper rules of law by the district court. The record demonstrates overt acts by the district judge reflecting great bias against Reserve Mining Company and substantial disregard for the mandate of of this court.

Miles Lord responded: [1]

I have become something of an advocate, that is my manner and that is something I can't change. The Senate approved me with that manner. I try not to use it on the bench.

[1] Quote from the *New York Times,* January 8, 1976.

APPENDICES

Mining, Beneficiation, and Pelletizing at Reserve Mining Company

BABBITT MINING OPERATION

Reserve obtains its raw material resource from a mine near Babbitt, Minnesota, on the eastern end of the Mesabi Iron Range. Refer to Figure 16. Reserve holds claim to approximately 1.2 billion tons of magnetic taconite containing 24–25% iron, or enough to supply the E.W. Davis Works at Silver Bay for 40 years at full production. Reserve's taconite deposit is about 9.9 miles long, 2800 feet wide, and 175 feet deep at its thickest part. Glacial overburden ranging from 2–20-feet thick covers most of the deposit, however, there is some surface outcropping.

Prior to actual mining, scrub brush and trees must be removed and overburden stripped to expose the taconite. Then a special jet-piercing rig is used to "burn" holes into the extremely hard taconite

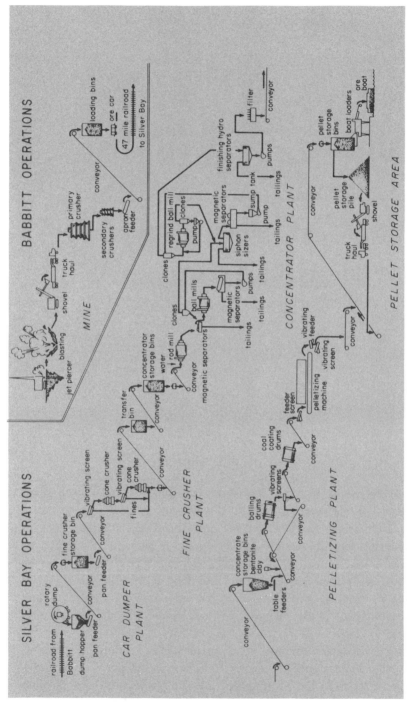

FIGURE 16   Taconite mining and beneficiation at Reserve Mining Company.

deposit. (Taconite is hard enough to cut glass.) A mixture of oxygen and kerosene is used to form an intensely hot (4300°F) flame that heats and cracks the rock. Then steam pressure and water from the rig make the rock brittle and drive out loosened particles. This jet-piercing rig can sink a 30–40-foot deep, seven-inch diameter hole in an hour. By contrast, conventional churn drills would progress only about one foot per hour. Holes are generally spaced 15–25 feet apart in a square pattern, charged with explosive, then detonated.

The large chunks of taconite rock resulting from the explosion are then loaded with electric shovels onto 90-ton, side-dump tractor trailers for transfer to primary crushers. The shovels are equipped with special 12-yard alloy steel dippers.

The two 60-inch gyratory crushers, powered by two 500 hp motors, reduce the ore to minus nine-inch chunks (i.e., the maximum size is nine inches) at the rate of 3500 tons per hour. The crushed ore is classified by a grizzly screen, then fed into three secondary crushers. These 30-inch gyratory secondary units further reduce the ore to minus four-inch chunks. This crushed ore is then loaded onto rail cars for transport 47 miles to Silver Bay via a company-owned railway.

Reserve's modern crushing plant is equipped with dust control equipment to minimize the escape of particulate matter into the surrounding environment.

BENEFICIATION

Railcars loaded with up to 85 long tons of raw ore are unloaded in less than two minutes at the Silver Bay plant by a giant rotary car dumper. Specially designed car couplings allow individual cars to be rotated without disengagement from the train.

The first step in the Silver Bay operation is further crushing to minus ¾-inch size. The finely crushed ore is then routed to one of 22 concentrating stations where water is introduced into the process. Each station has a capacity of processing 82,500 long tons per day of crude taconite, yielding approximately 27,500 long tons of concentrate and 55,000 long tons of tailings daily.

The concentration process essentially involves a series of three stages of grinding and five steps of separation. The ore first undergoes coarse crushing in rod mills, then magnetic separation is used to segregate particles rich in iron oxide from the lean or barren particles that become tailings. The first step results in approximately 63% of the tailings. Next, the iron-rich product is fed into ball mills, which grind the particles to intermediate size (as large as $\frac{3}{32}$ of an inch). A second magnetic separation process follows and produces higher-grade iron ore plus approximately 27% of the tailings.

Following the second crushing and separation stage, large particles are returned to the ball mill for further crushing, and appropriate-sized particles are routed to the third and fourth concentration steps. The third step involves hydroseparation wherein the heavier, iron-rich particles sink in relatively quiescent pools of water, and the iron-poor particles are carried in the water overflow to become part of the tailings (approximately 7% of the total tailings). The iron-rich particles in the hydroseparator *underflow* enter the fourth separation step, i.e. magnetic separators. This step results in another 2.5% of the total tailings.

Once again, the iron-rich material is sized; large particles are directed to the third grinding stage and appropriate-sized particles are routed to the finishing hydroseparator, which operates as described above. Heavier, iron-rich particles sink to the bottom of the tank and are pumped from the unit as final concentrate. Lighter, iron-poor particles flow over the top of the unit and are discharged as tailings. This step accounts for the final 0.5% of the total tailings produced during taconite beneficiation.

The concentrate is filtered to a 10.5–11.0% moisture content, then is conveyed to the pelletizing plant. At this stage the concentrate consists of up to 64.5% iron.

PELLETIZING

Concentrate is conveyed from storage bins to 9 × 30-foot concrete-lined steel balling drums, each with a capacity of 50 long tons per hour. Bentonite clay is added at the rate of 25 pounds per long ton of concentrate to add strength to the pellets before firing and to control the release of moisture during firing. The clay/concentrate mixture is introduced into horizontal-grate pelletizing machines where the pellets are fired at 2350°F, converting the magnetic iron to the hematite form. The pellets are fed to a roll screen, with undersized pellets (less than $1\frac{1}{32}$ inch) being returned to the head of the balling drum and finished pellets sent to product storage.

Pellets are stored in one of 10 bins, each with a capacity of 6000 tons, until loaded into an ore boat for transport to a steel mill.

Underwater Disposal Plan

Large thickeners and hydroseparators would be constructed and used to concentrate tailings from a 98.6% water content to a thick slurry. Chemical settling agents would be required to facilitate thickening. The thickened underflow, containing most of the tailings solids, would then be pumped through 14 eight-inch pipes submerged well below the thermocline level in the lake. Refer to Figure 17. Clarified overflow with low suspended solids content would be returned to Reserve's harbor near the existing water intake.

Estimated construction cost: $14 million (1971 estimate).

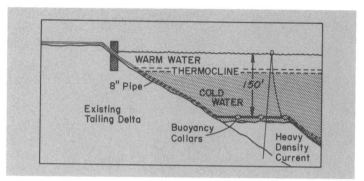

FIGURE 17   Deep pipe disposal plan.

Abbreviations
for Agencies
and Organizations

ABBREVIATIONS	AGENCY OR ORGANIZATION
MWPCC	Minnesota Water Pollution Control Commission
MPCA	Minnesota Pollution Control Agency
FWPCA	Federal Water Pollution Control Act
	also
	Federal Water Pollution Control Administration (predecessor agency to FWQA and EPA)
FWQA	Federal Water Quality Administration (successor to the FWPCA and predecessor of the EPA)
NWQL	EPA's National Water Quality Laboratory in Duluth, Minnesota

MECCA	Minnesota Environmental Control Citizens Association
DNR	(Wisconsin or Minnesota) Department of Natural Resources
WRC	Michigan Water Resources Commission
EPA	Environmental Protection Agency (successor to FWQA and FWPCA)
EQC	(Minnesota) Environmental Quality Council
BOM	Bureau of Mines

Summary
of Characters*

Murray Stein: Assistant Commissioner for Enforcement, Federal Water Pollution Control Administration, U.S.D.I., Washington, D.C.

Dr. Donald I. Mount: Director, National Water Quality Laboratory, Federal Water Pollution Control Administration, U.S.D.I., Duluth, Minnesota.

Dr. E. W. Davis: Director of the Mines Experiment Station at the University of Minnesota.

John A. Blatnik: U.S. Representative from the 8th Minnesota District.

* Affiliations reflect positions held during period of involvement in the Reserve case. Also, these individuals are all mentioned more than once in the text.

Charles Stoddard: Regional Coordinator of the United States Department of the Interior.

Max Edwards: Assistant Secretary of the Interior for Water Quality and Research.

Carl L. Klein: Assistant Secretary of the Interior for Water Quality.

David D. Dominick: Commissioner of the Federal Water Pollution Control Administration.

John P. Badalich: Executive Director, Minnesota Pollution Control Administration.

Thomas Frangos: Administrator, Wisconsin Department of Natural Resources.

Dr. Donald Baumgartner: Chief of the National Coastal Pollution Research Program for the FWPCA.

Dr. A. F. Bartsch: Director of the FWPCAs Pacific Northwest Water Laboratory.

Dr. Gary Glass: Chemist with the National Water Quality Laboratory in Duluth.

Edward M. Furness: President of the Reserve Mining Company.

Edward Schmid: Assistant to President Furness.

Dr. Louis Williams: Former research scientist with the NWQL; then a biology professor at the University of Alabama.

Dr. Kenneth Haley: Reserve's Vice President for Engineering.

Dr. G. Fred Lee: Professor of water chemistry at the University of Wisconsin.

Dr. Robert Bright: Associate Professor of geology and ecology at the University of Minnesota.

Grant Merritt: Director of the Conservation Group, MECCA, then Director of the State Pollution Control Agency, MPCA.

Edward Fride: Lead outside counsel for Reserve.

Dr. R. W. Andrew: A research scientist from the NWQL in Duluth.

Judge C. Luther Eckman: Lake County District Court, State of Minnesota.

Judge Donald Barbeau: Hennepin County District Court, State of Minnesota.

Judge Miles W. Lord: Federal District Court, District of Minnesota, 5th Division.

Dr. Phillip Cook: Research scientist in the enforcement branch of EPA, but assigned to the Duluth NWQL during the Reserve case.

Dr. Irving Selikoff: A cancer research specialist with the Environmental Sciences Laboratory at Mount Sinai School of Medicine in New York City. He was the government's (plaintiff) chief medical witness.

James R. Coleman: Assistant Director of the Division of Environmental Health for the Minnesota Department of Health.

Merlyn Woodle: A Reserve vice president.

Dr. Jack Zussman: Professor and Head of the Department of Geology at the University of Manchester, England.

Dr. Arnold Brown: Chairman of the Department of Pathology and Anatomy at the Mayo Clinic in Rochester, Minnesota.

Dr. Frederick Pooley: World-renowned scientist from Cardiff, Wales, and an expert in identifying physical and chemical properties of asbestos and asbestos-like fibers.

Dr. Paul Gross: Professor of pathology at the University of North Carolina.

References

1 / U.S. Department of the Interior, *Summary Report on Environmental Impacts of Taconite Waste Disposal in Lake Superior—Part I,* December 1968, p. 28.

2 / Minnesota Pollution Control Agency, *Report on Investigations of Water Quality of Lake Superior in the Vicinity of Silver Bay,* November 3–7, 1969, p. 1.

3 / Minnesota District Court (6th Judicial District), *Findings of Fact and Conclusions of Law and Order for Judgment,* by the Honorable C. Luther Eckman, December 15, 1970, p. 14.

4 / U.S. Department of Justice, *Specification of Scientific Charges (Civil Action No. 5-72 Civ. 19),* May 2, 1973, Claim No. 47.

5 / *St. Paul Dispatch,* June 15, 1973.

6 / *Minneapolis Tribune,* March 3, 1974.

7 / U.S. District Court (District of Minnesota, 5th Division), *Supplemental Memorandum (No. 5-72 Civil 14),* by the Honorable Miles W. Lord, May 11, 1974, p. 109.

8 / U.S. Court of Appeals (8th Circuit), *Order (No. 74-1291),* by Judges Bright, Ross, and Webster, filed June 4, 1974, p. 24.

9 / *World Book Encyclopedia,* Volume R (Chicago: Field Enterprises Educational Corp., 1974), p. 430.

10 / U.S.D.I.–FWPCA, *An Appraisal of Water Pollution in the Lake Superior Basin,* April 1969, p. 18.

11 / Transcript, second public *Hearing on Applications of Reserve Mining Company,* June 17, 1947, St. Paul, Minnesota, p. 35.

12 / Transcript, seventh public *Hearing on Applications of Reserve Mining Company,* September 30, 1947, St. Paul, Minnesota.

13 / Minnesota Department of Conservation, *Findings and Conclusions in the Matter of the Application of Reserve Mining Company for Certain Permits,* December 18, 1947, p. 3.

14 / Transcript, sixth public *Hearing on Applications of Reserve Mining Company,* September 4, 1947, St. Paul, Minnesota, p. 62.

15 / Transcript, second public *Hearing on Applications of Reserve Mining Company,* June 5, 1947, Duluth, Minnesota.

16 / *Duluth News-Tribune,* January 24, 1969.

17 / Ulrich, S.; Berg, J.J.; and Hedlund, D., *Superior Polluter,* Save Lake Superior Assn. and Northern Environmental Council, Duluth, Minnesota, October 1972.

18 / Minnesota District Court (6th District), *Memorandum* accompanying Judge C.L. Eckman's *Order,* December 15, 1970.

19 / Minnesota Supreme Court, *Mandate (Reserve Mining Company v. MPCA),* August 29, 1972.

20 / *St. Paul Dispatch,* June 15, 1973.

21 / *Duluth News-Tribune,* June 16, 1973.

22 / *Duluth Herald,* June 15, 1973.

23 / *Minneapolis Tribune,* June 16, 1973.

24 / *Minneapolis Tribune,* June 22, 1973.

25 / *Duluth News-Tribune,* June 30, 1973.

26 / *Duluth News-Tribune,* July 8, 1973.

27 / *Minneapolis Star,* July 10, 1973.

28 / *Duluth Herald,* March 18, 1974.

29 / *Duluth News-Tribune,* March 30, 1974.

30 / *Minneapolis Star,* April 10, 1974.

31 / Pontefract, R.D., and Cunningham, H.M., "Penetration of Asbestos Through the Digestive Tract of Rats," *Nature,* Vol. 243, 1973, p. 352.

32 / U.S. Court of Appeals (Eighth Circuit) *Order,* for *Reserve Mining Co.* v. *U.S.A.,* March 14, 1975.

33 / Mount, Donald I., "A Summary of the Studies Regarding the Effect of the Reserve Mining Company Discharge on Lake Superior," EPA–NWQL, Duluth, Minnesota, April 1973.

34 / Cabelli, V.J., *et al,* "Multiplication of Bacteria in Lake Superior Water Containing Taconite Tailings: Laboratory Studies" (EPA Report to the Federal District Court in April 1973).

35 / *Duluth News-Tribune,* March 16, 1975.

36 / "Concept Evaluation Report–Taconite Tailings Disposal" (prepared by Roy F. Weston, Inc., for the Environmental Protection Agency, October 27, 1971).

37 / *Minneapolis Tribune,* January 31, 1975.

38 / *Minneapolis Star,* December 26, 1974.

39 / *Minneapolis Star,* January 15, 1975.

40 / *Minneapolis Star,* January 29, 1975.

41 / Transcript, *Hearings before the Senate Commerce Committee on Toxic Substances Control Act,* 1973.

42 / Tihansky, D.P., and Kibbey, H.V., "A Cost-Risk-Benefit Analysis of Toxic Substances," *Journal of Environmental Systems,* Vol. 4, No. 2, Summer 1974, p. 117.

43 / *Chemicals and Health: Report of the Panel on Chemicals and Health of the President's Science Advisory Committee,* September, 1973.

44 / Cook, P.M.; Glass, G.; and Tucker, J.H., "Asbestiform Amphibole Minerals: Detection and Measurement of High Concentrations in Municipal Water Supplies," *Science,* Vol. 185, September 1974.

45 / McFarren, E.F.; Millette, J.R.; and Lishka, R.J., "Asbestos Analysis by Electron Microscope," presented at the *Second Annual Water Quality Technology Conference* of the American Water Works Association, December 1–4, 1974.

46 / *Los Angeles Times,* June 23, 1974.

47 / N. Candau, "DDT in Malaria Control and Eradication," *Journal of American Medical Association,* Vol. 209, August 18, 1969, p. 1096.

48 / Breslow, N.E., and Enstrom, J.E., "Geographic Correlation Between Cancer Mortality Rates and Alcohol-Tobacco Consumption in the United States," *J. National Cancer Institute,* Vol. 53, No. 3, September 1974.

49 / Wellford, H., "Behind the Meat Counter," *Atlantic,* October 1972.

50 / *Portland Oregonian,* March 22, 1975.

51 / *Duluth Herald,* January 16, 1975.

52 / *Portland Oregonian,* March 23, 1975.

Index

C

D

E

F